SCORING SECOND LANGUAGE SPOKEN AND WRITTEN PERFORMANCE

SCORING SECOND LANGUAGE SPOKEN AND WRITTEN PERFORMANCE

Issues, options and directions

Ute Knoch, Judith Fairbairn and Yan Jin

SHEFFIELD UK   BRISTOL CT

Published by Equinox Publishing Ltd.

UK: Office 415, The Workstation, 15 Paternoster Row, Sheffield, South Yorkshire, S1 2BX
USA: ISD, 70 Enterprise Drive, Bristol, CT 06010

www.equinoxpub.com

First published 2021

British Library Cataloguing-in-Publication Data
A catalogue record for this book is available from the British Library.

ISBN-13 978 1 78179 951 2 (hardback)
         978 1 78179 952 9 (paperback)
         978 1 78179 953 6 (ePDF)
         978 1 80050 038 9 (ePub)

Library of Congress Cataloging-in-Publication Data
Names: Knoch, Ute, author. | Fairbairn, Judith, author. | Jin, Yan, 1965- author.
Title: Scoring second language spoken and written performance : issues, options and directions / Ute Knoch, Judith Fairbairn, Yan Jin.
Description: Sheffield, UK ; Bristol, CT : Equinox Publishing Ltd, 2021. | Series: British Council monographs on modern language testing ; vol 4 | Includes bibliographical references and index. | Summary: "This book provides graduate students, researchers, test developers, other practitioners and teachers with an introduction to and an overview of the subject area - the scoring of second language performances"-- Provided by publisher.
Identifiers: LCCN 2020050328 (print) | LCCN 2020050329 (ebook) | ISBN 9781781799512 (hardback) | ISBN 9781781799529 (paperback) | ISBN 9781781799536 (pdf) | ISBN 9781800500389 (epub)
Subjects: LCSH: English language--Study and teaching--Foreign speakers--Evaluation. | Second language acquisition--Ability testing.
Classification: LCC PE1128.A2 .K587 2021 (print) | LCC PE1128.A2 (ebook) | DDC 428.0071--dc23
LC record available at https://lccn.loc.gov/2020050328
LC ebook record available at https://lccn.loc.gov/2020050329

Typeset by S.J.I. Services, New Delhi, India

CONTENTS

LIST OF FIGURES

Credits

LIST OF TABLES

INTRODUCTION

The ability to communicate effectively (through writing and speaking) is widely recognised as an important skill in many contexts and for many purposes – personal, educational and professional. Because these skills are considered important in second and foreign language learning contexts, they are often included in second or foreign language assessments. The scoring of such performance is, however, a complex undertaking and has attracted much attention, in both first and second language learning contexts. The increasing use of automated scoring systems has added to this complexity in recent years. It is therefore all the more surprising that there is no single monograph available that provides an overview of this topic area – the scoring of second language spoken and written performance. This book attempts to fill this gap, by drawing together the latest literature in the area. It focuses on issues relating to rater-mediated assessments and sets out consideration in relation to automated scoring and other technology-based systems which are increasingly used. We hope that this work will provide a useful introduction for graduate students, researchers, test developers, other practitioners and teachers to this topic which has in many ways dominated the field of language assessment over many decades.

What do we mean by spoken and written performance? We focus on the spoken or written responses students or test takers provide in response to a 'task' in a language assessment. A number of definitions have been put forward for tasks in the task-based language teaching literature (see, e.g., Bygate, Skehan & Swain, 2001; Ellis, 2003), and definitions have also been put forward for tasks in language assessment contexts (Bachman & Palmer, 1996; Davies et al., 1999; Skehan, 2000). For the purpose of this monograph, we would like to differentiate production tasks from more fixed item types such as multiple-choice, short responses or cloze tasks, where very little language is elicited from the test takers, and scoring is therefore more objective. We adopt the definition by Davies et al. (1999: 196) who defined tasks as:

a type of test item involving complex performance in a test of productive skills. Examples of writing test tasks are: writing an essay, drafting a business letter, and completing a summary of a text. Examples of speaking test tasks are: adopting a specific role in a role play, describing a photograph, and presenting an argument to a small group of peers.

Inherent in the definition above is that tasks can be broadly categorised as those that are independent, and therefore not reliant on some form of input, and integrated tasks, which require test takers to first read and/or listen to input material which is needed for the response. This monograph focuses on both types of tasks.

The book does not focus on any particular context, second or foreign language assessment or test-taker populations, although the attention is less on the formative classroom contexts where teachers mark performances to give feedback. The vast majority of the literature we draw on has concentrated on medium- to high-stakes assessment in a range of domains, for example, admissions, proficiency testing, completion of programmes or progression. Most of the literature that is cited in this monograph deals with the assessment of English, but this does not mean the same principles do not apply more broadly and transfer into the assessment of other languages. Although the main focus is on the assessment of second or foreign languages, we cite at times, where suitable, work that comes from first language (L1) contexts. The majority of the work involving scoring has been done in contexts where adults are assessed, but the principles introduced in this book would equally apply to the assessment of children or adolescents and are increasingly also used in this context.

Five scenarios: Rating practice in established testing contexts

To provide some background to the complexity of scoring constructed responses, and the different approaches taken by large-scale testing companies, it is helpful to consider five rating examples from five major language tests: the Test of English as a Foreign Language (TOEFL iBT), the Aptis test, the Pearson Test of English Academic (PTE), the College English Test (CET) and the Occupational English Test (OET).

The TOEFL iBT is, according to the developer's website, a 'standardized test to measure the English language ability of non-native speakers wishing to enrol in English-speaking universities' (Educational Testing Service, 2019). The test taker completes the tasks set by the test developer on the computer, and in the case of the spoken and written constructed responses included in the test, these are captured by the testing platform. The scoring of the speaking and writing performances is subsequently completed by two scorers: a human rater and an automated scoring platform. The two scores are averaged to arrive at a final score, and in the case of discrepancies, a third rater (a human rater) is consulted. The human raters draw on task-specific holistic rating scales, in which the raters only need to make one decision (that is, the aspects of the performance are described within one performance descriptor, rather than being broken up as is the case in analytic scales; see Chapter 5 for more details). The automated scoring platform, e-rater, used to score the TOEFL test is described in more detail in Chapter 6. Each constructed response, that is, each spoken and written task response provided by one test taker, is scored by different human raters to ensure maximum fairness to the test takers.

The Aptis test, developed by the British Council, is a computer-administered English-language test used in various contexts and for a range of purposes. The test comprises level-specific tasks for speaking and writing (four tasks for each test), which are linked to the Common European Framework of Reference for Languages (CEFR). The tasks are scored by human raters using holistic rating scales which were developed from the CEFR descriptors. Although each performance is only single-rated, each test is marked by four different raters. The Aptis test also has procedures in place for ongoing rater monitoring. Raters are regularly presented with control items, which measure their ongoing rating quality. If these control items (which have previously been scored by senior raters) are not rated to standard, then raters are suspended from further rating.

The Pearson Test of English (PTE) is a fully computer-administered and scored test used for various purposes, including to make university entrance decisions. The task types that are scored towards the speaking and writing sub-test scores are therefore more restricted than those in other tests to allow for fully automated scoring (please refer to Chapter 6 for more information on automated scoring). As no human raters are involved in the scoring process, no double ratings are conducted for the PTE Academic.

The College English Test (CET), a national English language testing system in China, has a number of constructed-response tasks: paragraph translation and essay writing in the paper-based CET; reading aloud, answering questions, presentation and pair discussion in the computer-based CET-Spoken English Test (CET-SET). Both paragraph translation and essay writing are single-scored by human raters on an online scoring platform in which a real-time training and quality-control procedure is in place to ensure the quality of scoring. Since 2016, the CET developer has been experimenting with a hybrid system which combines human scoring and automated scoring for paragraph translation and essay writing. The system for paragraph translation has been in trial implementation in several CET scoring centres since 2018 and the system for essay writing needs further validation before being operationally used. The CET-SET is scored using a combination of human scoring and automated scoring. Reading aloud is automatically scored by the computer. The remaining tasks are double-scored by human raters using an analytic scoring scale. Resolution is applied to performances with a certain level of discrepancy between the two raters. Currently, the CET developer is also experimenting with an automated scoring system which scores test-taker performances on all the speaking tasks.

The Occupational English Test (OET) is an English test for healthcare professionals and is accepted in various contexts globally to ascertain the English language proficiency of overseas-trained healthcare professionals. The OET is administered in pen-and-paper format and includes spoken role plays (of the healthcare professional interacting with a simulated patient) and a writing task (writing a letter of referral). All constructed responses are double-scored by human raters and if discrepancies between the scores continue to exist following a statistical analysis using Rasch measurement (see Chapter 2), a third or even a fourth rater is asked to score the performance. OET raters use analytic rating scales to score spoken and written response. These scales were developed with the input of health professionals and are designed to reflect what health professionals value in these performances. Rater quality is monitored by examining the rating performance of each rater in the Rasch analysis and raters are provided with feedback on their rating performance following each administration.

The five example scenarios described above provide an indication of the different choices test developers make when it comes to the scoring of constructed responses. Tests are either fully scored by human raters or by an automatic scoring engine, or scored by a combination of human raters and automated scoring. When human raters are involved, the scoring criteria may differ, and the number of raters and the score resolution techniques differ as well. When only one human rater is involved, the ongoing rater quality monitoring may be different to that in contexts where more than one rater is used. The examples, therefore, show just how complex the scoring of constructed responses is and it is our hope that this monograph will untangle and clarify some of these issues.

All test development work is underpinned by principles of validity and validation (Kane, 1992, 2006, 2016; Messick, 1989) and developers setting out to develop tests often draw on the principles of evidence-centred design (Mislevy & Yin, 2012) which requires the development of assessment design and use arguments early on in the process, and this includes the scoring methods. We discuss validity and validation in more detail in Chapter 7, but would like to stress that a consideration of validity is at the forefront of everything we describe in this book. Issues relating to scoring are also central to discussions of fairness in language testing (Kunnan, 2018; McNamara, Knoch & Fan, 2019; Xi, 2010b) which often focus on the technical qualities of language assessments, of which scoring processes are a central consideration.

Organisation of the book

In Chapter 1, we start by introducing the topic of raters and ratings. We provide a visual model that shows the complexity of the factors that influence rating quality in rater-mediated assessments, as well as some issues that are relevant to automated scoring. This model also provides an overview of many of the issues we introduce in the book. We then discuss the various rater effects that have been described in the literature and explore factors that may affect rating quality.

Chapter 2 focuses on measuring rater quality. We provide a detailed framework for classifying measures of rating quality and discuss the most commonly used indices and measurement techniques in more detail. The chapter concludes with a summary of what detailed information each rater index can provide about the rater effects described in Chapter 1.

In Chapter 3, we explore more qualitative aspects of the rating process – rater cognition. The chapter examines methodological considerations in collecting rater cognition data and then focuses on studies exploring rater decision-making.

Chapter 4 introduces approaches to enhancing rating and score quality, including work that has looked at rater recruitment, training, ongoing standardisation and monitoring of raters. The chapter also discusses various score resolution techniques that have been used and researched in language assessment contexts in some detail.

In Chapter 5, we look at scoring, in particular by using rating scales. We introduce various rating scale types and also examine rating scale development methods described in the literature. The chapter concludes by looking at one method increasingly used when scoring without specific scale descriptors – comparative judgement.

Technology in scoring is becoming an increasingly important topic, in particular through the introduction of automated scoring and feedback systems. In Chapter 6, we focus on such technological innovations. The chapter first examines the application of online marking, and then turns to automated scoring systems used for both speech and writing evaluation. The chapter outlines how such scoring systems work, and considers their advantages and disadvantages. Research on automated scoring systems is also presented to outline the current status of thinking in the field.

In the final chapter, we focus on the validation of scoring processes. More precisely, we examine in Chapter 7 how the conceptualisation of the validation of scoring processes has changed historically, introduce some key validation frameworks and then focus on some specific validation contexts: the validation of automatically-scored assessments, and the validation of classroom-based assessments.

Before we start, we would like to clarify the use of some terminology in this book. First of all, it may be surprising to some that the monograph is entitled 'Scoring second language spoken and written performance'. The book focuses on both second and foreign language contexts, but we don't feel that the issues relating to scoring are particularly different in the two contexts and we therefore refer to 'second' language constructed responses in this book, encompassing both contexts. Rater-mediated assessment refers to the use of human raters in the scoring process, as opposed to automated scoring systems. We use the terms raters, markers, judges and assessors interchangeably.

CHAPTER 1

UNDERSTANDING RATERS AND RATINGS

Introduction

In more and more educational assessment contexts, students are required to produce constructed responses to demonstrate their language ability. Such performances are more complex to score than, for example, multiple-choice items. Typically, such writing or speaking performances are evaluated by one or more raters who refer to rating criteria (also referred to as rating scales) when making their decisions (automated assessment will be described in Chapter 6). Raters are therefore central to arriving at a score that summarises the performance and this score later forms the basis for making decisions and drawing inferences about the student. Visually, if the performance (e.g., the written essay or the spoken response) is depicted on one side and the score is on the other side, then the raters can be seen as the mediating factor between these two aspects of the assessment situation. Raters, however, bring with them a variety of experiences, values and backgrounds, and, unlike automated scoring systems, do not necessarily act as interchangeable scoring machines. It is accepted that raters do not always agree with each other and that these differences may be due to a variety of factors and may be exhibited in different ways. In fact, every time a rater provides a score to a performance, the score is likely to misrepresent the true ability of the test taker to a certain extent.

In this chapter, we will examine in detail the factors that may influence a rating and the ways in which raters may differ. We start the chapter by setting out a model of the rating situation that we use to provide the structure for this and the following chapters in this book. We will then focus on two aspects of this model; first, we will describe a variety of rater effects that have been described in the literature and next we will examine a number of factors which have been shown to influence the quality of the ratings in judge-mediated assessments.

Understanding rating quality

A central concern in the context of rater-mediated language assessments is the quality of the ratings produced by raters. A plethora of research studies both from the educational assessment literature as well as from language assessment have therefore examined factors that may influence the quality of ratings, proposed and measured types of variability between raters, and described methods to minimise such variability.

McNamara (see, e.g., 1996; and later updated in McNamara et al., 2019) produced a simple diagram outlining the key aspects interacting in a performance assessment. He showed that the rating is produced by the rater while examining a performance in relation to the rating criteria. The performance itself is produced by the candidate interacting with the task (and possibly the interlocutor/examiner in the case of a spoken assessment). All these different building blocks or assessment facets in McNamara's model may impact the rating. For the purpose of this chapter, we have expanded McNamara's model to include a number of aspects influencing rating quality (Figure 1.1) and we will describe each of these aspects in more detail in this and the next two chapters.

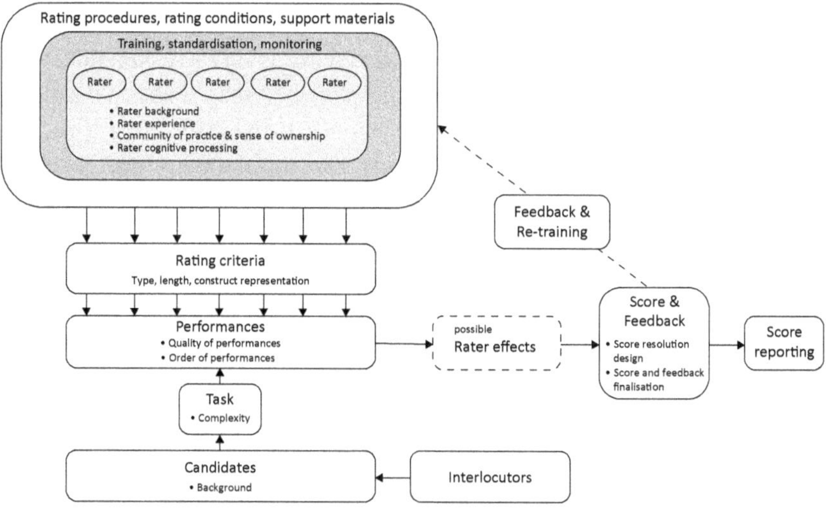

Figure 1.1: Factors influencing rating quality in rater-mediated assessment

As can be seen in Figure 1.1, raters bring different backgrounds and levels of experience to their rating practice. The raters as a group are influenced by the rating procedures used, the rating conditions in which they work, the rater training and the rating support materials available, as well as any standardisation and monitoring they experience as part of their rating practice. We have depicted the raters as a community of practice (Baird, Greatorex & Bell, 2004; Hall & Harding, 2002; Lindhardsen, 2018; Wenger, 1998) to show that this assessing is often done within an environment which provides a sense of a group, a common goal and an opportunity for conversations and discussions. In certain contexts, raters may be given the opportunity to get a sense of ownership of some aspects of the assessment (e.g., the scoring criteria). This sense of a community of practice may also affect rating behaviour as may rater cognitive processing.

The raters interact with the rating criteria (which may differ in layout, number of levels and construct representation) to evaluate the spoken or written performances. They may not only be influenced by the ability level displayed by the student (which is construct-relevant), but also by construct-irrelevant issues such as the quality of the performance they are presented with (e.g., the quality of the audio or the handwriting) or the order in which the performances are presented to the raters. Raters may also be influenced by certain candidate characteristics or the perceived task complexity, as well as the performance of any interlocutors involved in the performance.

Any of these aspects may result in the rater displaying one or more of a number of rater effects when finalising the scores (and feedback, if applicable) to test takers. In larger-scale or high-stakes situations, there are usually mechanisms for score or feedback finalisation, including the use of score resolution or checking techniques, before the score is reported. Based on the raters' performance, feedback and further training may be provided. In the following section, we will focus in detail on rater variability by describing a number of different rater effects that have been described in the literature. In the second part of this chapter, we will examine more closely some of the factors that may influence the quality of ratings. In particular, we will look at the two grey boxes relating to the raters, as well as factors relating to the test-taker performances, the task, the candidate and the interlocutors. We will only briefly comment on the rating criteria, as scoring criteria are covered in more depth in Chapter 5 of this book and procedures for rater training, monitoring, standardisation as well as score resolution techniques are covered in Chapter 4.

Examining rater variability – Exploring rater effects

We now turn to examining more closely a number of rater effects that have been described in the literature. Rater effects are commonly seen as a source of systematic variance which is associated with the raters and not the abilities of the candidates (Eckes, 2005). This means that any score variability is not related to the abilities of the candidates but rather of the raters. Rater effects are therefore unrelated to the construct being assessed and threaten the validity of the scores and resulting score interpretations. This means that every time a rater provides a score to a performance, the score slightly misrepresents the performance. The literature examining rater variability in language assessment as well as other contexts points to rater effects being prevalent across studies and contexts. What is more, rater variability can manifest itself in a variety of ways and is not easily removed with training (Eckes, 2005; Lumley & McNamara, 1995; O'Sullivan & Rignall, 2007; Weigle, 1998, 1999). Ideally, differences between raters should be so small following training that they do not have an influence on the resulting scores and score interpretations, but this has been shown to be impossible. This is not surprising considering that raters engage in a 'complex and error-prone cognitive process' (Cronbach, 1990: 584) to arrive at a final judgement. This problem led McNamara (1996) to conclude that variability between raters is a fact of life and that the best approach is to make raters internally consistent and then statistically adjust for the differences between raters.

In what ways, then, can rater variability manifest itself? A number of researchers have catalogued rater effects in varying detail (see, e.g., Eckes, 2011; McNamara, 1996; Myford & Wolfe, 2003). These and other authors have shown that raters can, for example, differ in terms of their leniency and harshness, their consistency, the way they interpret and use the rating criteria and how they interact with specific facets of the rating situation. Interestingly, the literature is not consistent in the terminology used to describe rater variability. As Myford & Wolfe (2003) point out, authors have used varying terminology, including rater effects, biases and errors and these terms are often not well defined and often used interchangeably. In this chapter we will use the term rater effects or rater variability to mean a group of effects which result in variability of ratings which is associated with the raters and not with the performance of the test takers. In the following sections, we would like to discuss each of these effects in more detail. In Chapter 2 we will describe how these effects can be identified using various statistical techniques.

Leniency and harshness

The leniency and severity effects, according to Myford & Wolfe (2003), were first discussed in the late 1920s and early 1930s (Ford, 1931; Kneeland, 1929 as cited in Myford & Wolfe, 2003) to describe raters that rate well above or well below the mid-point of a rating scale. Early researchers argued that leniency was part of human nature, because humans are generous to fellow humans, in particular if they know the people they are rating (which may be the case in many teaching contexts). Leniency and harshness can be examined in relation to agreed (or expert) ratings or in relation to a group of raters, as we will see in Chapter 2. For now, it is important to understand that leniency and harshness are systematic, that is, raters identified as lenient or harsh have a tendency to rate in this way systematically and across all criteria in a rating scale. However, as Wolfe, Jiao & Song (2015) point out, it is also important to remember that this is not an all-or-nothing behaviour by raters but rather a tendency. As we will see in below, leniency and harshness can also be exhibited selectively, in relation to particular criteria.

(In-)Consistency

Raters identified as rating inconsistently also do not rate according to previously agreed (expert) ratings or in line with a group of raters. But in this case, the difference to the benchmark ratings or to those of the other raters in the group is less systematic. A rater may at times rate too harshly, at other times too leniently and at other times to the standard. Importantly though, there are no clear patterns to this rating behaviour, resulting in inconsistent rank ordering of candidates when compared to either expert ratings or a group of raters (Wolfe, Jiao & Song, 2015). Inconsistent ratings have been described as the biggest threat to the validity of the scores (McNamara, 1996), as it is impossible to correct for such rating behaviour. Raters found to be rating inconsistently over a number of test administrations despite re-training efforts may need to be excluded from rating.

Halo effect

The halo effect manifests itself when raters do not distinguish between conceptually different categories on the rating scale but instead provide the same or very similar scores across the criteria in an analytic scale. Raters may be influenced by an overall impression of a performance or they may be influenced by the performance on a particular sub-skill or category and transfer the scores across to other traits on the scale. In studies on language assessment, for example, it has often been documented that raters tend to be influenced by the grammatical accuracy of a performance and then use the test taker's performance on this aspect as a guide for scores on other traits. The resulting score profiles of students are relatively flat (that is, very similar scores are awarded across categories) and the raters are usually identified as rating with too little variation. Interestingly, this rater effect may actually contribute to a picture of rater accuracy rather than inaccuracy (Myford & Wolfe, 2003) and therefore needs to be monitored carefully.

Some authors (e.g., Cooper, 1981; Murphy, 1982) have cautioned researchers to distinguish between valid halo and invalid halo. The latter situation may arise if traits are generally highly intercorrelated or related. It may also be the case that test takers exhibit even profiles across traits. In language assessment, due to the nature of the types of performances elicited in assessment, it is less common to find truly 'flat' performances across traits on a scale, although this may of course be possible.

Central tendency and restriction of range effects

In this section, we describe two related rater effects, the central tendency and the restriction of range effects. We discuss these together as they are based on similar principles and because they manifest themselves in similar ways in a statistical analysis. Raters exhibit a central tendency effect when they avoid the extreme categories of the rating scale and prefer to award scores near the mid-point of the scale. This has been shown to be a relatively fixed rating style for some raters and results in a bunching of scores around the mid-point, reducing the effectiveness of the scale and resulting in less discriminating ratings (Anastasi, 1988).

A restriction of range effect is closely related to the central tendency effect but differs in one way. Raters also use a restricted range of the rating scale but bunch the ratings not around the mid-point of the scale, but rather around a different point. For example, it may be possible that raters only provide scores in the two highest scale categories and rarely award any lower score levels.

Rater bias

Raters may also exhibit biases in relation to certain aspects of the rating situation. For example, raters have been shown to display interaction effects with facets such as candidate background or proficiency (e.g., Kondo-Brown, 2002), task type (Lynch & McNamara, 1998) or in relation to specific criteria (Knoch, 2011; Wigglesworth, 1993). For example, a rater may display a tendency of rating more harshly than expected when scoring a certain trait (criterion) on a rating scale or may be found to be rating more leniently than expected when scoring test takers from a certain L1 background. An analysis of interactions will routinely uncover a certain percentage of significant interactions, that is, raters are either rating unexpectedly harshly or leniently in relation to certain elements in such facets but may not display an overall severity effect.

While these biases are usually not routinely examined in most assessment contexts, assessment administrators may at times want to explore biases in relation to certain assessment aspects, for example, if a test has a high population of test takers from a certain background or if a new task is introduced.

Interpretation of scoring criteria

Raters may also differ in how they interpret the rating scale step structure and this has implications for the scores test takers receive. In Figure 1.2, for example, we have depicted three raters (Raters A, B and C) who all apply a four-point scale. However, as can be seen, the raters interpret the differences between scale steps differently and this will have score implications for the test takers. For Rater B, for example, the step from a score 1 to 2 is much smaller than for the other two raters.

Rater A:	1		2			3	4	
Rater B:	1	2	3		4			
Rater C:	1		2	3		4		

Figure 1.2: Interpretation of scale step structure
(based on McNamara et al., 2019)

While this sort of rating behaviour is rarely routinely analysed and shown to the raters, insights may help test administrators to better understand rating behaviour and to guide rater training and possible scale revisions.

Other rater effects

The literature has also described a number of lesser-studied rater effects and for the purpose of completeness we would like to mention these here briefly. We would like to note that many of these have not been studied extensively in language assessment contexts and may be difficult to detect. For a more detailed discussion of these effects, please refer to Myford & Wolfe (2003). The *logical error* can be seen as a sub-category of the halo effect. Raters who exhibit this assign similar ratings to traits that they deem to be logically related. The *proximity error* is found if raters assign similar ratings to traits that are positioned close to each other on the rating scale. Finally, an *order effect* is observed if raters rate performances encountered early in a rating session differently than those rated later. This may be due to rater fatigue or to a changing of standards throughout a rating session (Myford & Wolfe, 2003).

Following the description of the rater effects that have been described in the literature, we now turn to a more detailed discussion of the factors that may affect rating quality. We systematically describe the factors in Figure 1.1 in more detail, to examine what influence these factors may have on scoring behaviour.

Factors affecting rating quality

Rater-related factors

Figure 1.1 depicts the raters in the inner light-grey shaded box. It can be seen that the raters come with their own individual background and characteristics, and that they vary in rating and other relevant experience. Each of these factors (and the interaction of these) can influence rating quality. Similarly, whether the raters are provided the opportunity to form a community of practice and gain a sense of ownership of aspects of the assessment may also contribute to rating quality. We discuss each of these aspects in more detail below. A deeper understanding of how these factors influence rating quality is not only important for quality control and reporting purposes, but it can also help test administrators in rater recruitment, training and other practices around raters.

Rater experience

A significant body of research has investigated whether experience as raters impacts rating quality. Such research helps large-scale testing programmes to ensure rater quality through a more thorough understanding of what makes raters more reliable. In these studies, experience has been defined in a variety of ways. One group of studies has compared the rating behaviour of ***new and experienced raters*** (Attali, 2016; Barkaoui, 2010; Furneaux & Rignall, 2007; Lim, 2011; Shaw, 2002; Song & Caruso, 1996; Weigle, 1994, 1998). The findings from these studies are, however, inconclusive. Some studies found that inexperienced raters were more severe (Song & Caruso, 1996; Weigle, 1998) and less consistent (Weigle, 1994, 1998). Other studies, however, found that novice raters are more lenient (e.g., Barkaoui, 2010; Sweedler-Brown, 1985). There are also studies which found that the two groups of raters rated similarly in terms of leniency and consistency (e.g., Attali, 2016; Lim, 2011).

A more detailed picture of the rating behaviour of expert and novice raters emerges in studies that have also drawn on qualitative data or have looked at more longitudinal data. Lim (2011), for example, was able to show that novice raters moved closer to the group average in terms of leniency and harshness soon after starting operational rating and that the same patterns were also observed for consistency. Similar steady increases in rater agreement with agreed scores were also observed in studies by Furneaux & Rignall (2007) and Shaw (2002), although differences in rater severity persisted. Qualitative studies have provided more detailed insights into the rating behaviour of these two groups of raters. Cumming (1990) showed that experienced raters drew on a varied number of criteria when assessing writing, some of which were outside the assessment criteria, while novices were more limited on the criteria they used in their assessments. Barkaoui (2010) found differences in the assessment criteria the two rater groups emphasised in their rating of writing. Novice raters gave more emphasis to argumentation, while expert raters put more emphasis on accuracy. As was found in Cumming's (1990) study, the experts drew on evaluation criteria beyond the rating scale more often than the novices. Interestingly, Barkaoui also found that the results from the quantitative and qualitative analyses were not always aligned. While the quantitative findings suggested that linguistic accuracy played a more significant role in the rating of the experts, the qualitative data showed that the novices referred more frequently to linguistic accuracy when explaining their scores. Barkaoui offered possible suggestions for this discrepancy.

The differences in the findings can probably be attributed to methodological disparities. Firstly, the studies differed in how experts and novices were defined. Experience can be defined in the length of time rating as well as the amount of rating (Lim, 2011) and/or based on specific background features, such as professional background or teaching experience. Isaacs & Thompson (2013), for example, report that experts in the context of pronunciation assessment have been variously defined as phoneticians, speech therapists and ESL teachers. The studies also differed in the study contexts, the assessment tasks, the evaluation criteria, the participants as well as other rater factors that might interact with experience, including the first language of raters, their gender, age and own experience in completing the relevant assessment tasks.

A related body of research has compared the rating behaviour of trained and untrained raters. Shohamy, Gordon & Kraemer (1992), for example, compared the ratings on 50 compositions by 10 trained and 10 untrained raters. The results showed that, not surprisingly, the trained raters rated more reliably than the untrained raters. More recently, Duijm, Schoonen & Hulstijn (2017) compared the responsiveness of professional and non-professional raters on two aspects of spoken performance; fluency and accuracy. The study found that non-trained raters were more appreciative of higher performances on fluency while the trained raters were more focused on accuracy.

Rater background

Various rater background variables have been the focus of another group of studies into rater-related factors that may affect rating quality. Such studies are useful because apart from shedding light on possible causes of construct-irrelevant variance, they provide test administrators with useful information that can feed into rater recruitment as well as rater training. Among the variables that have been investigated are rater training, professional and educational background, teaching experience, gender, L1, place of residence and the raters' own exposure to the L1 of the test takers. We will now briefly review the findings of these studies.

The effect of ***rater training*** on rater quality has been studied by a number of researchers. Rater training has been shown to reduce some of the differences in rater severity and rater consistency (Shohamy et al., 1992; Weigle, 1994), though differences between raters continue to exist after training. We report on this research in more detail in Chapter 4 which focuses more closely on rater training and other efforts to increase rating quality.

We were only able to locate two studies examining a possible ***gender*** effect in rating. One could argue that the gender of a test taker is more apparent in a speaking test, although in writing an assessor may recognise the given name of a test taker. Haswell & Haswell (1996) examined this variable in the context of the grading of essays in the US college composition environment. They found evidence of a rater bias where raters scored essays written by students of their own sex more harshly. In a second language speaking context, more specifically in IELTS speaking, O'Loughlin (2007) was not able to find any gender-related bias either in the discourse produced by the interviewer raters or in the resulting scores.

A study conducted by Chalhoub-Deville & Wigglesworth (2005) examined whether the ***place of residence*** of raters has an impact on the scores provided in response to a speaking test. The aim of the study was to explore whether the ratings provided to speaking performances by different rater groups are comparable. They found significant differences between the different groups of raters (which were drawn from Australia, Canada, the UK and the US) but the effect sizes were small and therefore the impact on test takers relatively minor, providing test developers with some assurance that employing different rater groups across the globe is acceptable.

Within the context of the increasing internationalisation of assessments, and ongoing discussions about how to include a World Englishes view into testing, many large-scale assessments have investigated whether the ***linguistic background*** of raters plays a factor in rating quality. Many of these studies have focused on comparing rating quality of native speaker (NS) and non-native speaker (NNS) judges. The studies as a whole are inconclusive in their findings and this is not unsurprising given the different foci and designs, and in particular their operationalisation of who falls into NS and NNS groups. A group of studies have found that NNS are more severe in their ratings (e.g., Fayer & Krasinski, 1987; Marefat & Heydari, 2016; Santos, 1988); others that NS are more severe (e.g., Barnwell, 1989). A further group found that the quantitative scores of the two groups are similar (Connor-Linton, 1995; Johnson & Lim, 2009; Kim, 2009; Shi, 2001; Wei & Llosa, 2015; Xi & Mollaun, 2011; Zhang & Elder, 2011). These quantitative results only provide a partial picture, however. For this reason, some studies have also included qualitative components and it is in these studies that some interesting differences have emerged, even if the two groups of raters scored the performances similarly. In Zhang & Elder's (2011) study comparing NS of English and of Chinese (NNS group) in their ratings on the CET-SET (a speaking test), the NNS were more concerned with language while the NS were more focused on content. In the rating of writing, Lee (2009) and Marefat & Heydari (2016) found that NNS were more concerned with organisation and sentence structure (Lee, 2009) and grammar (Marefat & Heydari, 2016), mirroring the findings by Zhang & Elder (2011). Earlier studies by Connor-Linton (1995) and Shi (2001) also found that the two rater groups provided different reasons for their scores. Kim (2009) in the context of spoken assessment found that the NS teachers made more detailed judgements in the area of pronunciation, grammar and accuracy of information and Shi (2001) found that NS of English made more positive comments on written performance, while Chinese NNS of English identified more negative features.

A number of factors need to be considered when investigating differences between such groups of raters. First of all, it is inevitable that the findings might be obscured by the interaction of other factors, such as the educational or training backgrounds of the raters involved. It is also not clear how useful the distinction is between NS and NNS with the distinction having been questioned by a number of scholars (Davies, 1999; Kachru, 1982). This is because a rising number of second language speakers of English use English within their national borders for official or professional purposes. There is also increasing movement across borders which makes the distinction difficult to operationalise. As an alternative to the dichotomy, Kachru (1982, 1985) has proposed the distinction between Inner Circle countries, Outer Circle countries and the expanding circle, although this distinction may also not be useful if raters have moved between countries. Elder & Davies (1998) proposed that there may be a rater distance effect, where languages more distant to the raters' own may be more difficult to rate, but this is yet to be empirically shown in research on rating in language assessment. Most studies have included highly proficient NNS as raters, but none seem to discuss what the language proficiency threshold is that is necessary to be a capable rater, an issue which clearly deserves more attention and is important for recruitment purposes. Finally, we would also like to stress that the effect on rating quality by these different groups of raters may be stronger for speaking than for writing where exposure to the L1 of test takers may be more marked and provide raters with more advantages to understanding the spoken production of test takers (in particular in the assessment of pronunciation). It is this issue that we turn to next.

The effect of ***rater exposure to the L1 of the test takers*** has received more interest recently (Carey & Mannell, 2009; Carey, Manell & Dunn, 2011; Huang, 2013; Huang, Alegre & Eisenberg, 2016; Winke, Gass & Myford, 2013; Xi & Mollaun, 2009, 2011). The rationale behind these studies is that the pronunciation component of a speaking assessment may be understood differently depending on familiarity with the accent or the language variety more generally or because of certain attitudes towards a language. The rater's impression and thus the score on a speaking performance can therefore be positively or negatively influenced depending on the amount and type of exposure to the candidate's accent. Carey and colleagues (2009, 2011), for example, collected data from raters to see whether they had had prolonged exposure to one of three language varieties: Chinese, Korean and Indian English. They found that the pronunciation score on the IELTS speaking assessment was rated significantly higher when the interlanguage was familiar to the raters. Similar findings were also reported by Winke et al. (2013). Other studies examining this question (Huang, 2013; Huang et al., 2016; Xi & Mollaun, 2009, 2011) found no quantitative effect but raters in these studies mentioned that they felt they were influenced by their own familiarity of the language and were concerned about the impact of this on their ratings.

There are some factors to be considered in relation to these studies. The operationalisation of exposure differed. Some studies defined this as familiarity with the variety of language while others required the raters to have learned the L1 (possibly as a heritage learner). This may have had an impact on the results. Studies have generally focused on the ratings of pronunciation and have not yet examined whether there are effects on the ratings of the wider speaking construct. It is conceivable that exposure to the test takers' L1 may also influence the perception of rhetorical aspects of the language or other features, such as lexis and grammar. More research is clearly needed. What is clear from the studies that have been conducted is that an effect of exposure may be present and this is something that needs to be addressed in rater training activities.

A further rater-related factor investigated in research on rater effects is ***teaching experience***. This has been less researched. The studies we did find have generally compared the ratings of teachers with non-teachers; teaching experience was therefore operationalised as an all-or-nothing construct, while it is highly likely that more experienced raters would draw on their experience differently than relatively new raters. Huang (2013), for example, found no effect of teaching experience but the teachers in the study reported that their background impacted their ratings and the features they predominantly focused on in their ratings. Similarly, Erdosy (2003) found that raters with teaching experience may focus their evaluations on features relevant to their curricula. In the context of a spoken assessment, Hsieh (2011) examined the differences between ratings of linguistically naïve undergraduates and ESL teachers using an overall proficiency scale and a scale focusing on accentedness and comprehensibility. The teachers were found to be more lenient on these two aspects but there were no differences between the ratings of the two groups. An analysis of the written comments provided by the teachers, however, showed that the lay judges focused more on global qualities whereas the teachers focused on more specific qualities in the performances. Schoonen, Vergeer & Eiting (1997) also found an interesting effect for task when comparing language teachers' and 'lay' raters' rating performances written in response to a range of writing tasks. In a study in which these two groups rated three types of assessments on content and language use, they were able to show that the lay raters were less reliable when rating language usage but both groups were equally reliable when rating content. The more controlled a writing task was, the more reliable were the ratings of the lay raters.

Professional background of raters has also been investigated in relation to rating behaviour and quality. The first group of studies has compared the ratings of ESL teachers/lecturers with English faculty members (and other faculty members). Cumming (1990) reported that teachers of English to NS are more used to seeing relatively proficient performances and are therefore more likely to react more negatively to NNS errors. Similarly, Weigle & Boldt (2003) found that raters from English departments were more concerned with grammatical accuracy of students' writing while raters from the psychology department were more focused on content.

Also concerned with professional background is a group of studies conducted in the context of language assessments for professional purposes. Brown (1995), during the development of a test for Japanese tour guides, compared the ratings of native and near-native speakers of Japanese with tour-guiding experience and those with a background in teaching Japanese as a foreign language. No major overall differences between the two groups were found but there were significant differences on the ratings of individual criteria (the tour guides were harsher on task fulfilment, while the language teachers were harsher on accuracy). Brown argued that the findings revealed the different perceptions of what constitutes a good performance. Other studies investigating differences between language-trained assessors and raters with a relevant professional background have also found that the overall ratings were generally similar between the two groups but that the raters disagreed on some of the criteria (Elder, 1993; Lumley, 1998; Lumley & McNamara, 1995). What all of these studies lack is more qualitative data to gain a deeper understanding into the decision-making processes of raters and how they relate to the construct of these assessments.

In an attempt to account for a number of rater background variables and match these to rating profiles, Eckes (2008) put forward his rater types hypothesis in which he showed that raters display specific rating patterns and that these at least partially match various combinations of background variables. Eckes' work was preliminary and more large-scale investigations into the interplay of various background variables and rating behaviour are clearly needed.

Rater community of practice

Work on educational assessment has suggested that marking quality may be improved by a community of practice in which raters form a tight network, have the opportunity to partake in discussions with fellow raters and have access to marked benchmark examples (Baird et al., 2004; Hall & Harding, 2002; Wenger, 1998). This type of community may also create a sense of ownership in the group of raters. Baird et al. (2004) argue that because marking criteria are relatively abstract and standards do not reside in the assessment criteria, the knowledge of how to apply mark schemes in practice is negotiated by a group of individuals (or communicated down via senior examiners) and is based on tacit knowledge. Being involved in coordinators' meetings where changes to the rating criteria are negotiated also helps with the sense of being part of a team. Baird et al. (2004), in the context of GCSE English and History examiners in the UK, attempted to test this theory empirically and operationalised the features inherent in a community of practice as having access to benchmark samples or as having discussions between raters (as operationalised in three conditions: no coordination meeting, hierarchical coordination meeting and consensual coordination meeting). They found that neither procedure showed an improvement in rating quality. However, questionnaire responses showed that the raters valued aspects of the community of practice they were engaged in, including the coordination meetings where they were able to discuss harder-to-mark candidate responses.

Defining and measuring a community of practice is of course not unproblematic. Baird et al.'s study may not have been able to tap into the type of aspects which make such a community work and take ownership of the construct embodied within the assessment criteria. It is also not clear what fosters a community of practice that provides this sense of ownership. Nevertheless, we feel that more research, in particular in language assessment contexts, may be fruitful.

Rater cognitive processing

A final rater-related factor influencing rating quality is rater cognitive processing. This area has been studied in a large number of research projects since the early 1990s and so we discuss it in more depth in Chapter 3.

Rating procedures, rating conditions, support materials

Further factors influencing the quality of ratings are the rating procedures, the rating conditions and the support materials available to raters.

Rating procedures

The rating procedures used in an assessment might also influence rating quality, online rating being one such example. Raters now often work in isolation from home or from an office without being exposed to other raters and the opportunity to share experiences and problems. Raters may also experience headaches and eye strain when working for too long on a computer. Johnson & Nadas (2009) compared raters rating online and on paper and found that while the scores provided were similar, the cognitive load of marking on the computer is much higher. A lack of computing abilities also places a strain on some raters and may lead to a reduction in rating quality.

A further line of enquiry in this area relates to the scoring of spoken performances. Beltran (2016) investigated whether it made a difference for raters to rate from audio only or to have access to a video of the performance and therefore be able to have access to non-verbal behaviour, which is arguably also an important aspect of the speaking construct (see, e.g., Ducasse & Brown, 2009). The study found that there was no significant difference in the ratings; however raters preferred having access to the video of the performance.

Rating environment and conditions

The nature of the physical environment in which raters mark and the conditions under which they work can lead to reductions in rater quality. Black, Suto & Bramley (2011) note that anecdotal evidence from raters and assessment professionals describe clerical errors, problems with concentration and distraction because of noises and other interruptions. Raters may become fatigued if they are required to do too much rating in one session or over too many days (Ling, Mollaun & Xi, 2014; Myford & Wolfe, 2003; Penny, 2003). Ling et al. (2014) conducted a study examining fatigue of raters rating TOEFL iBT speaking tasks. They compared the rating quality of raters working under four different shift conditions and found that the raters working in a 6-hour shift with three 2-hour blocks displayed the highest level of rating quality. In a study focusing on the scoring of writing, Drave (2011) examined fatigue of raters rating written essays online. While all raters reported being fatigued, no significant effects were found on the raters' rating quality.

Related to the notion of fatigue is the idea of order effects. Researchers have proposed that the order in which candidates are rated may affect the ratings they receive, with candidates rated earlier on receiving higher ratings than those rated later in a session (Hopkins, 1998; Myford & Wolfe, 2003). Two studies examining this in the context of high-stakes school exams (Leckie & Baird, 2011; Pinot de Moira, Massey, Baird & Morrissy, 2002) however were not able to show such an effect empirically. A 'drift' in the ratings may also happen over a longer time period, sometimes over years. This means that ratings cannot be directly compared over years (Repp, Nieminen, Olinger & Brusca, 1988).

Rater support materials

Raters should be able to access additional support materials such as benchmark materials and materials clarifying task requirements or scoring rubrics as required. There is not much literature available on how widespread the use of such materials is and how they influence rating quality. In Chapter 2 we examine some issues with selecting scores for benchmark samples and how this creates an issue for rating accuracy, but in the context of this section, we would like to describe broader issues and the few relevant studies we have identified. Some discussion has centred around how benchmark samples are chosen and what levels of student performance they should best represent. Baird et al. (2004), in the context of national school examinations in the UK, found that the inclusion of cut-score examples resulted in slightly too lenient rating (but not significantly so) while more prototypical examples resulted in severe marking. It may also be helpful to include some more 'difficult to score' samples (Raczynski, Cohen, Engelhard & Lu, 2015; Wang, Engelhard, Raczynski, Song & Wolfe, 2017) with explanations of the rationale for how scores were awarded. Engelhard (1996) argues that the benchmarks should represent a range of typical performances. It has also been questioned how benchmark scores are best chosen; whether these should ideally be selected by senior examiners or whether a more demo-cratic approach is more helpful. In the context of language testing, Davis (2016) found in a study relating to the TOEFL iBT speaking test that the more accurate raters reviewed benchmark samples more often and took longer to make scoring decisions. In the context of a specific-purpose test for health professionals rated by linguistically-trained raters, Knoch et al. (2017) found that raters frequently requested access to sample answers to the task (a referral letter), citing a lack of knowledge of the discourse structure and the necessary information to be included in such letters. More research on the use of such sample materials would certainly be helpful.

Rater training, standardisation and monitoring

A further factor investigated in relation to rater quality is the impact of rater training, standardisation and ongoing monitoring. We have briefly touched on the effects of rater training in the section on rater background, but due to the importance of this area, we present both procedural consid-erations as well as a detailed picture of the related research in Chapter 4.

Rating criteria

The rating criteria represent an operationalisation of the theoretical con-struct of the assessment (Hamp-Lyons, 2011; McNamara, 2001) and pro-vide a 'lens' through which the raters evaluate a performance. A range of aspects of the rating criteria have been shown to affect rating quality. This includes the level of detail in the rating scale, the type of rating scale (e.g., holistic vs analytic scoring), how well the criteria are defined and differentiated, the number of scale categories as well as the number of levels in the scale. Because of the important role the rating criteria play in language performance assessment, we will examine these details more thoroughly in Chapter 5 of this monograph.

Candidate performances

Variation in the performances by candidates is in the first instance construct-relevant and therefore not a factor of interest in this chapter. However, there are some aspects of a candidate performance that can introduce construct-irrelevant variance into the rating context, and these are addressed in this section. We would like to focus on two aspects in particular, handwriting and audibility. The impact of poor ***handwriting*** on writing judgements has been examined in first language assessment context (see Brown, 2003b for a list of references to these studies) and it has been shown that poor handwriting does indeed have an impact on the scores awarded with better legibility resulting in higher scores. While it is intuitive that the impact of handwriting would follow this pattern, it is also possible that raters may give the benefit of the doubt to a writing sample that is difficult to read. Evidence of the problems created by poor handwriting during the rating process comes from verbal protocol studies of raters (see, e.g., Lumley, 2002), although this is not direct evidence that rating quality is at threat. Brown (2003b) conducted a study to empirically examine the impact of legibility in a second language assessment context. She compared handwritten and typed scripts and found that the handwritten scripts were advantaged in the ratings and that those scripts with poor legibility were the most advantaged.

Similar to handwriting, poor ***audibility*** of spoken samples can also introduce construct-irrelevant variance. McNamara & Lumley (1997) examined the impact of poor audibility on the rating of spoken interaction recorded as part of a screening test for health professionals (the Occupational English Test) and found a significant effect of audibility, with candidates rated from less audible tapes being rated more harshly. We were not able to find any other relevant research that examined the issue of audibility and background noise on rater quality, and feel that more research is necessary in this area.

Task characteristics

Task characteristics also have an influence on rating quality. In a recent synthesis of generalisability studies, In'nami & Koizumi (2016) showed that the interaction effect between task and rater is responsible for a significant amount of score variation. Hamp-Lyons and colleagues

(Hamp-Lyons, 1990; Hamp-Lyons & Matthias, 1994) showed that raters may use compensatory strategies when scoring topics they perceive as more difficult, consciously or unconsciously compensating students with higher scores. Studies have also found an interaction effect between task factors and rater variables. Schoonen et al. (1997), for example, showed that rater experience interacts with task complexity, in that inexperienced raters are able to rate with higher accuracy tasks that are more constrained (see also, Black et al., 2011). Weigle (1999) was also able to show that inexperienced raters were more severe on one task type (graph) than another (table).

Candidates

Characteristics of the test candidates have also been shown to have an impact on marking quality. Raters react differentially to performances from students of different backgrounds. Huang (2008), for example, was able to show that the essays from students of ESL backgrounds were rated with much more unwanted variance than those from native English students in a high-stakes provincial school examination in Canada. The desired variance was lower for ESL students and the observed generalisability coefficient (refer to Chapter 2 for a description of Generalisability theory) much lower. The author argued that this result raises serious fairness issues for the ESL students in the dataset. In a similar study conducted by Johnson & Van Brackle (2012) in the US, the authors compared raters' treatment of errors in three populations: African American writers, ESL writers and native English writers. The results pointed to 'linguistic discrimination' of African American errors and lenience to ESL errors, which is somewhat at odds with the findings by Huang (2008).

Because test-taker background is much more salient in spoken assessment, several researchers (e.g., Wei & Llosa, 2015; Winke et al., 2013; Yan, 2014) have investigated whether L1 background of students may impact on raters. The studies can be grouped into two groups, those that focused on candidate background without an interaction with rater background, and those that examined the interaction effect. Yan (2014), when evaluating rater performance for a local oral English proficiency test, found that the raters' severity varied depending on their speech perceptions of intelligibility of Indian and Chinese examinees. Hsu (2016), while not focused on examining rater quality, examined rater attitudes towards speech samples provided by Indian English speakers and found that raters displayed negative attitudes towards Indian English speakers.

We have already reported on studies that have examined the interaction effect between rater and candidate background above, in the section focusing on rater background. Such studies (e.g., Wei & Llosa, 2015; Winke et al., 2013) focused on the interaction of the raters' accent familiarity (defined in a number of ways) and the test takers' L1 background.

Other studies have examined effects on rating quality for gender (O'Loughlin, 2007) and candidate proficiency level (Yan, 2014). Yan found that rater quality differed at different proficiency levels; raters were more likely to agree on scores at higher proficiency levels and differed significantly more when rating lower-level candidates.

Interviewers or interlocutors

Interviewer and interlocutor effects have also been shown to affect rater accuracy. Brown & Hill (1998) and Brown (2003a, 2005) found that a rater's scores of test candidates' oral proficiency can be affected by the choice of interviewer. Brown (2005) was able to show that raters compensated for interviewer behaviour. Similar findings were made by McNamara & Lumley (1997) who analysed rater perceptions of interlocutor competence on the Occupational English Test. They found that perceived problems with the performance of the interlocutor led to higher ratings.

The issue of the impact of interlocutors on ratings is not limited to professional interlocutors employed by testing agencies but is also relevant to paired speaking tests, where several test candidates speak to each other and 'co-construct' the performance (Galaczi, 2004; May, 2009; Nakatsuhara, 2004). May (2009) was able to show, through a detailed analysis of rater notes, stimulated recall protocols, rater discussions and scores, how raters compensated or penalised candidates for their role in co-constructing interactional patterns.

Conclusion

Our summary of factors affecting rating quality shows that the topic is complex. We have attempted to present readers with a taste of the kind of studies that have been conducted in this context, but do not claim that this summary is complete. What can be seen is that studies have examined factors in isolation as well as the interaction of factors, for example, the interaction of rater background and experience, tasks, evaluation criteria or candidate background. The findings from these studies show that the interaction is complex and difficult to control. But what are the implications of these findings? Black et al. (2011) write about manipulatable and non-manipulatable factors. Those factors that can be manipulated (e.g., test question features and features of scoring criteria) can therefore be used to directly predict and control rating behaviour. Other factors are not completely manipulatable (but some aspects are), for example, the work environment of raters and the usability of rating technology. Other factors, in turn, are not directly manipulatable by the assessment team, or are only indirectly manipulatable (e.g., examinee response features and rater cognitive strategies).

Particular factors that influence rating quality pose a threat to fairness. For this reason, it is important for language testing providers to understand these factors and attempt to control these in various ways (e.g., through rater training or changes to the tasks) to ensure that all test candidates are provided with an equal opportunity to show their language ability.

CHAPTER 2

MEASURING RATING QUALITY

Introduction

In this chapter, we will focus more closely on different ways of measuring variability in ratings. A review of educational measurement and language assessment textbooks shows that measuring rater variability is far from straightforward, with no unitary technique presenting itself as the best approach for all situations and contexts. Instead, a review of the literature presents a vast number of statistical techniques which are continuously growing. The indices differ in the information they provide about raters and therefore it is often advisable to use a number of them in combination to gain the most detailed picture of rater behaviour. It is important to point out, as we did in the previous chapter, that complete accuracy or agreement between raters is rarely possible. For this reason, test administrators and researchers strive to minimise such variation as much as possible and through this practice ensure that the scores provided to students are the least influenced by this construct-irrelevant variation and most reflective of the test takers' true abilities. Results from the statistical techniques and measures presented in this chapter are used for various reasons in this context (Wind & Peterson, 2018), including to provide validity evidence about an assessment or assessment sub-test, to use the information for rater employment, monitoring and feedback, to make decisions about possible rating designs and score resolution techniques and to draw conclusions about the usefulness of the ratings for drawing inferences about the test takers.

A framework for classifying measures of rating quality

Our review of the literature uncovered a vast number of different indices or techniques for measuring rating quality and these have been classified in a number of ways (see, e.g., Brown, Glasswell & Harland, 2004; Engelhard, 2013; Stemler & Tsai, 2008; Wind & Peterson, 2018). In this chapter we broadly follow an amalgamation of Stemler & Tsai's and Wind & Peterson's classifications (see Table 2.1), focusing on measures commonly used in the language assessment literature as well as measures from the broader educational measurement literature that we find interesting to include here.

	Rater quality (without presence of expert/agreed rating)	Rater accuracy (comparison with expert/agreed rating)
Observed rating tradition		
Consensus	Percentage exact agreement with other rater(s) – One rater – Group of raters	Percentage exact agreement with expert rating – One rater – Group of raters
	Percentage adjacent (and exact) agreement with other rater(s) – One rater – Group of raters	Percentage adjacent (and exact) agreement with expert rating – One rater – Group of raters
	Cohen's weighted kappa (corrects for chance) for both exact and adjacent agreement – One rater – Group of raters	Cohen's weighted kappa (corrects for chance) for both exact and adjacent agreement – One rater – Group of raters
	Percentage agreement with mode	
		D^2 (distance accuracy) – mean square difference between observed and benchmark ratings
Consistency	Correlations (Pearson, Spearman) – One pair of raters – Averaged across pairs of raters to arrive at overall group index	Correlations (Pearson, Spearman) – One rater with expert scores – Each rater with expert scores and then averaged across raters
	Non-parametric rank correlation (Kendall's tau b) – One pair of raters – Averaged across pairs of raters to arrive at overall group index	Non-parametric rank correlation (Kendall's tau b) – One rater with expert scores – Each rater with expert scores and then averaged across raters
		Borman's DA
	Cronbach's alpha – for group of raters	
	Intra-class correlation	
	Factor analysis	
	Generalisability theory	

Scaled rating tradition	
Many-facet Rasch accuracy	Many-facet Rasch accuracy – Dichotomous – Polytomous

Table 2.1: Measures of rating quality

The measures we uncovered can be divided into two broad categories: (a) indices of rater quality or variability if no agreed ratings are available for comparison and (b) indices that provide an indication of rater accuracy if expert or agreed ratings are available. Some authors (e.g., Engelhard, 1996) have called the former group of indices 'indirect' measures of rating quality while the latter have been called 'direct'. Some measures are very similar across both categories, while there are some that only fall in one or the other category. Each of these categories can be further sub-divided into measures that fall into the observed rating tradition (and therefore be based on the practice of decomposing observed ratings into true scores and error components) and those that fall into the scaled tradition. The scaled rating tradition assumes that estimates should be based on the assumption that more than just the observed ratings for each rater should be used to compute the quality estimates but rather the information from all judges, across all candidates should be used. Those measures falling under the observed rating tradition can be further sub-divided into measures of consensus and consistency. We have summarised the indices and statistical techniques uncovered in our review of the literature in Table 2.1. In the rest of the chapter, we will describe each of these techniques in more detail and examine how useful each is to uncover the rater effects we have described in Chapter 1. If equivalent or highly similar measures are available for both rater quality and rater accuracy indices, we will describe these together.

The observed rating tradition

Engelhard (2013) proposed a framework for classifying measurement theories. The first major tradition he mentioned was the test-score tradition. This was later termed the observed rating tradition (see, e.g., Wind & Peterson, 2018). In this tradition, measurement traditions decompose observed ratings into true scores and errors. Wind & Peterson (2018: 4) list a number of measurement models which fall within this tradition, including classical test theory, analysis of variance, generalisability theory, regression models, traditional factor analysis and structural equation modelling. In the following section, we will review some of the most commonly used measures and techniques for establishing rating quality in language assessment and educational assessment based on this tradition.

Consensus measures in the observed rating tradition

Consensus estimates are used when it is of interest to show that raters can agree on a construct that is deemed to be subjective. The assumption is that if raters can agree in their judgements, they are applying the same underlying construct in their ratings. Below are some common consensus measures found in our review of the literature.

Percentage exact and adjacent agreement

The ***percentage exact agreement*** can be defined as the number of essays that received the exact same ratings by two raters, divided by the total number of essays (e.g., Brown et al., 2004; Eckes, 2011; Penny, Johnson & Gordon, 2000; Stemler & Tsai, 2008; Wind & Engelhard, 2014). The assumption is that if two raters are able to come to exact agreement when applying a rating scale, then this provides evidence that they are coming to the same interpretation of the construct (Stemler & Tsai, 2008). This is of course not necessarily true, as we will discuss later in this chapter.

If no agreed or expert ratings are available as comparison, the percentage exact agreement can be calculated for pairs of raters and then averaged across a group of raters. If agreed ratings are available, then the ratings of each rater can be compared against the 'true' scores. Averages of these agreement statistics for each rater can then also be created for a group of raters.

Let us review a simple example. In Table 2.2, we present a simple set of rating data. Two raters rated a set of ten essays.

The raters in Table 2.2 agreed in 5 of 10 ratings, taking their percentage exact agreement to 50%. So what would be acceptable values for the percentage exact agreement? Many textbooks mention that acceptable agreement rates should be around 80% for high-stakes situations, but in reality it is unusual to achieve such high levels. Brown et al. (2004), for example, reviewed a number of studies conducted in education and showed that the values usually ranged from 40% to 60%.

Essay	Rater 1	Rater 2
1	4	4
2	5	4
3	3	3
4	4	3
5	2	2
6	6	5
7	1	2
8	4	4
9	5	3
10	3	3

Table 2.2: Agreement data

The percentage exact agreement index is one of the most frequently used rater agreement indices, in language assessment and in educational assessment more broadly (Engelhard, 2013; Wind & Peterson, 2018). This is most likely due to a number of advantages of this index. For example, it is easy to calculate as it does not require any specific software package or statistical knowledge and it is also easy to explain to different stakeholder groups (Stemler & Tsai, 2008). A further advantage may be that a quick examination of a cross-tabulation of agreement statistics between raters may uncover those who are having problems applying the rating criteria. There are however, also a number of disadvantages of the percentage exact agreement statistic. First, the index may mask regularity in ratings as disagreement is viewed as random, unsystematic bias (Engelhard, 2013). For example, a pair of raters may never agree but nevertheless rate very similarly; one rater may always score performances one score point higher than the first rater, making the first rater more harsh. This type of variation is not identified by the percentage exact agreement index and therefore solely relying on agreement statistics does not reveal the full picture of rater behaviour. A further disadvantage is that this statistic needs to be calculated separately for each pair of judges, for each rating scale criterion and for performances on each task, and requires pairs of raters to be relatively neatly matched in their ratings. And, as Linacre (2002) points out, training raters to a point of forced agreement may lead to them consulting during rating sessions and may therefore reduce their statistical independence and threaten the validity of the scores they are providing. Consensus estimates such as the percentage exact agreement can also be inflated if the raters are required to use a very short scale. Finally, it does not show how far the raters are deviating from each other if they are not agreeing. For this reason, some practitioners and researchers prefer the percentage adjacent agreement statistic which we describe next.

The ***percentage adjacent agreement*** is designed to deal with the problem that it is very difficult to arrive at sufficiently high exact agreement results. It is defined as the percentage of times raters agree to within one unit on the score given to a performance (Penny et al., 2000; Stemler & Tsai, 2008). This means that judges are not required to come to exact agreement, so long as they do not differ by more than one point above or below the other judge or the expert ratings. As was the case with the percentage exact agreement, this index can also be calculated in relation to agreed ratings (as the percentage adjacent agreement with expert ratings for one rater or averaged for a group of raters) or as the percentage adjacent agreement for pairs of raters and then averaged for a group of raters. Reviewing the sample rating data presented in Table 2.2, the two raters would exhibit an adjacent agreement of 90%.

This index takes account of the fact that although raters do not always agree, they are often very close in their ratings, and this sort of behaviour should be taken into account. Ideally, however, this statistic works best if the scores of the two raters are distributed across score points on the scale and the disagreement is relatively randomly distributed, that is, one rater is not consistently rating lower than the other, as the statistic would then mask the regularity in the ratings. One major disadvantage of the percentage of adjacent agreement is that raters may start rating with a central tendency effect, that is, avoiding the outer scale band levels in fear of not reaching agreement. This is because it is much less likely that adjacent agreement is reached, for example, on a five-point scale, if raters avoid awarding 5s and 1s.

When using the adjacent agreement index, agreement values between 80% to 100% are commonly found in research studies (Brown et al., 2004).

Cohen's kappa and variations

Cohen's kappa index (Cohen, 1960) is used when we want to correct for agreement happening purely by chance. It is designed to estimate the degree of agreement between two raters (or a rater and an expert rating) and to determine whether the level of agreement is purely by chance (e.g., Brown et al., 2004; Stemler & Tsai, 2008), with values greater than .60 indicating substantial agreement not by chance. For a practical example of the calculation of Cohen's kappa, refer to Stemler (2001). A variation of the kappa index, the weighted version of kappa (Cohen, 1968) applies a linear weighting scheme, that is successively less weight is assigned to disagreement when scores are further apart (Eckes, 2011). The interpretation of the kappa index and its variations is as follows. It has a maximum possible value of 1 when agreement is perfect, a value of 0 that indicates no agreement higher than by chance and negative values that show agreement less than chance (e.g., Mun, 2005). While correcting for change agreement is advantageous, there are also some disadvantages with the kappa index. For example, as is the case with the other agreement indices, it can only be calculated for one rater pair at a time. Additionally, Uebersax (2002) argued that the interpretation of kappa is not always straightforward and that this makes it difficult to compare kappa values across different contexts. There are also several other variations of Cohen's kappa available (see, e.g., Agresti, 1996; Krippendorff, 2004). Krippendorff's alpha, for example, is able to deal with groups of raters and missing data. While some of these indices are difficult to calculate by hand, statistical packages are freely available or available at low costs to help with the calculation.

Percentage agreement with mode

The percentage agreement with mode is a consensus measure designed to deal with contexts in which no expert (agreed) ratings are available. It is calculated by counting the number of ratings which agree with the most frequently awarded score point by a group of raters and then dividing by the total number of ratings. This index was used by Harsch & Martin (2012) after being developed by Martin (2012) and is most useful if a group of raters rate the same performances, as is sometimes the case in research studies or in rater training contexts. The advantage of this index is that it does not require expert ratings to be available as it assumes that the most frequently awarded score point represents the 'best' rating. It therefore does not provide much indication of how well the raters are applying the scale as the construct of the test, but how well they are agreeing with each other. We feel that this measure is useful for certain contexts but requires more research to understand how it compares to other, more established rating quality indices. It is, however, less likely to be useful for operational rating contexts and probably more useful for research studies or rater monitoring or certification purposes.

D² (distance accuracy)

D^2 is an agreement index, that is, it can only be used if agreed ratings are available as comparison. It is defined as the mean square difference between the observed and benchmark ratings and averaged across test takers and rating scale criteria (Cronbach, 1955; Engelhard, 2013). We have not found any studies in language assessment contexts that have made use of this measure, but it has been used more broadly in studies on educational assessment. The index has the advantage that it provides an indication of how far the ratings deviate from the agreed score, but because the differences are squared, there is no indication of directionality, that is, if raters are awarding scores that are higher or lower than the benchmark rating. For this reason, particular rater effects are masked by this index.

Consistency measures in the observed rating tradition

The measures we have described above are all devised to report on agreement between raters. But as already noted, they do not provide any sense of regularity in the ratings if raters disagree. That is, the raters could be ranking the participants in exactly the same way, but never achieve agreement or even adjacent agreement. For this reason, it is also worthwhile calculating consistency measures if the observed rating tradition is followed. Consistency measures are based on the assumption that it is not necessary for raters to score performances identically, as long as they are classifying the performances in the same way (Stemler & Tsai 2008). Below, we present some of these measures of consistency.

Correlation coefficients (Pearson, Spearman, Kendall's tau-b)

Correlation coefficients indicate to what extent raters are ranking the test takers in the same manner. The **Pearson** correlation coefficient (also referred to as the product-moment correlation) examines the degree of linear relationship between the ratings of two judges or the ratings of a judge and the expert (e.g., Eckes, 2011). This is the most common index of inter-rater reliability (Stemler, 2007). The statistic is designed to show relationships between continuous, normally distributed variables. However, rating data based on scoring rubrics is usually based on ordinal data, which is rarely normally distributed. For this reason, there is concern that the results overestimate inter-rater reliability. Therefore, the **Spearman rank-order** correlation is more suitable as this is designed to be used with ordinal data (e.g., Penny et al., 2000; Stemler & Tsai, 2008).

Instead of using the observed scores, the Spearman rank-order coefficient is based on the ranks of the observed scores. Therefore, it is an indication of the monotonic relationship between two ordinal variables (Morgan, Zhu, Johnson & Hodge, 2014). However, the Spearman correlation does not adjust for tied ranks. For this reason, it may be better to use ***Kendall's tau-b*** in cases where many tied ranks are found (as is common in rating data). All correlation indices described above can range from −1 to 1, with higher positive values indicating a stronger correspondence (Eckes, 2011). Commonly found values for both Pearson and Spearman rank-order correlations are between .7 and .8 (Brown et al., 2004).

Returning to our simple sample dataset in Table 2.2 above, we calculated the three correlational indices as shown in Table 2.3.

Pearson	Spearman	Kendall's tau-b
.854	.813	.748

Table 2.3: Correlation indices

There are a number of advantages and disadvantages of using correlation coefficients. They have the advantage of avoiding the focus on exact agreement, as they allow for less stringent demands on the judges. A further advantage is that the correlation coefficients can easily be calculated as numerous free software packages (e.g., Excel) include this function. However, there are also a number of disadvantages. Rating scales are usually designed to represent the test construct and as such are designed to have an objective meaning at each score point. It is therefore desirable for raters to agree. In the case of short rating scales, with few band levels, consistency estimates are deflated due to limited variability. For this reason, it is recommended not to rely on consistency variables alone. It is also important for test administrators to further scrutinise the ratings of two raters, as pairs of raters may display high levels of consistency but not agree. This is usually the case if one of the raters is rating more leniently or harshly than the other, which may require adjustment of the scores. Finally, as correlation coefficients are limited to comparing two variables at a time, for example, the ratings of two raters on one criterion, a number of calculations may be necessary to arrive at a reliability score for a team of raters. The indices also require both raters to rate all cases, which is not always practical in real testing situations. Later in this chapter, we discuss alternative measures of consistency which can be used when more than two raters are involved.

Borman's DA (differential accuracy)

Borman's (1977) differential accuracy is calculated 'by correlating a rater's rating for each dimension with corresponding true scores across ratees, yielding a DA score for each dimension' (Sulsky & Balzer, 1988: 499). The overall DA score is computed by averaging the correlations using Fisher's r to z transformation. This measure only provides correlational information about the accuracy of the ratings and no information about the distance of the ratings to the expert ratings and is therefore also limited in the type of information it provides, in the same way as the correlation coefficients described above.

Cronbach's alpha

Cronbach's alpha (Crocker & Algina, 1986) examines whether there is a noticeable pattern of similarity in ranking of performances across a group of raters, rather than just examining the scores of two raters. If the Cronbach's alpha estimate is low, then this means that the majority of the variance in the ratings is due to error variance rather than true score variance (Crocker & Algina, 1986). While Cronbach's alpha is able to handle data from more than two raters, its major drawback is that all raters need to provide a rating for each case. If one of the raters does not provide ratings for an individual, that test taker will be excluded from the analysis. This may be problematic in many testing contexts as well as in research projects.

Intra-class correlation

The intra-class correlation coefficient is a further popular statistic used to estimate inter-rater reliability (Stemler & Tsai, 2008). This statistic is sensitive to two ways in which raters differ, consensus and consistency. For this reason, intra-class correlation coefficients will be low if either or both of these situations are problematic. The advantage is that this coefficient is sensitive to both these aspects and therefore provides test administrators with feedback. The disadvantage is that it is not immediately apparent which of these two areas is problematic and this makes it more difficult to provide feedback to raters. Furthermore, as Stemler & Tsai (2008) note, a disadvantage is that the intra-class correlation coefficient is sensitive to variance in the population of test takers, with results being lower if populations with less variance are rated. The final disadvantage is that the computation of this index is not straightforward and therefore a special software package is recommended.

Generalisability theory

Generalisability theory (or G-theory) (Cronbach, Gleser, Nanda & Rajaratnam, 1972) apportions variance in rater scores to tasks, raters and error as well as to interaction components and therefore provides an indicator of the amount of similarity in the raters' scores (Shavelson & Webb, 1991). This method is relatively commonly used in language assessment contexts (e.g., Huang, 2008, 2012; Lee & Kantor, 2007; Schoonen, 2005). It is a powerful technique as it takes into account the different sources of variation that can have an effect on test scores (Huang, 2008). The phi coefficient of dependability from G-theory is a special case of the intra-class correlation coefficient described above and can be used as an index of inter-rater dependability (Cherry & Meyer, 1993; Penny et al., 2000). This index is computed by specialised software packages (e.g., GENOVA developed by Crick & Brennan, 1983) from ratios of apportioned variances in the dataset and provides an estimation of the degree to which a score represents a 'true' score taking into account the effect of all judges' severity, their internal consistency and any interaction of task, rater and error. Technically, G-theory uses analysis of variance (ANOVA) to decompose the variance in the scores into the different sources, their interaction terms and the error terms.

G-theory includes two stages: (a) generalisability studies and (b) decision studies. G-studies are used to evaluate the relative importance of various sources of measurement error and changes in the measurement design. It is, for example, possible to explore what impact more raters would have on the dependability of the ratings. Decision studies allow the interpretation of score accuracy (Brennan, 2001). Generalisability coefficients range from 0 to 1, where a higher value indicates more reliability. Brown et al. (2004) note that coefficient values exceeding .80 are accepted as robust indication that judges are rating a common construct.

Factor analysis

According to Stemler & Tsai (2008), factor analysis is another technique that can be used to examine inter-rater reliability. In this method, a common factor analysis is applied to the ratings of a group of raters that have previously all rated a set of participants. Rater agreement is indicated in the shared variance and this should ideally be loading onto a single factor. The shared variance found in the first factor provides an indication of the extent to which raters' scores share a common construct. The loading of each rater on the first factor can be used to understand each rater's performance.

The disadvantage of this technique is that no information about individual rating behaviour is provided. While the summary score for each rater is useful, it does not provide any detailed diagnostic information about rating behaviour that can be used as feedback to the raters or to make decisions about rater employment. We were not able to find any studies in the language assessment literature that made use of factor analysis in this way, although Wind & Peterson (2018) found seven studies that made use of either factor analysis or structural equation modelling for the purpose of examining rating quality.

The scaled rating tradition

The second major tradition in Engelhard's (2013) framework for classifying measurement theories is the scaling tradition, later called the scaled rating tradition by Wind & Peterson (2018) in their review of the literature. In this tradition, rater quality is evaluated alongside student ability as well as other aspects (e.g., task difficulty) and these qualities are mapped onto an equal interval scale. Wind & Peterson (2018: 5) list a number of methods used in this tradition, including Rasch measurement theory, item response theory, nonparametric item response theory, multidimensional item response theory and others. For the purpose of this chapter, we will describe the use of Rasch measurement in this tradition, as this is one of the most frequently used methods in language assessment practice and research (McNamara & Knoch, 2012; McNamara et al., 2019; Wind & Peterson, 2018). Below we describe the use of many-facet Rasch measurement when no expert ratings are available as well as when agreed ratings are available.

Many-facet Rasch measurement – if no expert ratings are available for comparison

When used in the context of rater-scored assessments, Rasch models are a class of measurement models that make it possible to evaluate the impact that a number of possible variables (or facets) are having on the assessment outcome. While traditional Rasch models include only two facets (test takers and item difficulty), the many-facet Rasch model is able to model additional facets and it is this model that has been most frequently used to evaluate rater quality in rater-mediated assessments. The most common additional facet added is rater, but other facets can also be included, for example task, scoring criteria, interviewer or test method. Many-facet Rasch measurement (MFRM) is not only able to model the impact raters have on the scores reported to students but also can go one step further and provide 'fair' scores, which adjust for raters that are too lenient or too harsh or other facets that introduce difficulty into the assessment situation (e.g., tasks).

MFRM uses a probabilistic model to examine the probability of each score point in a dataset in light of the data as a whole. For example, it examines each rating produced by each rater in light of ratings by the other raters and is then able to produce an account of each facet in the analysis and how these facets relate to each other. Using a probabilistic model it provides us with an account of how probable the data it encounters is. Let us look at an example dataset to illustrate how many-facet Rasch measurement can be used to examine rater quality.

Our example dataset stems from a writing test which was taken by 45 test takers. Each candidate was double-rated by two raters (totally six raters were involved in the rating) on a six-point scale on three criteria: content, form and organisation. We used the computer program FACETS (Linacre, 2016) to conduct the analysis, but other software packages are also available.

Figure 2.1 shows the Wright map, one of the key pieces of output produced in a Rasch analysis and a helpful diagnosis when examining rater quality. In the left-hand column of the Wright map is the logit scale, which is an equal-interval 'ruler' with a mid-point at zero logits. The next column shows the candidates, plotted on the logit scale according to their ability. High-ability candidates are plotted higher up, lower-ability candidates are plotted lower down. The next column depicts the six raters. These are shown on the logit scale in terms of their severity. More severe raters are plotted higher up, more lenient raters lower down. The raters are centred around the zero logit point. We can see from this plot that the raters seem to differ substantially in terms of their severity, with Rater 1 being the harshest and Rater 4 the most lenient. The next column shows the three rating criteria. We can see that it was easier to receive a certain score point on content than it was on organisation and form. The final column shows the rating scale band levels. It can be seen that the raters did not use the whole range of the six-point rating scale, possibly reflecting the ability of the test takers.

```
+----------------------------------------------------------+
|Measr|+Candidate|-Rater|-Criterion                |Scale|
|-----+----------+------+--------------------------+-----|
|  5 +          +      +                           +  (6) |
|    |    *     |      |                           |     |
|    |          |      |                           |     |
|    |    *     |      |                           |     |
|    |          |      |                           |     |
|    |          |      |                           |     |
|    |          |      |                           |     |
|    |   ***    |      |                           |     |
|  4 +          +      +                           +     |
|    |          |      |                           |     |
|    |          |      |                           |     |
|    |   ****   |      |                           | --- |
|    |          |      |                           |     |
|    |          |      |                           |     |
|    |          |      |                           |     |
|    |          |      |                           |     |
|  3 +  *       +      +                           +     |
|    |          |      |                           |     |
|    |          |      |                           |     |
|    |          |      |                           |     |
|    |   **     |      |                           |     |
|    |   *      |      |                           |     |
|    |          |      |                           |     |
|  2 +          +      +                           +     |
|    |   ****   |      |                           |  5  |
|    |          |      |                           |     |
|    |   *      |      |                           |     |
|    |          |      |                           |     |
|    |   *      |      |                           |     |
|  1 +          + 1    +                           +     |
|    |          |      |                           |     |
|    | *******  |      |                           |     |
|    |          |      |                           |     |
|    | *****    | 3  6 | Form        Organisation  |     |
|    | *        |      |                           |     |
*  0 *  *       *      *                           * --- *
|    |          | 5    |                           |     |
|    |   ***    |      |                           |     |
|    |          | 2    |                           |     |
|    |   **     |      | Content                   |     |
|    |          |      |                           |     |
|    |   **     |      |                           |     |
| -1 +          + 4    +                           +     |
|    |  *       |      |                           |     |
|    |          |      |                           |     |
|    |  *       |      |                           |     |
|    |          |      |                           |     |
|    |  ***     |      |                           |  4  |
|    |          |      |                           |     |
| -2 +          +      +                           +  (3) |
|-----+----------+------+--------------------------+-----|
|Measr| * = 1    |-Rater|-Criterion                |Scale|
+----------------------------------------------------------+
```

Figure 2.1: Wright map

An MFRM analysis also produced detailed statistics about the raters and these are summarised in the rater measurement report which we have partially reproduced in Table 2.4. The 'Measure' column provides us with the raters' exact locations on the logit scale. We can see that the harshest rater is located about one logit above the zero point and the most lenient about one logit below the zero point. This sort of picture is relatively normal in real rating situations, but it does show that the raters are not rating interchangeably in terms of leniency and harshness. Infit and outfit statistics provide us with information about the variability in the ratings of the individual raters, and this is where we can search for evidence of raters that are rating inconsistently (i.e., with more variation than is expected by the Rasch model) or overly consistently (i.e., with less variation than is expected by the Rasch model). Infit statistics provide information about the more typical observations (once outliers are deleted), while outfit statistics include outlying observations. Mean square fit statistics have an expected value of 1. Raters rating with more variation have higher values and raters rating with less variation have lower values than 1. So what range of mean square values would be acceptable? McNamara (1996) proposed that raters falling between .7 and 1.3 are rating with appropriate variation. In our dataset, we have one rater identified with more variation than that in both infit and outfit mean square statistics, Rater 1. This rater is therefore 'misfitting'. This means that this rater is rating inconsistently. We can also see that this rater's observed exact agreement with other raters is much lower than what the programme would expect. There are also two raters, Raters 3 and 4, identified as rating with too little variation. To understand what rating patterns these two raters are displaying, it is necessary to return to the raw data and to scrutinise this more closely. In the case of Rater 4, we can see that this rater is displaying a halo effect. Almost all the ratings this rater provided are identical across the three scoring criteria. For example, the rater scored candidates as 4, 4, 4 or 5, 5, 5. Rater 3 on the other hand, has a different profile. This rater displayed some more variation in the ratings, but did not use the extreme categories of the rating scale, awarding only 4s and 5s, therefore displaying a restriction of range in the ratings. Neither of these two raters is degrading the measurement, but they are not providing all the possible information about the test takers and this results in less diagnostic information being available.

Rater	Measure	Infit mean square	Outfit mean square	Exact agreement observed %	Exact agreement expected %
1	.97	1.68	1.70	25.8	49.3
2	−.36	.76	.77	41.0	48.6
3	.31	.65	.64	55.6	48.6
4	−.98	.49	.48	52.8	48.0
5	−.16	.71	.71	60.6	52.1
6	.22	1.08	1.14	37.3	50.8

Table 2.4: Rater statistics

MFRM provides a myriad of other information about rater behaviour as part of an analysis. Apart from the information about rater leniency and harshness, inconsistency, halo and central tendency effect described here, the programme is also able to give information about rater biases (i.e., particular interaction patterns of raters with aspects of the rating situations, e.g., scoring criteria, tasks, students' background profiles, etc.) and raters' use of the scoring criteria. Detailed descriptions of these are beyond the scope of this chapter; we refer interested readers to a number of publications which have dealt with this, for example, Myford & Wolfe (2003, 2004), Eckes (2011), McNamara (1996) and McNamara et al., (2019).

MFRM is increasingly used to examine rater-mediated assessments and rater functioning. Its use has been increasing steadily in language assessment (see McNamara & Knoch, 2012; McNamara et al., 2019) and it was the only method we uncovered in our review of the literature that was able to identify all the rater effects we described in Chapter 1. However, it is also not without its drawbacks. To arrive at stable estimates of rater functioning, MFRM requires a certain minimum sample size and some expertise on the part of the data analyst. Neither of these is necessarily present in smaller assessment programmes.

Many-facet Rasch measurement accuracy

In the previous section, we demonstrated how MFRM can be used to identify some of the rater effects described in Chapter 1. For the dataset we described above, no benchmark ratings were available to which we could compare the raters' ratings and we therefore analysed the data without a comparison data set of expert or agreed ratings. Engelhard (1996; 2013) described a method in which MFRM can be used to examine rating accuracy. First an accuracy score is assigned to each rating. An accuracy score of zero is assigned when there is a difference between the rating assigned by a rater and the benchmark score. An accuracy score of one shows a perfect match with the benchmark rating. Using this dichotomous scoring system, MFRM can then be used to model 'rater accuracy' as a latent variable. Such an analysis is able to identify raters with high accuracy values, provide information about which benchmark performances are difficult to score, and which rating scale criteria are hard to score accurately. If the accuracy model was used, the Wright map would be slightly different to interpret, as depicted below (see Figure 2.2).

Logit scale	Rater accuracy	Benchmark performance	Scoring criteria accuracy
	High accuracy	Hard to be accurate	Hard to be accurate
4			
3			
2			
1			
0			
−1			
−2			
−3			
−4			
	Low accuracy	Easy to be accurate	Easy to be accurate

Figure 2.2 Wright map for rater accuracy

Engelhard's method of examining rater accuracy is limited due to the coding of the accuracy data. As all inaccurately scored ratings are coded as zero, information about the directionality and size of the difference is lost. Wang, Engelhard & Wolfe (2016) therefore expanded Engelhard's coding scheme to code for inaccurate below-expert ratings, accurate ratings and inaccurate above-expert ratings. They used the hyperbolic cosine model to analyse the data. (It is beyond the scope of this chapter to describe this model; we refer interested readers to Wang et al. (2016) for more details.) They were able to show that the model supported this type of analysis but also called for more research comparing different rater accuracy models. This call was taken up by Wolfe et al. (2015). They criticised the previous rater measurement models used as these did not account for distances between rater and agreed ratings. They tested two versions of the rater accuracy model, one with dichotomous data and one with polytomous data. They compared these models to a regular MFRM without expert ratings. Their findings showed that the rater accuracy models were able to 'detect, but not differentiate, rater severity and inaccuracy, but not rater centrality' (2015: 153). A regular MFRM analysis was able to uncover these rater effects but not in relation to accuracy ratings. More research in this area is clearly necessary.

The use of benchmark samples to establish rater accuracy

Establishing rater accuracy relies on the presence of accurate agreed ratings against which markers' accuracy can be compared. However, establishing such agreed scores is not without its problems. In Chapter 1 we discussed how such samples may be chosen to represent a range of performances but how the scores are established is another issue. Sulsky & Balzer (1988) point to considerable variation in the procedures used to obtain true scores. One very common method is to simply average all the scores provided by the raters but this method is far from ideal because it does not take into account the variation between the scores. Using the mode of the existing ratings as the most representative scores is a further method. Another method is to use expert raters (although the definition of an 'expert' rater is not standard in the literature). Obtaining benchmark scores from this group has varied. One method is to obtain consensus among experts (McIntyre, Smith & Hassett, 1984) but, as Sulsky & Balzer point out, this also does not show how large the disagreements between the experts were before consensus. Other more involved methods have been also been described (e.g., Borman, 1977), but as with all rater-mediated assessment, even the expert raters tend to disagree and it is important to keep the disagreement at a minimum. The validity of these ratings, however, forms an important basis on which rater accuracy is calculated and it is therefore important to review the procedures used.

Uncovering rater effects

Following the review of rater quality indices in this chapter, we would now like to return to the rater effects we described in Chapter 1 and comment on the ability of the indices to uncover these rater effects. Table 2.5 provides a summary of how well the different rater quality measures reviewed in this chapter are able to uncover the different rater effects. The table shows that only many-facet Rasch measurement is able to detect all the different rater effects we described in Chapter 1 (although two of the effects, halo and central tendency, require further scrutiny of the raw data). Most other measures are limited to one or two rater effects and many of these require further investigation.

	Rater effects					
Measure	**Leniency & Harshness**	**Consistency**	**Halo**	**Central tendency or restriction of range**	**Bias**	**Use of scoring criteria**
Percentage of exact and adjacent agreement, Cohen's kappa, percentage of agreement with mode, D^2	✓ (only with extensive further investigation)	✓ (only with extensive further investigation)	✗	✗	✗	✗
Correlational indices: Pearson, Spearman, Kendall tau-b	✓	✓	✗	✗	✗	✗
Cronbach's alpha & intra-class correlation	✓	✓ (at group level)	✗	✗	✗	✗
Factor analysis	✓	✓ (at group level with additional index for each rater from factor loading)	✗	✗	✗	✗
Generalisability theory	Only at rater group level	Only at rater group level	✗	✗	Only at group level	✗
Many-facet Rasch measurement	✓	✓	✓ (with further investigation)	✓ (with further investigation)	✓	✓
Many-facet Rasch measurement accuracy	✓ (detect but not differentiate)	✓ (detect but not differentiate)	✗	✗	✗	✗

Table 2.5: Rater quality measures – ability to detect rater effects

Using rater quality measures in the assessment cycle

In this chapter, we have presented a range of measures used to establish rater quality. We have divided these measures into two groups: those that can be used to establish rater quality in relation to agreed (or benchmark) ratings and those that are used if such ratings are not available. Here, we would like to briefly discuss how assessment administrators could make use of these two types of measures in the assessment cycle. We have identified three or potentially four instances in the assessment cycle where these rater quality measures may be used: (a) during rater training, (b) during certification following rater training, (c) during ongoing monitoring and (d) during re-training.

First of all, during rater training, raters may be asked to self-monitor their rating patterns using the percentage agreement statistic (with an additional cross-classification of rating patterns) to see whether they are rating too leniently or harshly. We do not believe that this is common practice in rater training sessions, but it may be valuable to raters while they are learning to understand the construct they are asked to assess and calibrate their own ratings to those of senior raters.

Following rater training, assessment managers or rater trainers would use an index which compares raters' ratings with agreed ratings to ensure that the raters are rating to the standard expected of an assessment system. As far as we know, relatively crude agreement indices are commonly used here and we would like to argue that more information about rater behaviour may be useful at this point to identify raters, for example, with very muted rating patterns. Conducting an additional analysis of MFRM on the new raters' data may be revealing of some of these rating patterns.

Once raters have been certified, it is crucial to conduct ongoing monitoring, in particular if raters are involved in high-stakes decisions. Here, we are aware of a variety of approaches to monitoring the quality of ratings (these will be further described in Chapter 4). There are two distinct approaches: one which regularly reviews rater behaviour following operational rating without comparing the ratings to expert ratings, and one in which control items are inserted into the ratings, which are previously rated by expert or senior raters. The former approach therefore requires measures which do not compare raters against expert ratings. In the latter approach to rater monitoring, decisions about rater behaviour (and possible exclusion from rating) are often done at the script level without too much attention given to the difficulty of different benchmark scripts.

As was shown in Engelhard's rater accuracy model, some benchmark performances are more difficult for raters to agree with. This information is rarely used by large-scale assessment companies making use of the latter system for accuracy monitoring. We feel that there is certainly room for the use of Engelhard's model to ensure that raters are not unfairly excluded from rating.

Finally, raters are usually regularly re-trained or re-standardised if an ongoing system of rater feedback or quality control is available. During these sessions, raters are also required to rate in line with agreed ratings provided by senior raters, and these are then usually compared using one of the accuracy measures presented in this chapter.

Conclusion

In this chapter, we have introduced a variety of measures that have been used to measure variability in ratings, both through the accuracy approach (which compares ratings to 'true' or expert ratings) and through the examination of rater variability by drawing on a dataset without expert ratings. We have shown that some of these measures or statistical techniques are more powerful and useful in identifying the rater effects we introduced in Chapter 1 and have concluded that different techniques may be more suitable in different situations in the assessment cycle.

There is however, often the assumption that if raters agree to a sufficiently high level, then they rate to the same construct. It is important to note, at this point, that this is not necessarily the case. A focus purely on the scores may not provide us with the full picture. For this, more qualitative techniques are required and we will look at the cognitive processes of raters in more detail in Chapter 3.

CHAPTER 3

RATER COGNITION

Introduction

In previous chapters, we reported that quantitative studies have found variability between raters and that some of that variability may be explained by a range of factors, such as rater background, experience, their familiarity with the background of the students or the rating scale used. We also showed that raters may attach varying levels of importance to different rating criteria. However, researchers working on these quantitative studies were able to show that not all variance can be accounted for and that individual rater variation may be attributable to the cognitive processes of individual raters. Mixed methods studies have also shown that despite agreeing on scores, raters may at times not agree on the underlying features in the performances to arrive at these scores (Douglas & Selinker, 1992). This may be due to the fact that rating scale descriptors are often brief and superficial (Cumming, Kantor, Powers, Santos & Taylor, 2000) and therefore require a level of interpretation by raters which may result in conflicting views of proficiency (Brown, Iwashita & McNamara, 2005). One way to gain a deeper understanding of rater decision-making is by conducting studies into rater cognition. Rater cognition refers to the mental processes raters engage when assigning scores to language performances (e.g., Cai, 2015). These processes may occur either at the conscious or unconscious level (Davis, 2012; Han, 2016). Raters may engage both cognitive and meta-cognitive strategies when rating (Purpura, 2012; Zhang, 2016) which can be linked to models of information-processing (Freedman & Calfee, 1983; Purpura, 2012).

Since the early 1990s, studies investigating raters' decision-making processes have become more frequent. These studies set out with a number of different goals and aims in mind. For example, some studies have been conducted with the aim of informing test development and validation, in particular the validation of scoring criteria. Others have set out to understand the criteria raters focus on and how these are weighted by raters. Several studies have examined the decision-making processes by raters, describing rating approaches and coming up with an overall model of the rating process. A further group of studies has examined areas of difficulties such as when raters cannot fit a performance into the descriptions on the rating scale, what happens when they encounter difficult-to-mark performances or what sort of construct-irrelevant features of the performance the rater may focus on when rating. Finally, a handful of studies have also set out to compare rating behaviour across two different types of rating scales or across two groups of raters, for example, experienced and inexperienced raters or accurate and inaccurate raters. The studies in this last group have attempted to link rater cognition to rater quality. They have implications for rating scale validation and revision, for rater selection, training and monitoring and for furthering our understanding of construct-irrelevant variation as larger test validation efforts. In this chapter, we will describe these studies in more detail and discuss the theoretical underpinnings of a handful of them. We will begin this chapter by discussing a number of methodological considerations in rater cognition studies.

Methodological considerations in rater cognition studies

A variety of qualitative methodologies have been used to gain a deeper insight into rater decision-making processes, with some studies also drawing on more than one approach. The most common methodology chosen is that of verbal protocols, both concurrent and retrospective, but other methods that have been used are focus group interviews, individual interviews, retrospective written reports, questionnaires and more recently eye-tracking methodology. Due to the frequency of verbal protocols in this type of research, we would like to briefly discuss some of the main methodological decisions, advantages and drawbacks of these. We will also briefly discuss eye-tracking as we anticipate that this methodology is becoming more frequent in our field. Because the use of the remaining methods has been so infrequent, we refer interested readers to more general publications on the use of these methods (e.g., Gass & Mackey, 2000).

Verbal protocols

A large number of studies have made use of verbal protocols in investigations of rater decision-making (e.g., Brown, 2000; Cumming, 1990; Cumming, Kantor & Powers, 2001, 2002; DeRemer, 1998; Erdosy, 2003; Lumley, 2002; Milanovic, Saville & Shen, 1996; Sakyi, 2000; Smith,

2000; Vaughan, 1991; Weigle, 1994, 1998; Wolfe, 1997). **Concurrent verbal protocols**, where a rater speaks out loud at the same time as completing the rating task, have been most widely used in the rating of written performances. The protocols provide 'real time' access to the raters' thoughts but some researchers have argued that they should not be used in situations where the primary task places a high cognitive load on the participant (Seamster, Redding & Kaempf, 2000) which it could be argued is the case for rating language performances.

Another possible method is the use of **retrospective verbal protocols**, or stimulated verbal recalls (Brown, 2000). These are particularly suited if the researcher wants to probe the reasons for doing particular actions. However, the methodology relies on participants remembering or being able to retrieve their original thought-processes. The advantage of retrospective verbal protocols is that they do not interfere with the rating process. This is particularly helpful for the rating of oral performances where raters would not be able to verbalise their thoughts without continuously stopping and starting the recording they are rating and therefore interrupting the listening and rating process. However, because of the delay in verbalisation, the drawback of retrospective protocols is that they rely on raters' working memory and it is quite possible that a number of the details in raters' thoughts will be lost because of the delay, in particular if the verbal protocols are not produced immediately after rating a performance. Green (1998) proposes two possibilities – raters may 'tidy up their thought processes' or they might say what they think the researcher wants to hear. Raters may, for example, claim that they are conforming to the rating scales, when in fact, they are not. Brown (2000), in a study which collected retrospective verbal protocols from IELTS speaking raters, describes how the raters were specifically advised not to say what is expected. Raters were told that they were the experts and that conforming to the scales was downplayed. Nevertheless, retrospective verbal protocols may provide less access to the rating process and may result in more data on what aspects of the performance the raters paid attention to (Brown et al., 2005). Other drawbacks relate to the time-consuming nature of transcription and analysis of verbal report data and the risk that the researcher may introduce subjectivity during the coding and analysis process.

Despite some of the drawbacks of the two variations of verbal protocols described above, their validity and reliability has been tested in a number of studies (e.g., Barkaoui, 2011b; Gass & Mackey, 2000) and they are therefore accepted as viable data collection methodologies which provide 'an avenue through which to gain insights into an individual's thought and decision-making processes which is not possible to obtain through other research tools' (May, 2006: 30) It is important to remember, however, that it may provide a slightly limited picture into the raters' thoughts. Lumley (2002), for example, cautioned that just because a particular feature on the scale or in a test-taker performance has not been mentioned by a rater, does not mean the rater did not consider it in their rating. This relates directly to one of the two main concerns that have been voiced about verbal protocols, especially regarding *veridicality*, that is, whether the participants' verbal reports are true and complete. The other concerns relates to *reactivity*, that is, whether the reporting process may alter in the process of being observed.

Regardless of the verbal protocol methodology chosen, raters need to be trained to verbalise their thought-processes. Detailed training procedures are presented in Ericsson & Simon (1993) and Barkaoui (2011b). Typically, raters are presented with some background information about verbal protocols, including information about why they are used. Raters may be presented with some modelling and then usually practise the procedure and receive some feedback before they conduct the think-aloud protocols for the study.

Eye-tracking

As an alternative to verbal protocols, eye-tracking can provide data on raters' cognitive processes which may not be accessed by thinking aloud. It provides information about raters' focal attention and the amount of time they fixate on something. Eye-tracking is a commonly used methodology in psychology and cognitive science and has recently become increasingly popular in research on language assessment. The rationale behind eye-tracking is that there is a direct link between eye-movement and the human mind (e.g., Pollatsek, Reichle & Rayner, 2006). Winke & Lim (2015) conducted a study in which they examined what aspects in the rating scale raters focused on when rating written essays. Fixation indicated cognitive processing as raters read and re-read the wording in the criteria in relation to the particular essay being read. They posited that the reading of the rating scale in the study is directly related to the scoring process, not the internalisation of the rating scale, on which the raters have already been thoroughly trained. Longer fixations may pinpoint scoring points with which a rater may struggle or they may signal greater care taken in the rating process. In particular, the researchers examined: (1) time to first fixation on the scoring rubric, (2) total fixation duration (the sum of all eye fixations on an area of interest) and (3) visit counts, which measure the number of eye visits to an area of interest. For a subset of the raters, they also created heatmaps (a visual summary of the rater's eye movements across a single use of the rubric) and gaze plots (sequence and position of eye fixations on the rubric). When using this methodology, the authors were able to show that raters used the analytic rating scale in the sequence of the scale categories, that raters paid very little attention to mechanics and that the amount of time spent looking at an aspect on the scale resulted in an increase in inter-rater reliability. We feel that this methodology has potential to provide interesting insights into raters' mental processes in future studies.

There are, however, also some drawbacks associated with using eye-tracking. First, the equipment is costly to purchase and maintain. Raters might be conscious of having their eye movements tracked and this may contaminate the data. Eye-tracking is also less useful for scoring speaking performances. Finally, eye-tracking data are also not easy to analyse.

Rater decision-making

Studies examining the decision-making of raters of second or foreign language performances have had different foci over the years. One group of studies has described what elements of the performance raters focus on and how these elements have been weighted. Others have set out to describe the overall rating approach or the general decision-making behaviours by raters. In this section, we summarise the key studies we identified in this area.

Focus of rating

Several studies have examined the elements that raters focus on when rating. The majority of these studies were conducted on the assessment of writing, although some studies also focused on speaking. Research on the elements that raters focus on is helpful in rating scale development if the raters are asked to verbalise such features without a scale or in the context of test validation when an existing scale is in place. In the latter case, the data can be used for scale revision and to identify construct-irrelevant aspects in the raters' thought processes or to gain an understanding of the weighting of these features in raters' minds.

Milanovic et al. (1996) employed various methods to access the complexity of raters' cognitive processes, including group interviews, retrospective written reports on thought processes and verbal reports. They identified a list of eleven essay elements which raters focused on: length, legibility, grammar, structure, communicative effectiveness, tone, vocabulary, spelling, content, task realisation and punctuation. In a study focusing on the rating of spoken performances, Brown et al. (2005) found that the most commonly mentioned categories included linguistic resources, phonology, fluency and content. Within each of these aspects, raters also commented on a number of specific performance features. And despite agreeing on the aspects to focus on, raters seemed to disagree on the performance levels they assigned. This was in particular the case for certain features of the performances, where for example some raters thought that re-use of vocabulary from the input was a feature of higher-ability test takers while others thought that higher-ability test takers should be able to paraphrase or use other strategies not to re-use the vocabulary. Similar findings were also made by Brown (2000) who found that raters disagreed on the performance level of test takers who made use of self-correction, circumlocution and self-clarification. She also found that different raters privileged different aspects in the performance with some found to be more performance-oriented (that is, focusing on the features of the performance in relation to the scoring criteria) and others more inference-oriented (drawing conclusions about the test taker's ability to cope in contexts beyond the testing situation). Brown (2006), in a study on rater behaviour in the IELTS speaking test, found that raters adhered to the criteria in the rating scale, with more quantifiable aspects such as amount of hesitation, and error density and type more frequently mentioned. Rather than focusing on the elements salient to raters in spoken performances, May (2006, 2009, 2011) and Ducasse (2010) were interested in examining the features of interactional competence that raters noticed in paired speaking tests. May found that the main features salient to raters were non-verbal communication, interactional listening comprehension and interactional management (e.g., topic change and turn organisation).

The majority of studies investigating elements raters focus on when rating identified that raters also focused on criteria not represented in the rating scale. We have already touched on this when reporting on Brown's (2000) finding that some raters drew on making inferences about test-taker behaviour outside of the test domain to reach their scoring decisions and this type of decision-making when rating seems common across contexts. Pollitt & Murray (1996) found that raters take into account candidates' perceived maturity and willingness or reluctance to converse and Meiron (1998) found that raters focused on creativity and humour, both aspects not represented in the scale criteria. Brown (2003a, 2005) also noticed that the raters took note of the performance of the interviewer and even reported compensating for what they felt was inappropriate interviewer behaviour. Similarly, Orr (2002) found that some of the raters in his study focused on a range of non-criterion-related information, such as the way the candidates presented themselves and communicative success and failure. May (2006) found that raters had a tendency for 'fleshing out' the criteria in the rating scale with features that were not explicitly mentioned. She found that as many as 30% of rater comments related to non-criterion-related aspects (these included features such as the first impression of the candidate, the confidence of test takers as well as the complexity and logic of the candidates' ideas). The identification of such features can help test developers with the validation of their tests. The identification of features in the verbal protocols not represented in the scale criteria may lead to revisions of the criteria. In the studies above, several of the features may be deemed construct-relevant (e.g., the complexity and logic of ideas put forward by test takers) while others may be construct-irrelevant (e.g., the humour of test takers) and may be explicitly targeted in rater training activities. Either way, the data show that these sorts of behaviours can only be uncovered through the use of qualitative methods; quantitative studies fall short in this area.

Research on the focus of raters' attention has also examined whether raters weigh any elements of the performance more heavily than others. This is particularly of interest when holistic rating scales are used where raters are required to make judgements about the elements most crucial to a specific performance level and particular aspects in scoring rubric may be more salient to raters. Milanovic et al. (1996) found that the raters in their study varied widely in their weighting of particular elements in the written performances. For example, some raters focused heavily on vocabulary while others did not lend much weight to this aspect. In the context of spoken assessment, Brown (2000) found that the verbal report data showed that the IELTS holistic speaking scale used at the time was problematic for raters as different criteria seemed more salient at different proficiency levels and that different examiners focused on different aspects in the performance, privileging certain aspects over others. In a follow-up study examining the use of the newly introduced analytic rating scales a few years later, Brown (2006) found that the differences in weighting patterns across raters were largely resolved by the new rating scale.

Raters' weighting patterns have also informed studies attempting to establish rater types. Cai (2015), for example, identified three types of raters in the context of an EFL speaking test – form-oriented, balanced and content-oriented raters. Verbal protocols were used to confirm the weighting patterns identified in a quantitative analysis. The author argued that identifying weighting patterns in raters' rating processes is a crucial insight into unbalanced construct-representation where some criteria are given overweight (higher than justified or expected) or underweight (lower than justified or expected) emphasis. Reduced weighting of some criteria can lead to construct under-representation and may be a threat to test validity. Evidence of weighting by raters was also found by Winke & Lim (2015) in their study employing eye-tracking technology. The eye-tracking results quite clearly showed that some raters focused more extensively on some criteria on the scale (e.g., organisation) over others (e.g., mechanics). The researchers were able to link this extra attention to better reliability statistics.

Wolfe, Kao & Ranney (1998) built the scoring focus as a key aspect of their rater cognition model and hypothesised that the scoring focus of raters may in part influence the scoring proficiency of raters. In their empirical study, they were able to show that more proficient raters tended to use top-down approaches to rating focusing on more general performance features while less proficient raters tended to focus on more specific performance features. Eckes (2008) advanced the rater type hypothesis in which he posited that experienced raters fall into various types or classes of raters which differ depending on the weighting they assign to different criteria. He identified a number of groups of raters that assigned more weight to some criteria while others were typified by assigning less weight to certain criteria.

Rater decision-making behaviours

In the previous section, we described aspects of the performance that raters focus on when rating, including implicit criteria not represented in rating scales. A further group of studies has focused on rater decision-making behaviours, which include both the criteria and any strategies used by raters to arrive at their rating decisions. Cumming (1990) and Cumming et al. (2001, 2002) identified 27 decision-making behaviours that emerged from think-aloud data of raters not using a rating scale. They grouped these into three categories of focus: (1) a self-monitoring focus (where readers read and re-read the essay or compared the essay with others), (2) a rhetorical and ideational focus (where raters assessed aspects such as content and organisation) and (3) a language focus (where assessors considered accuracy, lexis, complexity etc.). The authors concluded that scoring criteria should be balanced between the different areas of focus. The work by Cumming and colleagues was different from previous work in the area as it classified rater decision-making strategies into two dimensions – focus and strategy. They identified the three foci described above as well as the two types of strategies (interpretation and judgement strategies). Interpretation strategies are used to make sense of the written text at hand while judgement strategies are used to evaluate the qualities of the text. This model therefore described the raters' decision-making processes in a more detailed manner than previous work.

Lumley (2002), in his study of four raters rating writing samples from an Australian proficiency test, found that although raters generally followed a similar path in rating (reading an essay – assigning a score – reconsidering assigned score), the relationship between the writing sample, the raters' intuitive impressions and the scoring criteria remained obscure and that raters came up with a variety of individual strategies and decision-making behaviours to compensate for this problem. He concluded that rater training may be able to help raters produce more consistent results.

More recently, Baker (2012) tried to get a more detailed understanding of individual differences in rater decision-making by designing and administering the General Decision Making Style Inventory questionnaire (Scott & Bruce, 1995) to six raters. She collected information on (a) how often raters deferred their score decision and (b) whether they underused fail levels. She also collected write-aloud protocols from the raters. The aim of the study was to explore whether individual decision-making styles for each of the raters could be created based on the different data sources and whether there is a relationship between the decision-making behaviours and the scores awarded to the written texts. Through this work, Baker was able to identify some discrepancies between the quantitative data and the qualitative data which were insightful. She was also able to uncover some difficult-to-mark scripts and in this way explain some of the quantitative results. She concluded that more of this rich, qualitative work is needed to expand on the exploratory nature of her study.

Work on the scoring of integrated tasks is less common. In one study, Gebril & Plakans (2014) explored the decision-making behaviours. The authors used the different foci and strategies identified by Cumming et al. (2001, 2002) and applied these to the rating of integrated reading to write tasks. They found that the nature of the tasks required raters to conduct more self-monitoring. They also noticed that raters needed to draw on additional processes when rating, including locating source information, citation mechanics and determining the quality of source use. The third of these findings was particularly an issue in higher-level essays. At lower score levels, raters were more concerned with language-related problems rather than source use.

From rating approaches and styles to models of rating

The work done by Eckes (2008) and Cai (2015) in classifying raters into different types is related to another group of studies that have set out to investigate more than the features in a performance that raters focus on. The aim of these studies was to gain an understanding of the overall process of rating, from reviewing a performance to assigning a score. One seminal study in this area was conducted by Vaughan (1991). Vaughan identified several characteristic rating styles, such as the 'first-impression-dominates style', the 'two-category style' and the 'grammar-oriented style'. She was able to show that raters, despite undergoing the same training, differed in their individual approaches to rating essays. Similarly, Milanovic et al. (1996) identified four marking approaches, namely the two-scan/read, the pragmatic two-scan/read, the read through and the provisional mark approach. Similarly, Smith (2000) grouped six raters' verbal reports into three approaches, two of which were the same as those identified earlier: 'the read-through-once-then-scan', 'the performance criteria-focused' and 'the first-impression dominates' approach. Interestingly, Smith also found that raters falling into 'the first-impression-dominates' approach commented the least on extraneous features compared with the other styles of raters, and those falling into the 'performance criteria-focused' group commented the least on textual features. Wolfe & Ranney (1996) extended this work by examining whether rater proficiency influenced the rating approaches and styles of raters. They found that more proficient raters seemed to read the text without interruption and then evaluated it (interpret-then-evaluate), while less proficient raters seemed to go through an alternating cycle of reading and evaluating portions of the text (interpret-evaluate-interpret-evaluate). They also found less variability in more proficient raters' reading styles. Han (2016) criticised the kind of work that has been done in identifying rater reading styles for a lack of theoretical underpinning from work in information-processing such as similar work done by researchers of examination marking processes (e.g., Suto, Crisp & Greatorex, 2008; Suto & Greatorex, 2008)

Sakyi (2000), based on his research on holistic scoring, built a tentative model of the holistic scoring process. In this model, he posited that content and language figured prominently as two kinds of factors affecting the formation of a general impression of an essay. Other aspects he included in his model were the raters' personal biases and their personal monitoring processes. Wolfe (1997) also advanced a rater cognition model, which he thought comprises two interrelated components. The first component is the framework of scoring which comprises the cognitive processes through which a text image is created, compared to the scoring criteria and used as a basis for decision-making. The second component, which he called the framework for writing, is a mental representation of the scoring criteria in the rating scale. He argued that both these components may differ across raters, as raters may differ in the text image they create in their minds and in the way they view the scoring criteria that describe the writing and how they weigh them (Wolfe, Kao & Ranney, 1998). Finally, Bejar (2012) put forward a comprehensive model of the assessment of constructed responses which draws on existing theories and research findings on human information processing. Despite the work described above on creating a model for rating, there is no such model available representing the cognition of speaking raters (Han, 2016) and, as has been argued by Davis (2012), simply transferring the work done on the assessment of writing is problematic.

Benefits of rater cognition research

As mentioned earlier in this chapter, research on rater cognition has had a number of benefits. Such studies have provided researchers with a detailed window into raters' thought processes while rating and with that it has been possible to uncover aspects of rating which may not have become apparent while drawing on quantitative data alone. In these studies, interesting discrepancies between quantitative and qualitative findings have emerged which make it clear that more in-depth rater cognition research is needed to establish validity. The studies have also shown that cognitive processing may differ when performances at different proficiency levels are rated. Insights into raters' attempts to rate difficult-to-rate performances have provided useful information for rater training. Finally, such studies have also given us helpful information for rating scale validation. All of these areas will be discussed in this section.

Studies on cognitive processes of raters were often able to uncover interesting ***discrepancies between quantitative and qualitative findings*** or confirm and explain quantitative findings. Baker (2012) when examining rater decision-making styles noted in several cases that the fit statistics were in line with the qualitative decision-making styles of the raters but in some cases this was not the case, which is interesting. Orr (2002) was also able to show that despite agreeing on the scores, raters perceived the quality of the performances in the Cambridge First Certificate in English very differently. He argued that misapplication of the rating scale and a focus on non-criterion information can complicate the scoring. And although differences in scores were not perceived, the construct on which these scores are based are different and therefore threaten the validity of the interpretations that can be made based on the scores.

Some studies (e.g. Pollitt & Murray, 1996; Gebril & Plakans, 2014) found that raters change their focus when rating performances at different ***proficiency levels***. Pollitt & Murray as well as Gebril & Plakans, for example, found that at the lower levels, raters focused more on language in general or grammatical accuracy more specifically. At higher levels, the focus was more likely to be on sociolinguistic or stylistic competence (Pollitt & Murray, 1996) and source use (Gebril & Plakans, 2014). Similar findings to those of Pollitt & Murray were also made by Brown et al. (2005) in relation to individual categories on the rating scale. Such findings have important implications for rating scale design and rater training activities.

Qualitative investigations have also given an insight into how raters deal with ***difficult-to-rate performances***, including when an essay does not match the features described in the rating scale. Lumley (2002, 2005), for example, showed that individual monitoring processes came into play when raters tried to reconcile their global impression of a script, specifically, difficult-to-rate features in a writing script and the rating scale descriptors. In such circumstances, raters drew on their opinions and schemata to arrive at a score. Baker (2012) also reported on a writing sample where particular key information was missing which required raters to make a decision whether this was serious enough to warrant a fail mark. Problems were also found in papers that were either overlength or underlength and often to a degree that required raters to count the words to notice this. She argued that such difficult-to-rate papers were much more frequent than anticipated, and resulted in raters having to make decisions which may go beyond the descriptors in the rating scale. Work in this area can directly feed into rater training and rating scale validation activities.

Studies into cognitive processes of raters also provide a much richer insight into ***disagreements between raters*** than quantitative analysis allows for. Brown et al. (2005), for example, found instances where judges seemed to diverge in what aspects of a candidate performance they interpreted as an indication of proficiency. This was, for example, in relation to the re-use of source materials in the integrated tasks. While some raters valued the re-use of input material, others preferred it if test takers attempted paraphrasing. Another source of discrepancies was around disfluencies and speech repair. Some judges saw repair as test takers' ability to correct their own performances whereas others judged it as interfering with comprehensibility. Raters also disagreed on what constitutes 'key' information in the content of the source text. Also related to the rating of spoken performance, Joe, Harmes & Hickerson (2011) report that the use of notecards by speakers was interpreted differently by different raters. Some raters noted a heavy reliance on notecards by speakers, or the mishandling of notecards, while other raters did not comment on the use of notecards. However, as reported above in the section on methodology, even if a behaviour is not reported by raters, it does not mean it did not come into play in their decision-making. A clearer understanding of when and why raters disagree can provide valuable information for task design, rating scale revisions and rater training.

Work on rater cognition has also provided a very helpful insight into how raters engage with ***rating scales*** in the rating process and what the impact of the scales is on construct-irrelevant rating behaviour. Two studies conducted by Brown (2000, 2006) focusing on the IELTS speaking test, were able to compare raters' thought processes when rating with a holistic scale (Brown, 2000) and the newly introduced analytic scale (Brown, 2006). She was able to show that the analytic rating scale resulted in far fewer instances of raters commenting on aspects of performance not included in the scale which was in marked contrast to the study conducted in 2000 where experienced raters often drew on inference-based decisions. A number of studies since have directly set out to compare rating behaviours across holistic and analytic rating scales in a variety of contexts. Li & He (2015) compared rating behaviour of CET-6 raters when using the CET-6 rating scale and when using an analytic scale specifically designed for the study. They found that raters focused more on general language quality and non-scale related features when rating holistically and when rating using the analytic scale, more attention was given to coherence and grammar. Wiseman (2008), when comparing essay scoring processes across a holistic and an analytic scale, found that the analytic scale reduced raters' engagement with the essays. Barkaoui's (2007) study comparing four raters' essay-rating processes when using the two types of scales resulted in a number of key findings. Drawing on Cumming et al.'s (2001) distinction between judgement and interpretation strategies, Barkaoui found that raters used more judgement strategies (e.g., strategies to formulate a rating) and self-monitoring strategies when using the analytic scale and more interpretation strategies (e.g., strategies to comprehend the essay) when rating holistically. As was the case with previous studies, raters used the criteria of the rating scale more when rating analytically. When rating holistically, they drew more on self-generated criteria and on the comparison of writing samples to each other. In later work, Barkaoui (2010) added the variable of rater experience into the investigation. He found that the impact of rater experience was not significant when it came to the use of the two rating scales. With holistic scales, novices often focused on a number of linguistic features while when rating analytically, they were able to distribute their focus across all scoring categories. The findings of these studies have direct relevance to rating scale designers and implications for the validation of test scores and inferences. They can also feed directly back into the design of rater training packages.

Linking rater cognition to theory

Han (2016) has criticised research into rater cognitive processes for their lack of theoretical underpinning. He suggests that studies in this area should draw more closely on existing theories and research on human information processing to explain what goes on in raters' minds when assessing. Some work in this area has already been conducted. Bejar (2012), for example, put forward a comprehensive model of the assessment of constructed responses which draws on existing theories and research findings on human information processing. Han (2016) also puts forward a cognitive model of rater cognition specifically for L2 speaking assessment which draws on Purpura's (2014) models of the architecture of human information processing and the interface of cognitive competence and L2 processing. Any such models need to be empirically validated by future research. Han (2016) claims that such a model could helpfully feed into rater training and rater awareness-raising but whether this influences rater behaviour is yet to be established. Nevertheless, more theoretically-sound models are needed, which can be applied to a range of contexts and rating situations, and validation of such models needs to be undertaken.

Conclusion

In this chapter we have explored more qualitative methodologies to gain an insight into rater decision-making processes. The existing research in this area has shown that drawing on such research, in addition to more quantitatively-focused studies, can be beneficial to uncover rater behaviours and thought processes which may otherwise be hidden. Uncovering reasons for score discrepancies of raters can be helpful for rater training as well as rating scale revisions.

CHAPTER 4

APPROACHES TO ENHANCING RATING AND SCORE QUALITY

Introduction

We have seen in previous chapters that human ratings are inherently unreliable. To enhance rating and score quality, test developers and administrators need to address two areas. The first area deals with a priori aspects such as the recruitment, training, standardisation and monitoring of examiners. Examiners need to be recruited who have the underlying knowledge to develop the language assessment skills required to fully understand and be able to apply the principles behind the scoring construct. They must then be trained so that they come to an agreed and consistent interpretation of the rating descriptors representing this construct. They must also be standardised and monitored on an ongoing basis to ensure quality rating. The second area that needs to be considered for enhancing score quality is the resolution of score differences between raters following test administrations. This chapter explores both areas.

Before we consider techniques to enhance rating quality further, it is important to point out that a number of authors (Huot, 1990; Moss, 1992) have argued that we should not strive to force raters to rate similarly, that in fact the different positions they bring to the rating process are valuable and reflective of real-life readers and listeners. This position, however, has been difficult to defend in the case of large-scale tests in particular, where score uses are often highly consequential for test takers.

Recruitment

The choice to recruit raters or interlocutors depends on the type of language test. In a semi-direct speaking test where the test taker speaks to a pre-recorded prompt either online or by phone, the response is marked by a rater and there is no interaction between the test taker and the rater. In some face-to-face tests (e.g., in the Cambridge FCE speaking test) one person works primarily as the interlocutor and engages with the test taker by asking the test prompts, while the other person focuses on observing and rating. In the IELTS test, an examiner fills both the rating and inter-locutor roles simultaneously.

For the rater role, the ability to accurately and reliably rate writing and/or speaking responses is required. It can be difficult to assess this ability at the recruitment stage. Instead, a qualification in language teaching, a university degree and teaching experience as minimum professional requirements are often used as evidence of the capability to rate writing and/or speaking responses following training. Interestingly, we were not able to uncover any research that examines whether these qualifications lead to the best results in marking.

Requirements for interlocutor recruitment often differ to those for raters. Research into interactional competence shows that the discourse between the interlocutor and test taker is co-constructed and the behaviour of the interlocutor can impact on test-taker performance in a number of ways (Brown, 2003a, 2012; Fulcher & Davidson, 2007; McNamara, 1996; Nakatsuhara, 2008). For some researchers, this variation in interlocu-tor performance creates a richer, wider and more valid sociolinguistic-interactional construct. With expert interviewing skills, it is argued that interlocutors can 'bias for best' and support the test taker to such an extent that the test taker is able to perform to the best of their abilities (Fox, 2004; Swain, 2001). However, subjective variation in the inter-locutor test delivery style and content can also be seen as unfair to test takers, especially when the purpose of the test is to make high-stakes decisions which are life-changing. In these testing situations, a narrower psycholinguistic-individualistic construct is sometimes preferred, where test takers are assessed on their ability to produce context-free, fluent, accurate and complex language (Fulcher, 2015; Roever & Kasper, 2018).

For high-stakes tests such as IELTS, interlocutors use controlled scripts with a narrow construct where variables in test delivery are controlled (Seedhouse & Egbert, 2006). No research has specifically been done on the best background characteristics of interlocutors, but looking for pre-vious interviewing experience might be helpful. We are not aware of any research into what qualifications or background interlocutors should have, although we feel that more research into this area is clearly needed.

Training

Training is another crucial aspect of rating quality. Raters must fully understand the principles behind the construct and come to an agreed and consistent interpretation of the descriptors. The type and quality of training can have a direct impact on rating accuracy (Hamp-Lyons, 1995).

Training and rater reliability

Empirical studies on the effects different approaches to training have on rating reliability are limited but rater training in general has been shown to improve intra- and inter-rater reliability by helping raters (a) understand the task demands and test-taker characteristics, (b) increase the understanding of the rating scale criteria and descriptors, (c) reduce extreme marking severity or leniency, (d) increase self-consistency and (e) reduce individual biases (Davis, 2016; Shohamy, Gordon & Kraemer, 1992; Weigle, 2002).

Davis' (2016) study showed that while rater reliability improved with training, there was little effect on rater severity, a result confirmed in other studies (Lim, 2011; Weigle, 1998). Some researchers have queried the emphasis on rating consensus (Lumley & McNamara, 1995; McNamara, 1996; Weigle, 1994), suggesting that the goal of perfect inter-rater reliability decreases the validity of the marking because it may require that raters ignore their personal intuitions or decision-making styles. In such cases, the rating will be unnatural for the rater and therefore not valid or reliable. These researchers believe that it might be better to determine the severity or leniency of a rater and confirm that they have acceptable internal consistency and then adjust the final scores using multifaceted Rasch analysis or similar methods. The aim of training, therefore, should not be on achieving high levels of inter-rater reliability but on making raters more self-consistent. Other researchers argue that if raters follow their personal decision-making style, it might improve the validity of the rating but could decrease the construct validity of the assessment (Brown, 2012; Fulcher, 2015). Raters might focus on areas of the performance that are not included in the rating scales and inferences made about what a test taker can do could therefore be false.

The assessment context determines if the validity of the rating or the validity of the decision-making should take precedence, which then determines the type of training that should be conducted. For high-stakes tests that make life-changing decisions about test takers, rating score reliability is most important and a top-down approach to rater training is appropriate. In classroom formative assessment, allowing more idiosyncratic rater decision-making and the formation of a community of practice might be more acceptable (Brown, 2012). Let us now explore these two methods in more detail below, before describing online rater training.

Top-down training

The top-down model of training is where raters are asked to conform with a 'gold standard' set by a testing organisation. In this model, training normally consists of two parts: a training element with benchmark responses for each proficiency level and for each task type which exemplify the standard, along with practice samples and discussion; and secondly an accreditation or certification.

The recommended procedures for training new raters in this top-down model should include the following elements (Alderson, Clapham & Wall, 1995; Brown, 2012; Elder, Barkhuizen, Knoch & Von Randow, 2007; Shaw, 2002; Weigle, 2002):

- Introduction and clarification of the task demands and test taker characteristics.
- Introduction of the rating scale(s).
- Review of one set of benchmark performances from each proficiency level, along with comprehensive feedback. At this stage performances are clearly introduced as representing a specific level on the scale. The benchmark performances should be as unambiguous as possible and illustrate clear performances at each level and for each task type. The purpose is for raters to familiarise themselves with the marking scale(s) and ask questions, using the benchmark performances for discussion.
- Review of a further set of response samples from each proficiency level, ordered randomly. The rater should not see the marks and feedback, or any of their colleagues' marks, until they have marked the response, so that they are not influenced in their decision-making. The responses should be discussed as a group and raters encouraged to re-rate the samples until there is no longer a discrepancy. The purpose is to gain experience using the marking scale(s) and fully internalise the marking scale(s) so raters must be able to return to all of the samples as many times as they want (Brown & Jaquith, 2011). Raters who review benchmark responses more often are more accurate, according to Davis (2016). A possible explanation for this finding is that the benchmark responses help raters align their rating perceptions to the rating scale and relevant features of performance.

Weigle (2002) notes that between three and ten samples should be used for each set and Alderson et al. (1995) recommend that twenty responses should be used overall, including five scripts that are difficult-to-rate.

- Accreditation: Accreditation ratings should include between eight and ten samples for each task type. Decisions need to be made whether raters are allowed more than one attempt at accreditation (Brown & Jaquith, 2011) and how a 'pass' on the accreditation is determined. Accreditation is further discussed later in this chapter.

Suggested guidelines for the selection of benchmark samples to be used during rater training are as follows. The samples should have responses that are fairly straightforward to rate and also include problem responses, along with guidelines on how to mark these, so that raters approach these responses in the same manner (Weigle, 1994). Examples of difficult-to-rate responses include:

- Off-topic responses
- Memorised responses
- Excessively short or long responses
- Borderline cases (especially when a pass or fail decision is to be made)
- Unbalanced task performances on different criteria, sometimes called jagged profiles (e.g., very fluent or complex responses that lack vocabulary or grammar accuracy or excellent grammar accuracy but poor pronunciation)
- Illegible writing or inaudible speaking tests
- Responses that copy the prompt.

Community of practice training

While the guidelines for training presented above are suitable for high-stakes contexts, they are probably not common in assessment for learning contexts. Another model of rater training emphasises more of a 'community of practice' (COP) approach where standards are negotiated by the raters during training. It has been shown that communication between raters improves reliability because the contact boosts confidence, provides a platform to discuss interpretations of the rating scales, allows raters to share experiences and information, and promotes professional development. It is through this communication that standards are set and reliability improved (Shaw, 2004; Watts, 2006; Wenger, 1998; Wenger & Snyder, 2000; Wenger, Snyder & McDermott, 2002).

In this rater training model, various rater decision-making styles are accepted. Raters might disagree on their scores but their perspectives are equally valid. Through the community of practice, consensus-building is used to develop agreement on test-taker performance (Brown, 2012). Having such a resource is especially important for new raters who may have decision-making styles or internal criteria that are different to the construct of the test being marked (Fairbairn, 2015; Jolle, 2014). It is noteworthy that Shaw (2002) and Watts (2006) propose communities of practice for raters for the sake of greater reliability. However, what has not yet been achieved in the research is exactly how to link a community of practice to better rating quality (Baird et al., 2004).

Training raters online

Rater training can be done face-to-face or online and each mode of training has its benefits and drawbacks. Raters are more likely to quickly develop a sense of community in face-to-face training, which has been shown to be important for rater reliability. However, face-to-face training has been criticised on the grounds that training sessions can be intimidating, force raters to work at the same speed, and be impracticable and expensive for globally dispersed teams. Training online is often more convenient and gives raters time to think and review performances at their own pace and at a convenient time (Elder et al., 2007). In an online environment, there is no limit to the number of samples that raters can access, although the temptation is to provide too much information in an online course (Watts, 2006).

In online training, there may also be less pressure to conform to the group, especially if participants can study at their own pace whenever they like (asymmetric training). Symmetric training by comparison means that participants attend sessions at the same time, with similar to face-to-face training, making the development of the community of practice more likely to occur. For asymmetric training, participants have time to think at their own pace without the immediate peer pressure which occurs in face-to-face or symmetric training. In an online context, it can be more difficult to manage symmetric training, especially if the training cohort is globally dispersed. In reality, a combination of symmetric and asymmetric training is likely to be the best option with activities that raters can do in their own time supplemented by some online lectures, webinars and video conferences at set times to develop the community of practice.

Brown & Jaquith (2011) found that raters preferred online training because the lack of interaction did not allow stronger personalities to take over or shy ones to feel uncomfortable, but the online trained raters performed less well than a comparison face-to-face trained group. It could be that peer pressure produces rater convergence, which might be more difficult to accomplish online where shy personalities have more time to think and develop counter-arguments (Watts, 2006). However, Knoch, Read & von Randow (2007) found that online training was marginally more successful. The key to these contrasting findings could be a finding by Elder et al. (2007), which showed that raters who were more positive about online training showed more improvement than raters who were less so. Raters who are more comfortable working online and remotely, who can type at speed on a keyboard and can express themselves as well in written format as in spoken format may be more suited to training online. The training platform also needs to work; if there are technical difficulties loading tests, for example, raters will not enjoy the experience (Brown & Jaquith, 2011). More research is needed into online training and rater convergence with respect to how much of the training can be asymmetric, how long it should last and the best online tools.

Elder et al. (2007) also state that online training should not be used as an alternative to face-to-face training for new raters. Studies examining this question (Knoch, Fairbairn & Huismann, 2015, 2016) have found no statistically significant difference between the accreditation results when training new raters online and face-to-face but it should be noted that the online raters had all been recruited based on having good online skills and were comfortable with the training format.

Rater standardisation

Following initial certification, raters must be regularly standardised as the results from training have been shown to last for only a limited time (Lumley & McNamara, 1995). One way to standardise raters is through exposing them to benchmark responses that illustrate various levels of performance on the rating scale at specific times (for example once a year), prior to the next operational rating session, continuously, or when rating has been found to be not to standard.

Normally, benchmark responses are chosen by expert raters and agreed by a panel. In a number of high-stakes testing contexts, performances which achieve the greatest agreement are selected as benchmarks (Alderson, 2000).

During the training process, raters who review benchmark responses more often are more accurate according to Davis (2016) but the finding is not always supported once training is complete. Baird et al. (2004) found that raters who were not provided with benchmark responses for writing responses were more accurate. They compared three groups of raters:

- Group 1 used a marking scale only
- Group 2 used a marking scale and benchmark performances at the mid-band (marks in the middle of the rating scale band level)
- Group 3 used a marking scale and benchmark performances at the cut scores (at the bottom end of the rating scale band).

Group 2 raters, who received mid-band benchmark performances, were more severe than Groups 1 and 3 but it could be that the mid-band benchmark performances were interpreted as cut-score performances. Interestingly, the most accurate rating was produced by the group that only used the rating scale (Group 1) raising the possibility that using benchmark performances may not help to standardise raters. If benchmark performances are to be used for standardisation, Baird et al. (2004) note they need to be chosen for the full range of the rating band: a performance from just above the cut score to the band below, a performance in the mid-range, and one just below the cut-score to the band above.

An added complication, according to Sadler (1987), is that benchmark responses tend to exemplify only some features of the expected performance and usually do not explicitly match all the criteria in the rating scale. The performances can then encourage raters to focus or prioritise different parts of the rating scale, depending on the choice of benchmark performances. Wenger (1998) notes that implicit information must be included in rater standardisation, which is the instinctive and commonly held knowledge by professionals in the field of language assessment (Sadler, 2011). It is not possible to put everything into the rating scales and therefore a community of practice can be where the implicit part of standardisation is nurtured (Watts, 2006; Wenger & Snyder, 2000).

Rater monitoring

There are several approaches that testing organisations use for monitoring rating quality in live marking. The first method is to use senior or expert raters to evaluate rating quality. Senior examiners review a random selection of scored performances, double-mark the performances and give feedback on the ratings and speaking test delivery. Follow-up monitoring is conducted if rating is not to an agreed standard. Robust standardisation across these senior examiner trainers is crucial for such a system to work.

Another option is to have all raters mark the same control items during live marking (Engelhard, Wang & Wind, 2018; Patterson, Wind & Engelhard, 2017). The marks on these control items can then be used to track intra-rater reliability and to identify raters who are making decisions that are different to the group. The control item system also works as a self-standardisation system in that raters can review their reliability statistics across task types and access materials to help improve performance. A similar system is in place for the Aptis test, developed by the British Council (O'Sullivan & Dunlea, 2015). While senior raters are marking live tests, they can put forward responses that exemplify a specific level and would make good control items. A second rater checks the mark and if the mark is agreed, the item enters the system as a control item. When raters are marking responses, control items are randomly interspersed amongst the live items at a rate of 5%. Currently the statistics calculate percentage exact accuracy and adjacent accuracy, but a system using many-facet Rasch analysis could be set up to arrive at a more robust understanding of rating accuracy (Eckes, 2015).

There are mixed findings on the usefulness of giving feedback on rating performance during live marking. Some research finds that raters are able to modify their rating through feedback, while others find little or no improvement (Elder et al., 2005; Knoch, 2011; Wigglesworth, 1993). This research, however, has not looked at providing feedback during the marking period, but rather afterwards. There is a risk that raters may over-react to feedback or over-generalise the feedback inappropriately to other tasks or responses. It also makes it difficult to conduct many-facet Rasch analysis adjustments to scores if the feedback causes raters to become internally inconsistent. In a study conducted by Knoch (2011), raters tended to not feel they could use the feedback to improve their rating and subsequent ratings did not improve. Raters were positive about receiving the feedback but it appears that some raters were not able to internalise the feedback properly. One way forward might be to identify rater types as developed by Eckes (2012) and tailor the feedback to match the decision-making process or personalities of the raters. More research is needed, especially on the effectiveness of computer-assisted automatic feedback for online rated tests.

Ongoing rater monitoring is important also to avoid rater drift or differential rater functioning over time, which can take place if raters rate over several hours or days or even longer time periods (Wolfe, Moulder & Myford, 2001). Rater drift is often subtle and difficult to detect and it is important to be aware of this occurring. Methods have been proposed to identify rater drift (Wolfe et al., 2001) as well as how to provide feedback to raters who are exhibiting this behaviour (e.g., Hoskens & Wilson, 2001).

Score resolution methods

Despite all the efforts put into rater training and monitoring, rater differences often still persist. For this reason it is common practice to double-rate speaking and writing performances to help ensure accurate scoring and subsequented score interpretation (Johnson, Penny, Gordon, Shumate & Fisher, 2005). Ideally, exact agreement is reached by the two raters but scores can differ resulting in the need for a score resolution procedure. There are benefits and drawbacks to different score resolution methods with implications for score interpretation.

Evidence for the generalisability (or reliability) of scores is part of the process for making a case for test validity. The argument-based framework (Kane, 1992, 2013) and socio-cognitive model (O'Sullivan, 2011; Weir, 2005) for test validation both explicitly discuss test scores as a key element in the validation process (see Chapter 7).

This section will describe and critique various score resolution methods that are used to help arrive at more reliable final test-taker marks. We will first look at averaging two scores and then investigate how to integrate a third rater into the process, after which we examine the negotiation model where raters discuss their differences and come to an agreed score, and finally consider the confidence scoring model.

Averaging two scores

One score resolution method is to average the scores from two raters. This method involves summing the scores and then using the summed score or dividing by two to get a final average score. The benefit of this model is that it is relatively easy and inexpensive to implement and can therefore be used in small-scale test situations. When using this method, one needs to consider whether the two scores need to be adjacent. If the scores are adjacent, it could be assumed that the test taker is at the cut-score of the two levels, but if the scores are not adjacent there is a clear difference in judgement by the raters and averaging the scores may not be sufficient to arrive at a fair final score.

There is another problem with this model – it may result in half scores. For example, on a 0–5 holistic scale where descriptors are provided for each point on the scale, if one rater gives a score of 3 and another rater gives a score of 4, after the score resolution procedure, the final score would be 3.5. How should the score be reported and interpreted if the half score does not correspond to a level on the rating scale? Even more problematic is if the pass cut-score is a 4 and the test taker fails based on one rater's decision (Johnson, Penny, Fisher & Kuhs, 2003). To overcome the issue of half scores, descriptors could be developed for the additional score levels but it can be very difficult to create meaningful descriptors across additional levels. Another risk with half scores is in the validity of the score. A score of 3.5 may look more precise than scores of 3 or 4 but we cannot be sure whether the enhanced precision has construct validity if the meaning of a 3.5 is difficult to define or is undefined.

Another drawback of this score resolution method is that lenient raters could be paired with lenient raters resulting in scores that are too high (or conversely too low if severe raters are paired with severe raters). Test administrators can overcome this problem by pairing raters who are known to be lenient with raters who are known to be severe. However, implementing such a system is expensive and difficult to manage and there is also a likelihood of a central tendency effect, particularly for rating scales that use odd-numbered scale points (Penny & Johnson, 2011). The model reduces extreme rating, which impacts on the interpretation of the scores as there are fewer very high- or very low-level test-taker performances, with scores bunched in the middle.

Another option is to enter all scores into a many-facet Rasch model and adjust the scores based on the fair average generated by this model. Myford & Wolfe (2002) found that using this option scores would change for about one-third of performances by less than half a point, and by more than half a point for two-thirds of test takers on a 9-point scale.

Johnson, Penny & Gordon (2000) note that averaging two scores is the least reliable score resolution method, apart from single rating, for the reasons mentioned in this section. They recommend using a third rater as an adjudicator, arbitrator or moderator and feed this third person into the score resolution process.

Incorporating scores from a third rater

When using a third rater, there are four approaches on how to incorporate the third score (Johnson et al., 2005; Weigle, 1998). They each have their benefits and drawbacks and impact on test reliability, construct and interpretation in different ways.

The first sub-model is to have the third rater mark the test blindly and then average the three scores, with the three raters contributing equally to the final score. Test precision is enhanced by having three judgements on a performance, but the issues raised in the previous section are still problematic, including the need for even more descriptors to describe levels of performance. This model is very marginally more reliable than the averaging of two scores, yet because of the even more pronounced central tendency effect, there is an even greater impact on pass rates (Johnson et al., 2000).

The second sub-model uses the third rater to review the two original ratings and then select one of the two original ratings as the final rating. By seeing the original marks one issue that could arise is that there is a chance the third rater could be influenced by the scores. The second issue is that the third rater is normally chosen for their scoring accuracy and not necessarily for their decision-making skills (Lim, 2011). This model is an either/or decision by the third rater rather than a blind assessment of the performance, which threatens score validity.

The third sub-model is to have the third rater conduct a blind review of the test-taker response and then combine the third score with the closer of the two original scores, while the more discrepant original score is discarded (Weigle, 1998). The third rater is not influenced by seeing the original marks because they are marking blindly, the final score fits into the rating scale and the central tendency issue is also eliminated. The main issue with this model is in the choice of the third rater who ulti-mately chooses the final score. As previously mentioned, the third rater is often chosen because they have high rater reliability statistics or more experience. High rater reliability statistics demonstrate accurate scoring outcomes, but these statistics do not include any information on the types of decisions a rater makes (Jolle, 2014). It is quite possible for the third rater to display scoring strategies that cause the score to be invalid, for example rater bias towards a type of test taker or task. Furthermore, as

Cumming (1990) notes, an experienced rater is no guarantee of rating accuracy.

The fourth and final model replaces both original marks with the mark of an expert rater. Of course, if the third rater has an extreme score or some sort of bias, the two original raters do not mitigate the extreme score.

Rater negotiation

Rater negotiation entails two raters, when there has been a disagreement on the score, discussing the performance and arriving at a consensus score (Johnson et al., 2005). The benefit of this model is that it involves raters discussing task constructs and rating scales related to specific test-taker performances and therefore encourages rater standardisation and a more precise understanding of the rating scales and the test construct. Trace, Janssen & Meier (2017) found that the negotiation model did not change rater severity but reduced rater bias and led to a more nuanced understanding of the rating scales. They also found that raters reported that this knowledge was carried over into their classrooms contributing to positive washback and better test validity. The one downside of this model is that rating sessions are longer and can be impractical for large-scale testing in terms of both cost and time.

Johnson et al. (2005) compared the averaging-two-scores model with the negotiation model and did not find significant differences in rater reliability. Raters marked using both holistic and analytic rating scales and were instructed to resolve discrepant scores by discussing how the content, personal expression and surface features of the writing sample supported their choice. The raters could choose one of the two scores as the final score or average the scores. Although this research did not find any increase in rating accuracy, the researchers did find the activity supported professional development and ongoing rater training.

One drawback of rater negotiation is that researchers have found evidence of rater dominance where raters are not equally engaged or have unequal power in the negotiation. Interestingly, in the Johnson et al. (2005) study, rater dominance only occurred with holistic scales. The hypothesis is that with more decisions required for analytic rating, non-dominant raters could feel surer of themselves when negotiating individual criteria.

More research is needed particularly around how decisions are agreed between raters with different levels of dominance, decision-making styles and experience, and also which rating scale criteria benefit most from negotiation. Most studies have been small-scale and classroom-based, and it would be interesting to explore how a negotiation model could be operationalised in large-scale tests.

Confidence scoring model

More recently, a confidence scoring model has been developed. In this model, raters mark the response using rating scales and then give a score on how confident they are with their score. The system then uses a confidence scoring algorithm to arrive at a final score (Jin, Mak & Zhou, 2012). In the research by Jin et al. (2012) which used an 11-point (0–10) confidence scoring system, if raters were very confident in their scores, they would assign a score of 10 for their confidence indicator. Such a system could be useful for highlighting responses that require re-rating and decrease the need for everything to be multiple-marked. This research found the rating to be more dependable compared to double-marking but the confidence scoring method has not yet been operationalised in large-scale, high-stakes testing.

Conclusion

In this chapter, we examined two key important areas relating to score quality. The first focused on quality control before and during scoring, including rater recruitment, training, standardisation and ongoing rater monitoring. The second centred on various score resolution methods which can be used when score discrepancies between two or more raters are identified. We have documented these methods in one chapter in the hope that this will be a useful source for practitioners as well as graduate researchers interested in these topic areas.

CHAPTER 5

RATER-MEDIATED JUDGEMENT WITH OR WITHOUT RATING SCALES

Introduction

In the previous chapter, we discussed methods that can be used to enhance rating and score quality. One of these methods, which we will focus on in this chapter, is the use of rating scales, which provide descriptions of candidate discourse at different score levels. These descriptions can help raters identify features in candidate discourse that match these descriptions. The development and use of rating scales, just like scoring more generally, is complex and we have therefore decided to devote a chapter to this topic. We introduce various rating scale types and discuss how the purpose and context of the assessment should determine the rating scale used. We then turn our attention to rating scale development. We show that the key scale development methods presented in the literature are not reflective of actual practice. We therefore argue for a more eclectic approach to scale development and the need for awareness of how different methods affect the scales' ability to reflect the context of the assessment and the resulting implications for generalisability. We then present some of the key scale development methods found in the literature to provide readers with a toolkit to draw on in their own scale development activities. This chapter concludes with a rating method which is typically operationalised without the use of rating scales – comparative judgement.

Rating scale types

The two most commonly used types of rating scales in L2 performance assessments are holistic and analytic rating scales, but there are a number of other scale formats that have been used in the field. In this section, we describe the most common scale types and formats, as well as the contexts in which they may be used. We argue that the scale type should match the purpose of the assessment.

Analytic and holistic rating scales

When rating with an analytic rating scale, raters are required to consider different aspects of a performance separately, and to provide scores on sub-scales for each of these aspects. For example, a writing performance may be scored on content, grammar and vocabulary, and organisation. Scores may be averaged afterwards, but this is typically not the role of the raters. In the case of holistic rating scales (or holistic scoring), raters are not presented with separate sub-scales for different aspects of writing, but are rather asked to provide a single, integrated score for the performance. Holistic scales typically provide descriptions of different score levels that encompass various aspects of performances that might be rated to the different levels. Raters are therefore required to provide a score based on a more global impression of the performance as a whole.

The advantages and disadvantages of these two scale formats have been extensively discussed over the years. Holistic scoring is considered to have the advantage that test takers are less likely to be criticised for poor performance on a single aspect (e.g., poor organisation). The approach is considered to be emphasising what test takers have done well, rather than focusing on deficiencies (e.g., White, 1985). At the same time, holistic scoring is faster and therefore more efficient and cheaper than analytic scoring. There are also some drawbacks to holistic scoring. First, depending on the purpose of the assessment, it has been argued that just providing one score to students (and other score users) may not provide sufficient information about strengths and weaknesses in the performance. Foreign language and L2 users have been shown to often display uneven profiles in their performances where, for example, the pronunciation or fluency of a speaker is not as well developed as their grammatical control. Such uneven profiles can be masked by holistic scoring, as various aspects of a performance are lumped together into one performance level. Some research has also shown that holistic scoring may correlate highly with superficial aspects of a performance, for example, handwriting in the case of written tests (e.g., Sloan & McGinnis, 1982).

Analytic scoring, on the other hand, helps raters focus on various aspects of a performance. This is helpful as it guides raters to notice different performance features in more detail, helps in the training of raters, provides more detailed feedback to learners and highlights uneven performance profiles (Hamp-Lyons, 1991; Weigle, 2002). White (1985) has, however, argued that analytic scoring requires raters to read in an inauthentic fashion. There is also no guarantee that raters differentiate between the different scale categories as some studies have shown that raters may read holistically and then assign the same scores across sub-scales (Weigle, 2002).

Research comparing the two rating scale types has focused on comparisons of rater reliability, rater experience and the rating processes displayed by raters. In terms of reliability, several studies have shown that holistic scoring results in higher inter-rater agreement (e.g., Barkaoui, 2007; O'Loughlin, 1994). This may be because analytic rating requires more decisions which will then result in less inter-rater agreement (Bejar, 2012; Schoonen, 2005). On the other hand, several studies have also found that holistic scoring results in lower inter-rater reliability, possibly due to raters struggling to fit writers' uneven profiles into one performance category (Cumming, 1990; Perkins, 1983). In a more recent study, Barkaoui (2011a) found that raters were less severe and more self-consistent when scoring analytically and exhibited higher inter-rater reliability when scoring holistically. Rater experience has also been investigated when comparing holistic and analytic scoring. Barkaoui (2011a) found more misfit for inexperienced raters when rating holistically, suggesting that holistic scoring may require a higher level of practice to differentiate between levels reliably. In terms of the rating process, Barkaoui (2010) showed that raters referred more often to the essay they were rating when scoring according to a holistic scale, while they referred more often to the scale when scoring analytically. Seedhouse, Harris, Naeb & Ustunel (2014) also noted the high cognitive load in trying to match a speaking response to an analytic scale, indicating that cognitively, analytic scoring is more demanding and may therefore require higher levels of experience and expertise. Rater cognition is also directly related to the construct that the two rating scales assess. While raters may agree on a score, they may disagree on the reasons why they chose this level (Lumley, 2005; Weigle, 2002). Wolfe (2006) argues that this phenomenon may be related to raters having different mental images of a test taker's performance and mapping this image onto different mental images of the rating scale.

Other rating scale formats

While holistic and analytic rating scales are the most prominently used and researched scale formats in our field, there are also others. One such scale format, which has mostly been used in classroom-based assessment, is the empirically derived, binary-choice, boundary definition (EBB) type of scale which was first introduced by Upshur and Turner in the mid-1990s (Turner & Upshur, 2002; Upshur & Turner, 1995,

1999). EBB scales require the rater to make a series of yes/no decisions before arriving at a final score for a performance. Because of these yes/no decisions, which lead through a decision-tree format scale to a final score, EBB scales are thought to require less interpretation by raters, and therefore may result in relatively high inter-rater reliability. These scales are not without their problems though. First, because they are developed based on teachers' review of performance samples from a specific context, they have relatively low generalisability beyond the context they are developed for. These scales therefore lack theoretical underpinnings. Certain aspects of the construct under investigation are prioritised and therefore more heavily weighted – the first yes/no decision has more impact on the score than the last one.

Another scale format that is popular in classroom contexts is the diagnostic rating scale. Diagnostic rating scales are typically also used in classroom contexts to identify test takers' strengths and weaknesses. A key feature of diagnostic scales is that the construct represented in the scale is described in much more detail than in other types of scales, requiring raters to look for more features in the performance and to make more decisions. Recent examples of diagnostic scales were developed by Y.-H. Kim (2011) and Wagner (2015) both in the context of writing assessment. Kim (2011) developed and validated an empirically-derived descriptor-based diagnostic (EDD) checklist to use in classrooms. To develop the checklist, the author had nine teachers provide think-aloud verbal protocols while assessing ten TOEFL iBT essays on two topics. The verbal data were coded, reviewed and fine-tuned by a second panel into 35 EDD descriptors. The 35 EDD descriptors were next categorised into five writing skills: content fulfilment, organisational effectiveness, grammatical knowledge, vocabulary use and mechanics. FACETS analysis showed raters rank-ordered the writing responses in similar manner using this checklist and the checklist rank-order correlated well with the TOEFL writing scores rank-order. Twelve of the descriptors showed weak diagnostic power in separating test takers into mastery and non-mastery categories. There were also some cases where two test takers had the same TOEFL rating score but one of the test takers mastered all the five skills while the other mastered none, which would be confusing feedback to test takers, and highlights the care that is needed when providing test takers with diagnostic feedback.

Wagner (2015) developed a diagnostic rating scale linked to a high school curriculum in Canada. The development of the rating scale was informed by both empirical and theoretical scale development approaches. Both ESL teachers and ESL students were involved in the development of the criteria, and Wagner drew on a variety of scale development approaches (theories, curriculum, ESL writing products) to underpin her diagnostic scale. The scale included 30 descriptors, organised into six sub-skill areas.

In the context of speaking assessment, Nakatsuhara, May, Lam & Galaczi (2018) developed a very detailed diagnostic checklist of interactional competence, featuring both a full list of detailed descriptions and feedback, as well as a more concise version which can be used by teachers. The scale was developed based on verbal protocols that were elicited from experienced raters, who were asked to comment on recorded, paired interactions at different score levels.

Research on diagnostic rating scales in L2 contexts is still in its infancy. A variety of questions need to be investigated, including whether rater reliability can be achieved at the sub-skill level, what cognitive processes raters draw on when scoring performances with such scales, how students engage with the feedback based on such scale descriptors, and whether teachers can make use of the feedback they receive about their learners.

Rating scale development in second language assessment

In the late 1990s and early 2000s, several authors (Brindley, 1998; McNamara, 1996; Turner, 2000; Upshur & Turner, 1995) suggested that it is surprising that despite rating criteria forming such an integral and important part in the scoring process, there is so little information published on how these are constructed and validated. This situation has very much changed. In recent years a plethora of studies have been published describing the rating scale development process in great detail and providing a detailed insight into the wide range of methods used to develop scales (see, e.g., Banerjee, Yan, Chapman & Elliott, 2015; Ewert & Shin, 2015; Fulcher, Davidson & Kemp, 2011; Galaczi, ffrench, Hubbard & Green, 2011; Harsch & Martin, 2012; Hirai & Koizumi, 2013; Isaacs & Thomson, 2013; Isaacs, Trofimovich & Foote, 2017; Knoch, 2009; Lallmamode, Daud & Abu Kassim, 2016; Mendoza & Knoch, 2018; Rakedzon & Baram-Tsabari, 2017; Turner, 2000; Turner & Upshur, 2002).

What these studies have shown is that rating scales are rarely developed and then used without further modification. In fact, regular monitoring of scale performance and subsequent revisions to scales is very common.

We have depicted this process in Figure 5.1. Scale criteria are commonly developed through a series of steps, which we will describe in more detail in this chapter. The cycle starts with the development of a new scale or the revision of an existing scale. Following this is usually a stage in which the existing criteria are reviewed, or a draft scale is piloted. This commonly results in revision and then use of the scale. This cycle may be repeated several times, sometimes over many years. There is, therefore, often no clear demarcation of when scale development finishes and validation activities start, and we therefore would like to argue that the two activities usually go hand-in-hand. For the purpose of this monograph, we describe these two activities separately – scale development activities are presented in this chapter, and validation activities are presented in Chapter 7. However, only in some contexts can these two activities be completely separated.

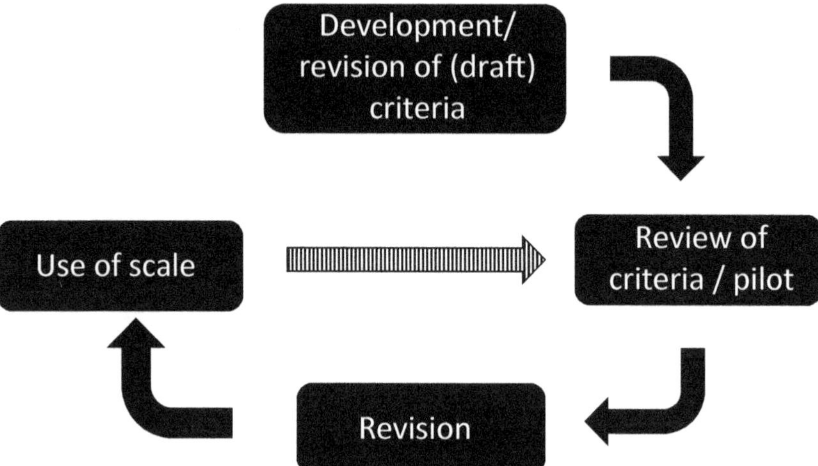

Figure 5.1: Scale development/revision cycle

Approaches to rating scale development

So how are rating scales for second/foreign language assessments developed? Galazci et al. (2011) point out that scale development is complex and multidimensional and, as a result, a range of different approaches are available to test developers. A number of publications have described these approaches to rating scale development (Council of Europe, 2001; Fulcher, 2003; Fulcher et al., 2011). They have done this by grouping different scale development methods and giving labels to these approaches.

In this section, we will describe these approaches. A review of the many recently published studies on scale development, however, shows that these groupings do not adequately represent common practice in rating scale development which frequently draws on a range of methods to develop scales, and mixes more than one of these approaches in one scale design project. Nevertheless, we feel that an understanding of these broad approaches is useful and we therefore review them in this section.

Fulcher (2003) described two main approaches to scale development: intuitive methods and empirical methods. He divided *intuitive methods* into three further sub-categories: (1) expert judgement, (2) committee, and (3) experiential. Expert judgment involves an individual, either a teacher or a language tester, writing a new scale based on various sources, for example, other rating scales, a teaching syllabus or the results of a needs analysis. The committee method is similar to expert judgement, but relies on a group of people to design the scale. Finally, the experiential method may start with either expert judgement or a committee and the scale is then refined in various iterations to reflect a shared understanding among scale users.

The *empirical methods* were also divided into three sub-categories: (1) data-driven scale development, (2) empirically derived, binary-choice, boundary definition (EBB) scales and (3) scaling descriptors. In data-driven scale development, the scale developer examines performances on the task and identifies key aspects of performances to include in the scale. The performances may be divided into different levels either based on a previous rating scale used or based on raters' or teachers' intuition of what constitutes a better or worse performance on the task and scale descriptors are created based on the analysis of performance features. EBB scales are developed by a group of teachers and raters who group performances into levels and then discuss the key features distinguishing these levels. A more detailed description of this method is presented below. The final method, scaling descriptors, requires the collection of scale descriptors from a range of rating scales. Once this has happened, experts, such as teachers, are asked to rank these in order of difficulty. The results are then analysed statistically and the hierarchical scale is created based on the quantitative results.

A very similar categorisation of rating scale approaches was made by the Council of Europe (2001) which grouped methods, just like Fulcher (2003), into either intuitive, qualitative or quantitative methods. The intuitive methods described are identical to those in Fulcher's taxonomy.

Qualitative methods include (1) 'key concepts: formulation', where raters are asked to recreate a draft scale that has been cut up, (2) 'key concepts: performances', a method which requires raters to identify key performances for levels and match these to the descriptors, (3) primary trait in which performances are ranked and then the key trait or construct that determines this ordering is identified, (4) binary decisions, which refers to the EBB scales described above, (5) comparative judgements where raters are asked to discuss pairs of performances with the aim of identifying key features that differentiate performance levels and (6) sorting tasks, which requires informants to sort draft descriptors into categories, at the same time accepting, editing or rejecting descriptors. The Council of Europe (2001) describes three quantitative methods. The first is discriminant analysis, which follows a discourse analysis of previously rated performances and is designed to determine the features which have the most impact on the scores awarded. The second quantitative method described is multidimensional scaling which examines which analytic scale categories are most significant in the score. The final method, item response theory, is a family of models which includes many-facet Rasch measurement. We described this method in Chapter 2 in relation to rater quality, but this method is also powerful in examining rating scale functioning.

The final taxonomy of scale development approaches was presented more recently by Fulcher et al. (2011). They divided scale development methods into the measurement-driven approach and the performance data-driven approach. Measurement-driven approaches include methods that do not rely on the analysis of performance samples (and are driven by a statistical method to arrive at band levels). They include the a priori method, which was previously called the intuitive method. Another scale development in this approach is the scaling descriptors approach, which we have briefly described above (and will describe more below). This was used to create the Common European Framework of Reference for Languages. Fulcher et al. (2011) criticise measurement-driven approaches for their lack of sensitivity to the communicative context, with a high level of abstraction which results in a disjunct between the score and the score meaning. They therefore argue for an approach which is more sensitive to the performance features. The performance data-based methods address this limitation. Here methods such as conversation analysis or discourse analysis are used to carefully describe features of the performance which are then incorporated into the rating scale. A further method in this approach is the development of EBB scales.

As can be seen from the description above, authors have attempted to group different scale development methods into approaches, mainly drawing a distinction between methods that rely on actual test-taker performances to develop the scales and a range of other methods which rely more on the experts and their understanding of the construct to develop the scoring criteria. However, through a review of the studies we have found describing scale development projects, we would like to argue that these groupings do not reflect the bulk of scale development studies published in the literature in recent years. Most studies we have identified seem to rely on a mix of methods to develop and refine the scales, more often than not drawing on methods from a range of these approaches. This is in line with a number of authors who have argued for a combination of scale development methods in an iterative process. Interestingly, none of the descriptions of the approaches we have reviewed above seems to incorporate approaches which draw on theoretical models of language development. This exclusion may cause potential scale developers to undervalue a theoretically-based approach to scale development.

In this chapter, we would like to argue that rather than grouping methods into broader approaches, it may be more useful to potential scale developers to be presented with a list of possible methods, with their associated advantages and disadvantages, and to be mindful how the method(s) chosen takes into account the context the scale is used in and therefore impacts the generalisability of the scale. Let us explain this in more detail by thinking about two scale development methods: review of other scales and data-driven scale development. If scale developers collect some existing scales from other contexts and create the new criteria based on these scales, the resulting scale is likely to be relatively context-free and therefore more likely to be applicable to a range of prompts and also more generalisable to performance outside of the specific task used in an assessment. However, the scale may incorporate the type of vague terminology that has been criticised in some rating scales (see section on Problems with rating scales, below) and may not reflect the type of language used in test-taker performances. Scales developed using a data-driven method account for this latter problem in that the results from a detailed analysis of the discourse can be incorporated into the scale descriptors to ensure the scale is reflective of candidate discourse. However, the drawback of this method is that the resulting scale might be limited to discourse on the specific task or prompt which was analysed and hence generalisability may be limited.

Not all scale development methods which we describe in this chapter fall on either end of this dichotomy between context-free methods and context-sensitive methods; many methods fall somewhere in-between and the distance to either end of this continuum is also determined by how the specific method is implemented. For example, a data-driven procedure can be moved more towards the context-free end of the scale by the inclusion of performances from a wider range of task types in the analysis. Similarly, the review of other scales can be moved to the more context-sensitive end of the continuum by including only scales that were developed for very similar contexts. The point we are trying to make is that no method is necessarily fixed on the continuum; scale developers should however always consider the impact of the scale development method(s) chosen on the generalisability of the resulting scores.

Scale development methods

We have argued above that while a number of authors have grouped rating scale development methods into broader approaches, we feel that these approaches may be seen as dichotomies to new scale developers and therefore limit the range of methods they may draw on. We also feel that none of the groupings of approaches we have reviewed included all the methods we uncovered in our review of the literature. For this reason, we have chosen to describe each method separately in this chapter. We have attempted to include all the different methods we uncovered in our review of the literature. It is important to remember that many of these methods are not sufficient by themselves, that is, it is unlikely a functional scale can be developed by using just one of these methods. For this reason, test developers and researchers often combine approaches in an iterative process of developing draft criteria, piloting the criteria, examining the results of the pilot, and so on. Our list of methods is not presented in any particular order but is intended as a list of options in the scale developer's toolkit.

Review of theories or other literature

A careful review of relevant theories and models of language or language development can form the basis for the descriptors incorporated in a rating scale. A number of studies have used this method as a starting point. For example, Knoch (2009) reviewed a number of theories/models of communicative competence, writing and rater decision-making to create a taxonomy of possible criteria to include in her diagnostic rating scale. Similarly, East (2009) drew on theories of communicative competence as a starting point for his scale. The advantage of drawing on such theories is that a scale is underpinned by a theoretical framework and is therefore not likely to be criticised for being atheoretical. However, researchers drawing on this method have generally found that no theoretical models are available that describe language performance in writing, speaking or integrated skills sufficiently to serve as the basis for such development. Scale developers have therefore either created taxonomies of aspects adopted from different theoretical models or have supplemented this method with other methods. On a continuum from context-free to context-sensitive, this method is located on the context-free end. This is because such theories are often developed to be general and not context-dependent. Scale development can also include a review of the relevant literature. This is similar to a review of theories, but can be used when no theory is available. For example, Deygers & van Gorp (2015) used this method to gain a better understanding of the construct of academic language proficiency. Based on this literature review, they created a draft scale. Similarly, Struthers, Lapadat & MacMillan (2013) conducted a detailed literature review on cohesion in children's writing before developing their draft rating scale.

Review of existing scales

A number of studies (e.g., Chan, Inoue & Taylor, 2015; East, 2009; Isaacs et al., 2017; Lallmamode et al., 2016) have used existing scales as a starting point. The studies do not often describe in detail how features from these scales were incorporated into the new scale, but they differ in the types of scales they have drawn on. For example, East (2009) reviewed the Jacobs, Zinkgraf, Wormuth, Hartfield & Hughey (1981) scale, a very general scale which has been used for a large variety of purposes since its development. The use of this scale can also be classified as context-free. Isaacs et al. (2017), on the other hand, used a scale they themselves developed for a previous study as the starting point. We can therefore assume that this scale is much more sensitive to the context focused on in the project. There are a number of advantages and disadvantages of drawing on existing scales. One benefit is that previous scales provide instant access to scale descriptors as well as to descriptor wording. However, because there is usually no documentation of the development of these scales, they are likely to include flaws which will then be incorporated into the new scale. Amongst these problems may be that the wording of the descriptors may not reflect the performances in the new context which can lead to issues with subsequent rating quality.

Review of a teaching syllabus

Classroom-based rating scales can be made more context-sensitive by incorporating a careful review of the teaching syllabus into the scale development process (see Rakedzon & Baram-Tsabari, 2017 for one such example). None of the studies we identified described clearly how the teaching syllabus was reflected in the scale; however, this method is arguably highly context-sensitive when placed on a continuum from context-free to context-sensitive. As is the case with context-sensitive scale development methods, the generalisability of the scale is subsequently more limited when transported to other contexts.

Test developer intuition

A further method draws on the intuitions of test developers, either individually or in groups. This method is usually used a priori, when a draft scale is developed and may or may not be combined with other methods, such as the review of theories or other scales. Test developers design a scale without reference to candidate performances in this case, relying on their own experience and impressions of the kind of language test takers produce at different score levels. The disadvantage of this method is that because the developer is not referencing the descriptions in the scale to real test performances, the descriptions may not match the candidate discourse. Scales based on intuitions have also been criticised for being vague and abstract (Mickan, 2003; Upshur & Turner, 1995). However, if this is only the first step in the scale development process, and the scale is later referenced to actual candidate performances, this may be a valid starting point, in particular if the developers also make reference to theoretical frameworks as part of the process. Because the developer is not looking at actual candidate performances, the scale may be context-free; however this depends on how familiar the developer is with the context.

Descriptor scaling

Descriptor scaling, as described, is the method that underlies the development of the Common European Framework of Reference for Languages (Council of Europe, 2001). To develop the scales on the CEFR, rating scale descriptors from a range of scales were collected and then presented to teachers taken out of the context of the original scale. Teachers judged how difficult it would be for a learner to achieve each descriptor. This quantitative information was then statistically analysed to identify a hierarchy in the descriptors and to identify descriptors that were misfitting. Descriptor scaling cannot be done without drawing on a statistical method. This method falls on the context-free end of the continuum as many rating scales from a diverse range of contexts are used to mine for descriptors. For a fuller description of descriptor scaling we recommend readers refer to North (2003).

Rater verbal protocols

Rater verbal protocols have been used at two stages of the rating scale development or revision process. Some studies asked raters to verbalise their thoughts while judging essays without accessing a rating scale. These thoughts were transcribed, analysed and coded to identify aspects of writing which were then included in the rating scale. One such example was H. J. Kim's (2011) study where the verbal protocols provided the information needed to create the draft descriptors. In Galazci et al.'s (2011) study, verbal protocols were used to examine the functioning of the first draft scale which was subsequently revised before a larger trial. Similarly, Zhao (2013) used insights from rater verbal protocols, interviews and quantitative methods to revise a preliminary rating scale for authorial voice. Rater verbal protocols may also be used to refine more established scoring rubrics and to understand how raters interpret the rubric and use this information in rater training sessions. Where this method falls on a continuum from context-free to context-sensitive, depends on the methodology chosen. If raters are, for example, insiders in the context to which the assessment is extrapolated, then this method is context-sensitive, but if raters are drawn from a more general context, then the method is relatively context-free. The comments elicited should ensure that the scale is relevant to the discourse produced, although we are not aware of any studies that have detailed how the comments from verbal protocols are then translated into scale descriptors.

Rater feedback – Interviews, focus group discussions, surveys

The elicitation of rater verbal protocols is time-consuming, and although these comments are rich, a number of studies have elicited rater comments less directly, through interviews with raters, focus group discussions or surveys (Banerjee et al., 2015; Chan et al., 2015; Chen & Liu, 2016; Galaczi et al., 2011; Janssen, Meier & Trace, 2015; Knoch, 2009). Each of these will provide different challenges and differ in the level of depth of the comments, and will depend on how the data collection is designed. Focus group discussions, for example, will provide the richest data if the raters discuss a performance they have just rated, instead of relying on a memory of their impression of descriptors used a few days ago. Surveys can be administered to larger groups of participants, but may elicit data that is more superficial. Nevertheless, all of these data-collection methods are helpful to inform scale design and revision.

Input by other experts (teachers, domain experts, students)

Input may be sought from other stakeholders aside from raters. For example, in a classroom-based assessment, the descriptors may be based on the insights of experienced teachers who may not be the end-users of the scale. Similarly, in an assessment for specific purposes, descriptors may be based on the 'indigenous criteria' (Jacoby, 1998; Jacoby & McNamara, 1999) of domain insiders. For example, in a study by Knoch et al. (2017), indigenous criteria for the writing section of the Occupational English Test (OET) were elicited from health professionals (in this case doctors and nurses). These domain experts were shown examples of referral letters extracted from real patient records and commented on the strengths and weaknesses of these documents. Based on these comments, the research team, which also included domain experts, created a rating scale for the OET writing assessment which was later trialled. Finally, students may be asked to provide feedback on descriptors. Morozov (2011), for example, used this method in a writing classroom setting. Students were asked to provide feedback on the usefulness of the criteria for their learning. Students preferred more detailed descriptors.

Descriptor ordering or sorting

Both descriptor ordering and sorting are methods listed in the CEFR (Council of Europe, 2001) as possible scale development methods. Both rely on draft descriptors being available. Descriptor ordering requires raters or other users of the scale to reconstruct the scale after it has been taken apart. Following this exercise, a discussion would ensue about reasons for problems when identifying the correct ordering – this discussion may then result in revisions to the scale. This method was used in the Eurocentres certification scales (Council of Europe, 2001). Descriptor sorting requires participants to sort descriptors according to categories (or underlying traits) and according to level. Based on this exercise, changes to scale descriptors may be made. As with descriptor scaling, this method is relatively context-free, although the participants in the session may increase the context-sensitivity.

Review/analysis of performance samples by raters/test developers

The inclusion of performance samples from the assessment in question in the rating scale design process is what is referred to as the data-driven approach or the empirical approach to rating scale development (Fulcher, 1996). This method, however, can be implemented in a variety of ways. It can involve a careful discourse analysis of performance samples which then feeds either into the development of a new scale or into the revision of an existing scale. Or, performance samples are reviewed by raters to create/revise a scale. Let us describe each of these in turn.

The former method, which involves a discourse analysis of performances, can be time-consuming but is rich. It has the advantage that it is highly context-sensitive and that the resulting scale descriptors are grounded in real student performances. But, depending on how it is performed, it may be difficult to translate the findings from the discourse analysis into descriptors that are useable by raters. Some studies have relied on more 'qualitative' discourse analyses (e.g. Fulcher, 1996) and this has resulted in richer scale criteria. More 'quantitative' discourse analyses (e.g., Knoch, Macqueen & O'Hagan, 2014) are possibly less useful for the creation of a rating scale but may help validation or revision efforts. In recent years, researchers have at times drawn on automated text analysis programmes such as Coh-metrix (Graesser, McNamara & Kulikowich, 2011) to help in this process (see e.g., Banerjee et al., 2015). It is always important to remember some key points about this type of analysis. First, if the descriptors are based on candidate discourse, the resulting descriptors will be highly sensitive to the context of the assessment, but the resulting scale may be limited in generalisability. Second, the discourse analysis will determine the construct that is represented in the scale. If the discourse measures used in the analysis do not fully capture the construct, then the rating scale will subsequently under-represent the construct. Studies drawing on discourse-analytic measures that count different features at different score levels are likely to under-represent the construct in question. This is because many key features of spoken or written performances cannot (yet) be measured in this way. Finally, if the performances are analysed based on previous scores, then it is important to remember the cyclical nature of the scale development. The scores may have been based on a scale that needs revising but they now form the basis of the categorisation of discourse features for the new scale. It is helpful if test developers keep this problem in mind.

Raters or test developers may also be involved in reviewing performance samples to create, verify or refine draft rating scales or to select performance samples as benchmark samples of different score levels. One such method requires raters or other informants to examine performances and rank order these into levels. Once the rank ordering has been completed, the participants are asked to describe the principle on which this rank ordering was created. This method is designed to highlight the key features at particular levels and these features are then represented in the rating scale. There are a number of variants to this method. One requires raters to sort performances into different piles, rather than simply ordering them. Another requires raters to make comparative judgements of two performances and the discussion of the raters is then used to formulate descriptors. A further method, the creation of EBB scales (Upshur & Turner, 1995, 1999) described briefly above, requires a group of teachers or raters to sort performances into piles of higher and lower performances. Then, these piles are examined to identify key features that define each level. Then, critical questions that define each level are devised. A flowchart of yes/no choices is developed and in this way each performance is allocated to a final score. The EBB scales therefore rely on rater/teacher intuition as well as empirical evidence through the use of performance samples. The final method in this group requires raters to match performances to key descriptors at performance levels in an effort to ensure congruence between the descriptor wording and performances. This careful exercise may result in revisions to the wording of descriptors.

Statistical methods

Many rating scale development projects have drawn on statistical methods. These methods have varied in their underlying assumptions and in the purposes for which they were employed. It is beyond the scope of this chapter to describe any of the methods in detail, but we would like to briefly introduce some of the methods used in the studies that we have sampled.

Many studies have made use of **many-facet Rasch measurement** (MFRM) to examine the properties of the rating scale. MFRM makes it possible to examine not only the properties of the rating scale overall, but also of any sub-scales if an analytic scale is used. Rasch measurement can be compared to a magnifying glass which makes it possible to examine the finest details in a rating situation. MFRM can provide information about how the criteria in a scale are functioning and whether they are all working together to measure the same underlying trait. It can also provide information about how raters are applying the sub-scales and whether any band levels are not being used sufficiently. For a full description of how rating scale information can be analysed using MFRM, interested readers are referred to Linacre (1999) and McNamara et al. (2019).

Factor analytic techniques have been used in a number of rating scale development studies (e.g., Hirai & Koizumi, 2013; Knoch, 2009; Zhao, 2013) to examine whether a rating scale is measuring one underlying dimension or more than one dimension can be detected. Results from such an analysis are important as they can have important implications for score reporting.

Discriminant analysis can be used to explore whether any discourse-analytic measures chosen for a discourse analysis are significant in determining the rating given by raters. Those key features can then be incorporated in descriptors (see, e.g., Fulcher, 1996; Banerjee et al., 2015).

Chalhoub-Deville (1995) used ***multidimensional scaling*** to examine the relationship between analytic rating scales and see which of the scales are most strongly determining level. This descriptive technique may be useful for scale developers as it may provide information about possible issues with sub-scales.

Statistical techniques are often used following a pilot of the rating scale or to examine scale behaviour in an existing assessment. These methods are usually used in combination with other methods we have described above.

Combining methods

Earlier in this chapter, we suggested that methods to scale development may need to be combined and that the approaches we described earlier may be too restrictive and not representative of the combinations chosen by recent studies. The mixed approach to rating scale development is therefore becoming increasingly recognised (Banerjee et al., 2015; Becker, 2016; Galaczi et al., 2011; Knoch, 2009). In this section, we will briefly describe two studies (Galazci et al., 2011; Knoch, 2009) that have drawn on a mixed approach to show examples of how researchers have combined the methods we described above.

Galazci et al. (2011) describe the process of revising a set of assessment scales for a large-scale speaking assessment related to the CEFR. The scale revision process was divided into three phases: (1) establishing the design principles, (2) componential analysis and (3) operational analysis. During the first phase, four individuals reviewed the current literature in relation to the four assessment criteria and in light of the CEFR. These experts were asked to identify any potential issues with these criteria. The project team then administered a questionnaire to oral examiners to elicit their experience with the previous rating scales and their input on strengths and weaknesses of the scale. The design principles were also informed by a Conversation Analysis study which analysed the previous scales against test performances. These three data sources then informed the design of the draft descriptors. In the second phase, speaking examiners were asked to map the draft descriptors to the CEFR and an MFRM analysis was used to establish the difficulty of the descriptors based on this mapping exercise. Misfitting descriptors were identified and revised based on this analysis. Focus group consultations with experienced examiners as well as a verbal protocol study with eight examiners were also held. These data sources then led to the revisions of the draft descriptors. In the third phase, full trials of the new scale were conducted and analysed using MFRM. Following these trials, the scale was finalised.

Knoch (2009) developed a diagnostic rating scale for a university post-entry writing assessment. She started out by conducting a literature review of any relevant theories or theoretical frameworks relevant to writing. She then created a taxonomy of criteria to be included in the rating scale. She analysed a large number of writing samples using discourse-analytic measures and grouped the results of this analysis according to the score levels derived from ratings on the previous scale. The discourse measures used were mapped to the criteria identified in the literature review. The results from the analysis then informed the development of the rating scale. Raters rated 100 performances each and participated in an interview about their perceptions of the scale. The quantitative results were analysed using MFRM and factor analysis. Following the results of the study, the scale was revised.

The two studies described above illustrate the different paths chosen by scale developers and how different methods are combined in different contexts. What is clear from both studies is that the researchers did not stick strictly to any of the approaches described above but rather drew on a number of methods to develop or revise scales.

Construct representation in rating scales

Why is the meticulous construction of a scoring rubric so important? A number of authors have argued that the rating scale and the rating criteria act as the de facto test construct (e.g., McNamara, 2002) with others arguing that this view is too simplistic as the construct is produced by a complex interplay of tasks, performance conditions, raters and the rating scale, and the rating scale therefore only represents an impoverished view of the construct (North, 2003). Jamieson (2014) noted that it is helpful to consider the scope of the construct and make a distinction between (a) a theoretical construct and (b) an operational model of the construct chosen for a particular test (see also Chalhoub-Deville, 1997). The operational model should be clearly related to the theoretical construct (which is more abstract) but also incorporate contextual aspects. A similar distinction between theoretical and operational construct was made by Knoch & Macqueen (2019), but the distinction was taken even further by also including the stated construct, which is the construct that test users can see. The rating criteria, then, characterise the aspects of the construct which can be scored in a performance. The test developer should explain how the criteria relate to the operational mode of the construct and how this relates to the theoretical construct (Jamieson, 2014). The rating criteria also often form a part of the stated construct, as it is common practice to make these available to test users as part of the published test materials (e.g., on a test's website).

A review of the literature outlining test development projects shows that many of these studies have engaged with the theoretical construct at the beginning of their project, generally through a review of the literature, although other methods such as teacher or rater input were also used to create the criteria. A criticism of drawing on informants or discourse analyses to represent the construct has been that this inevitably results in an atheoretical, impoverished construct which is more related to the context and therefore less transferrable or generalisable. One of the key considerations in assessment design is how well the construct is covered and this is represented in a scoring rubric. One danger of not taking theoretical models into account when developing an assessment is that it may result in a construct-under-representation of the trait in question. We refer readers interested in examining how the construct has been represented in rating scale development studies, to some of the references listed, for speaking (e.g., Babaii, Taghaddomi & Pashmforoosh, 2016), writing (Banerjee et al., 2015; Berge et al., 2017; Hawkey & Barker, 2004), reading-to-write (Chan et al., 2015; Ewert & Shin, 2015; Shin & Ewert, 2015), content in writing (Bae, Bentler & Lee, 2016), pragmatic competence (Chen & Liu, 2016), voice/stance (DiPardo, Storms & Selland, 2011; Zhao, 2013), lexis (Fritz & Ruegg, 2013), grammatical ability (Neumann, 2014), cohesion (Struthers et al., 2013); spoken fluency (Fulcher, 1996), interactional competence in service encounters (Fulcher et al., 2011), comprehensibility (Isaacs et al., 2017) and functional adequacy (Kuiken & Vedder, 2017).

More recently, Knoch, Deygers & Khamboonruang (in press) examined published scale development studies by drawing on a systematic review. They were able to identify eleven different sources of scale construct used by scale developers. They grouped these sources into test internal and test external and argued that each source may have different effects on score generalisability and the precision of post-test predictions that can be made about test takers. They put forward a model of construct sources that can be used by scale developers, as well as for scale validation activities.

Problems with rating scales

A number of criticisms have been levelled at commonly used rating scales. Apart from the criticisms of scales being developed a priori and without reference to theoretical models (Brindley, 1991; Fulcher, 1996; North, 1995; North & Schneider, 1998), some scales have been criticised for their lack of correspondence to what learners produce in their performances (e.g., Fulcher, 1996; Upshur & Turner, 1995) or the lack of congruence to the task used to elicit the performance (Turner & Upshur, 2002). Researchers have also criticised the inconsistency of scales to findings from second language acquisition. Most scales assume linear development of language ability, although studies have shown that this is not always justified (see, e.g., Meisel, Clahsen & Pienemann, 1981). In fact, Brindley (1998) has argued that there is a noticeable lack of intersection between the work done in second language acquisition and the kind of representation of progression in rating scales (see also Bachman & Cohen, 1998).

Another group of criticisms relates to the level descriptors. For example, the level descriptors have been criticised for often being interdependent and hard to distinguish (Turner & Upshur, 2002; Upshur & Turner, 1995) which may be caused by the relative wording that is often used as well as subjective and imprecise terminology (Mickan, 2003; Upshur & Turner, 1995). Finally, some researchers have noted that raters at times struggle to distinguish sufficiently between sub-scales on an analytic scale and this phenomenon has also been noted in quantitative studies which showed sub-scales being highly correlated (Sawaki, 2007; Xi & Mollaun, 2006).

It is worthwhile that test developers keep these potential problems in mind during the development phase and consider how these issues can be addressed to ensure that raters do not encounter problems applying the rating scales.

Other considerations in scale development

So far in this chapter, we have presented the main rating scale development approaches and methods. We would now like to briefly list some other considerations in rating scale development. Researchers need to decide what type of rating scale they would like to develop. In this chapter we reviewed a number of different scale types which have been used in second language assessment contexts, including holistic and analytic scales, as well as diagnostic scales and decision-tree designs. It is important that the scale relates directly to the purpose. It would not be sensible, for example, to design a holistic scale for a context where diagnostic information is required or designing a diagnostic scale when only one score will be reported to learners.

A further consideration is the number of band levels that will be included in the scale. North (2003) shows that there is a tension between having enough levels to show progress and discriminate between different learners and raters being able to distinguish between the levels reliably. An early study by Miller (1956) shows that raters can only differentiate between about seven levels (plus or minus two). It is also important to consider the construct in a band scale and into how many levels this can be distinguished. Some categories may not lend themselves to be 'cut' into as many levels as others.

Finally, the way the descriptors are formulated has received considerable attention in the research literature. North (2003) has distinguished between three different approaches to formulating descriptors. In the abstract formulation, descriptors are formulated using qualifiers and quantifiers, such as 'a lot' or 'some', which may make it difficult for raters to distinguish between levels. Concrete formulation relates to descriptors that provide more detailed information about what raters should look for in performances. Finally, an objective formulation style relates to scales that seek objectivity by relating bands to countable features, like the number of mistakes.

Comparative judgement – Scoring without a rating scale

Thus far we have focused on scoring using rating scales. While this is the most common approach in scoring second language assessments, not all rating is conducted using rating scales. Recent years have seen renewed interest in the method of comparative judgement first proposed by Thurstone (1927) for work in psychophysics. The method was first used for foreign language speaking assessment by Pollitt & Murray (1996) and the method has since been used by British school examination boards for various purposes (but has received less interest in the area of ESL).

When rating using comparative judgement, raters are presented with two performances at a time (usually on a computer) and are asked to select the better of the two performances. The computer algorithm, following a large number of such judgements, then organises the performances from strongest to weakest by aggregating the data. The underlying premise of comparative judgement is that humans are much better at making comparisons than attempting absolute judgements in isolation.

Proponents of this method have noted a number of advantages of comparative judgement. Studies have shown that this method is marked by high reliability, which is usually higher than in comparison studies drawing on ratings using rating scales (see, e.g., Bramley, 2007; Pollitt, 2012). This is because these forced comparisons can mitigate a number of the rater effects we looked at in Chapter 1. For example, raters are not able to display central tendency effects and lenience and harshness, as these are moderated through the method. Studies have also shown that the method can be successfully implemented by untrained raters or raters regardless of their rater background. The method is cost-effective, as raters can make their judgements in less time than when applying a rating scale.

However, there are also a number of clear drawbacks to comparative judgement. Firstly, it is not always clear what construct raters draw on when operationalising comparative judgement. There is a chance that the decisions raters make are based on surface features, such as the length of an essay or the handwriting. The method essentially results in norm-referenced decisions, without a specified cut-score, where in many contexts a criterion-referenced decision on a rating scale is more appropriate. Depending on the purpose of the test, there is also no mechanism to provide feedback to test takers based on the judgements. Comparative judgement is also not as efficient as it may seem on the surface. While scoring time per performance is likely to be shorter, many more judgements are needed to arrive at sufficiently reliable results. Some studies have put this number at over 25 judgements per performance (e.g., Steedle & Ferrara, 2016).

To increase efficiency, the method of adaptive comparative judgement (ACJ) has been proposed. This rating method is similar to adaptive testing, in that after the first rating round, raters are provided with performances which are matched – raters are asked to compare two 'winners' from the first round or two 'losers'. Each essay is therefore compared to a sub-set in the group, rather than the whole corpus. The algorithm underlying ACJ is based on well established statistical models, such as the Rasch model. But even with the adaptive model, more pairings are required than when rating with a rating scale. Opponents of ACJ have also criticised that this technique over-inflates the reliability results (Bramley, 2015).

Finally, a further variation of comparative judgement, called randomly distributed comparative judgement, has been proposed by Wheadon (2015). In this variation, random pairings are maintained and each essay is marked the same number of times without any pair being repeated. This is described as less likely to over-inflate reliability.

Conclusion

In this chapter, we have examined some of the methods that have been used for scale development in the second language assessment literature. We have argued that the approaches to scale development put forward do not relate to actual practice and we have therefore presented individual methods and have shown how some sample research projects have combined methods to develop or revise scales. We next turn to the use of technology in second language performance assessment scoring, in particular the use of automated scoring systems and other technological advances in scoring.

CHAPTER 6

TECHNOLOGY IN SCORING

Introduction

Automated essay scoring and evaluation dates back more than half a century – in 1966, Ellis Page, then a high school English teacher, published the article 'The imminence of grading essays by computer'. Six years later, Page and his colleagues at the University of Connecticut in the US developed the first essay grading program, called Project Essay Grade (PEG). In the early 1990s, William Wresch, chair of Department of Mathematics and Computing at the University of Wisconsin, lamented that '(T)he fact that 25 years have now passed since the original studies were published and no high schools or colleges use computer essay grading sums up the reaction to these studies' (Wresch, 1993: 49). Admittedly, computer technologies at the time were less developed, and there was little interest in using computers for the purpose of scoring student essays.

Over the past two decades, significant progress has been made in the development and use of automated scoring and evaluation 'in response to the increasing demand for more efficient constructed-response scoring and the maturation of computer technologies' (Williamson, Xi & Breyer, 2012: 4). In recent years, with the rapid advances in the fields of artificial intelligence and natural language processing, automated essay scoring (AES) and automated writing evaluation (AWE) in which evaluative feedback is provided have been implemented in both large-scale and classroom contexts. Scoring engines have been developed, including, for example, Criterion by the Educational Testing Service (ETS) (www.ets.org/criterion), MyAccess! and IntelliMetric by Vantage Learning (www.vantagelearning.com) and Intelligent Essay Assessor (IEA) by Pearson Knowledge Technologies (www.pearsonkt.com). Most AES or AWE applications were designed to evaluate English, but progress has also been made in the evaluation of Japanese, Hebrew, Bahasa Malay, Chinese, French, German and Spanish (Deane, 2013; Shermis, Burstein, Higgins & Zechner, 2010).

Until the 1990s, the majority of automated scoring engines were developed for writing assessments. The application of automated scoring and evaluation for speech-based assessments is relatively recent. SpeechRater was the first scoring engine of speaking performances (Xi, Higgins, Zechner & Williamson, 2008). The system was developed by the ETS to provide test takers with feedback on their TOEFL preparation tests. The speaking assessments of Pearson's tests, including PTE Academic, PTE General (www.pearsonpte.com) and Versant tests (www.versanttest. com), are machine-mediated and machine-scored, using the technology provided by Pearson Knowledge Technologies. Other large-scale computer-mediated speaking assessments such as TOEFL iBT (www. ets.org/toefl/ibt) and Aptis (www.britishcouncil.org/exam/aptis) are currently scored by human raters.

In this chapter, we present an overview of automated scoring and evaluation of writing and speaking. Before delving into the topic, we will briefly review an equally important but less 'intelligent' technological application for scoring language assessments, that is, online marking of constructed-response items.

The application of online marking

The history of using computer technology for scoring language assessments dates back to the early 1970s when optical mark reader (OMR) systems were developed and used for scoring multiple-choice questions automatically. Following the automated scoring of selected-response items, the technology of online marking was developed for computer-based human scoring of constructed-response items, including free-response items such as extended essay writing. Before the invention of online marking, markers were required to collect examinees' scripts and mark them in a designated venue and then return the scripts to test centres for data capturing and processing. With online marking, examinees' handwritten scripts, if not directly typed on a computer, are first scanned and the images are distributed to raters for marking. In high-stakes testing contexts, the distribution is usually completed through a secure intranet system.

In this section, we will first describe the workflow of online marking and the benefits brought about by the technology. Then, we will review the research of issues involved in online marking. A note about the terminology: in the UK and Hong Kong Special Administrative Region of China, the term 'onscreen marking' is more often used whereas in the US and

Mainland China, 'online marking' is preferred. Occasionally 'e-marking' is used to refer to online or onscreen marking. In this chapter, these terms are used interchangeably.

The workflow of online marking

The workflow of online marking consists of several major components. According to Hong Kong Examinations and Assessment Authority (2015), the HKEAA OSM system works as follows: (1) Examinations completed by candidates; (2) Examination scripts collected from examination centres; (3) Examination scripts scanned and images saved; (4) Images of examination scripts distributed to markers for marking via a secure intranet system; and finally, (5) Marks and annotations by markers captured by the OSM system. Figure 6.1 shows in some detail the main components that feature in most online marking systems.

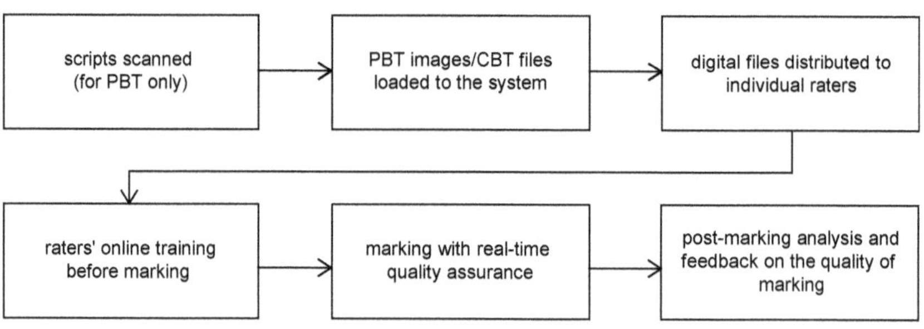

Figure 6.1: The workflow of online marking

In the case of paper-based testing (PBT), online marking starts with the scanning of scripts, i.e., candidates' responses to constructed-response items. The resulting digital images are then loaded to an internet or intranet system and distributed to individual raters. For computer-based tests (CBT), including a computer-based speaking test, digital files of candidates' responses are loaded to the marking system after the test is completed. Raters are required to receive online training before operational marking, in which they study benchmark performances and score some pre-selected sample scripts or audio clips. Raters who meet the basic requirement in the training session start their marking by downloading the scripts or audio clips first and then score them online. Marking can be done either at a secure place of raters' own choice or at a testing centre. During the process of marking, real-time quality assurance measures are implemented to control the quality of marking. Post-marking analysis also needs to be conducted to check the quality of marking. Feedback is provided to raters for improvement in their future marking performances.

Operational online marking systems may vary in some of the components. The Cambridge Assessment scoris® assessor marking system, for example, has two sub-systems: for individual markers, the system presents 'a secure online environment in which they can receive, view and mark exam scripts on their own home computers' (Cooze, 2011: 13); for examination boards, the system provides 'a web-delivered workflow system, which controls the process of allocating exam scripts to markers, collecting marks and monitoring the quality and consistency of markers' work' (ibid.). During the process of marking, the system allows examiners to use zoom tools to facilitate reading, mark annotations electronically and note comments.

Quality control procedures also vary from one system to another. Information about the exact quality assurance measures taken by an online marking system is not easy to retrieve, but there are some commonly used measures (see the next section for more details). In the Chinese College English Test (CET) online marking system for its written test (Jin & Yang, 2011), such measures include statistical analyses of the scores awarded by individual raters or groups of raters (e.g., mean, standard deviation, score distribution) and statistics of rater performance (e.g., speed of rating, times of correction, etc.). When marking is in progress, feedback is provided to the leader of each marking group, instead of individual raters, so as to avoid unnecessary rater anxiety and fluctuation in strictness or leniency. When needed, raters will be required by their group leader to receive another round of compulsory training and re-mark some of the scripts.

The benefits of online marking

Quoting Raikes, Greatorex & Shaw (2004), Fowles (2011: 4) commented on the gains achieved by marking online: '(T)he online marking by examiners of scanned scripts can be seen as a hybrid system' which is 'a way of realising some of the benefits of digital scripts in a context where paper is likely to remain important for many years to come'. The so-called hybrid system capitalises on the technological advances to improve the quality, efficiency, security and fairness of marking constructed-response items.

The most important benefit of online marking is the potential to enhance the quality of marking by such means as better standardisation processes, online training and real-time quality control using item seeding and double-marking. Standardisation is an essential prerequisite for quality assurance. In an online mode, virtually all the administrative work such as script distribution and collection, training and re-training, and control of the rating speed is automatically performed by the computer, making it much easier to standardise the rating processes.

Quality assurance measures can be built into an online marking system to monitor individual raters and groups of raters in real time. Scripts with expert scores (or gold standard scripts) are often used as 'anchors' to check raters' performance. These scripts are blended with and seeded in normal scripts. Discrepancies between raters' scores and expert scores on the anchored scripts are checked for quality control purposes. Double-marking in a paper-based mode is not easy to implement due to the difficulty in handling paper scripts. Online marking makes it much more convenient for scripts to be double-marked, checked for discrepancies between the two scores and submitted for the jurisdiction of a third rater if necessary. Real-time quality checks of this kind allow early intervention to ensure inter- and intra-rater consistencies as well as inter- and intra-centre consistencies when there are multiple marking centres. Furthermore, the flexibility of online marking makes it possible for raters to be assigned to mark different tasks. In such a case, the same test taker's performances on several tasks of a test (particularly a speaking test) can be marked by different raters, thus enhancing the marking reliability at the test level.

Secondly, online marking helps improve the efficiency of the marking process and delivers test results in a fast, secure and cost-effective manner. For test providers, the use of an online marking system can greatly reduce their administrative workload, especially in the case of paper-based testing. Such administrative work includes (1) before marking: collecting and storing scripts, covering test takers' ID to ensure anonymity, and distributing scripts; (2) after marking: copying the scores given by raters to answer sheets or computer systems, and storing and tracking the scripts for verification purposes. In paper-based testing, the security of online marking can be more stringent than that of traditional onsite paper-based scoring because it is much more secure to transfer, store and distribute digitised files than paper materials.

Finally, in an online marking mode, scripts or audio clips can be randomly distributed to individual raters, which is essential for using statistics as measures of quality assurance, because random sampling is a prerequisite for statistical analysis. More importantly, random distribution also contributes to test fairness because bias against test takers with a certain socio-cultural or language background can be avoided.

Research on online marking

An immediate concern of online marking is whether the application of the technology jeopardises test validity. As Fowles (2011: 2) put it, '(I)f tests are re-designed or modified in any way to make them more suitable for e-marking there is a danger that validity could be an issue.' To explore whether test validity would be compromised, test developers should look for 'any evidence of assessment schemes being developed and shaped by what technology can offer' (ibid.). In reality, however, the issue of validity is seldom directly addressed by studies of online marking, which are largely centred on the following practical concerns: usability of online marking systems, comparability of online marking with paper-based marking in terms of score differences (i.e., marking accuracy) and reliability across marking modes, and the impact of online marking on raters' behaviour, including their perceptions of online marking and the rating criteria they attend to when rating online.

In the late 1990s, studies were conducted by ETS to evaluate the efficacy of its Online Scoring Network (OSN) system for marking extended essays (e.g., Powers & Farnum, 1997; Powers, Farnum, Grant & Kubota, 1997) and free-response questions in Advanced Placement exams (e.g., Zhang, Powers, Wright & Morgan, 2003). In these studies, raters were invited to mark samples of essays and responses on screen and on paper after a general OSN training. Data were also collected using survey questionnaires. The results revealed that raters were generally positive about their experiences of online marking and that there were no significant differences in scores awarded in the two modes. Suggestions on some aspects of the OSN system were made to improve its user-friendliness and technical qualities such as connection with the website and download speed.

In Mainland China, the CET online marking system was evaluated in terms of its user-friendliness, marking reliability, raters' decision-making processes and the effectiveness of online quality control measures. Wang (2004a, 2004b, 2015) conducted his doctoral study on the validation of the CET online marking system. Wang (2004a) provided a detailed description of the workflow and main features of the prototype CET online marking system. Wang (2004b) reported a comparative study of online marking and traditional paper-based marking. In the study, 14 certified raters were invited to score 1341 CET essays in two modes. The results showed that both inter- and intra-rater consistencies were improved in the online mode of marking. In his following studies (2005, 2015), Wang collected more evidence through surveys and interviews to evaluate the usefulness and user-friendliness of the CET online system. Huang (2007) collected data from 52 raters through a questionnaire survey and interviews following an operational CET online marking session. The results produced evidence supporting the general acceptance of the CET online marking system and raters' positive feedback on the reliability and efficiency of marking online. Suggestions on how the system could be improved were provided by the raters, relating to the presentation of the scripts, the amount and the type of feedback to raters, the control of marking speed, and so on.

Coniam (2009, 2011, 2013) and Coniam & Yeung (2010) reported a series of studies examining onscreen marking in the context of Hong Kong public examination. Coniam (2009, 2011) examined the marking reliability and raters' attitudes towards onscreen marking of extended essays in English Language examinations. The study showed that raters were reliable in both modes of marking. It was also found that raters had been ready for the new marking medium, i.e., onscreen marking, in 2009, and by 2011, onscreen marking was becoming increasingly accepted. Coniam & Yeung (2010) revealed even more positive attitudes towards onscreen marking among raters of Liberal Studies than the raters of English language examinations in the previous study. Coniam (2013) investigated the attitudes and perceptions of a group of younger raters, undergraduate language or linguistics students, who marked short, objective answer questions in the Hong Kong Advanced Level Examination Use of English. The findings indicated an increasing acceptance of onscreen marking, especially by young tablet-owners, who were used to reading on the tablet.

Research of Cambridge Assessment's scoris® assessor marking system revealed that examiners employed different behaviours when marking in different modes. They navigated through essays and made annotations in different ways. The differences, however, did not influence marking reliability and accuracy. Geranpayeh (2011), for example, invited eight senior examiners to score CAE writing papers using a 5-point holistic scale in two modes (paper-based versus onscreen). The results of FACETS analysis showed that the mode of marking had no impact on examiners' marking; the results of a feedback questionnaire and interview data analyses showed that the examiners had little problem in using the onscreen marking system once they received initial training.

Following this review of online marking, we will move on to the more 'intelligent' application of computer technology for language assessment: automated scoring and evaluation. We will describe the mechanism of automated scoring, and discuss the benefits and challenges of automated scoring technologies. We will also review existing research and point out the way forward for the field of automated scoring and evaluation of writing and speaking.

How does automated scoring and evaluation work?

Shermis & Burstein (2003, 2013) present a complete picture of the evolution and the state-of-the-art of automated essay scoring and evaluation technology across a number of disciplines: teaching pedagogy, educational measurement, cognitive science and computational linguistics. Although the development of an automated scoring system has a seemingly straightforward goal: producing scores similar to those of human raters, automated scoring is an essentially cross-disciplinary area. In this section, instead of going into the detail about the highly technical procedures of automated scoring systems, we will provide a non-technical description of how an automated scoring system works to achieve the goal of matching human scores.

Automated essay scoring

Drawing on Ruth & Murphy's (1984) understanding of the major elements at play in direct, on-demand, timed writing assessments, Deane (2013: 11) described the rating process of 'current-generation AES systems'. The process follows a three-stage model of automated essay scoring, which is parallel to human scoring but with some new added elements. Below is a more detailed description of each stage.

The first stage is a sampling process for model student responses. At this stage, human raters who have been found to consistently produce high-quality scores, or expert raters, score a training sample of up to several hundred to thousands of responses. For a prompt-specific scoring engine, models specific to a particular writing prompt are generated using prompt-specific samples for machine training. When a generic engine is to be developed, samples of the right genre would serve the purpose. The actual number of samples for machine training depends on 'the complexity of the writing task, the rating scales, and the type of modelling techniques applied' (Van Moere & Downey, 2016: 343).

The second stage is a model design process that builds the elements needed to implement a general or prompt-specific scoring model. In this process, an AES system generates a scoring model by 'learning' the criteria of human rating and inferring the pooled judgements of human raters. It is important that a sufficient number of responses at each score point on the rating scale of the assessment are used to train the engine. To build the scoring model, the system identifies a number of features and weights the features or clusters of features. For prompt-specific models, a unique set of features is developed for each prompt, whereas generic models apply the same set of features and feature weighting to responses on all prompts. Feature scores or trait scores (scores of clustered features) are regressed using multiple regression against human scores, and finally, a total score that would best predict human scores in the training sample is computed.

When the model is established, a second sample of human-scored essays is required for validating the scoring model. When the model functions satisfactorily, the automated scoring system enters the third and final stage of operational rating. At this stage, the system analyses all the responses to identify text features, assign a score to each response using the model and, where required, generate feedback.

To evaluate the content relevance of an essay, some programs employ a natural language processing technique called Latent Semantic Analysis (LSA). The technique enables the engine to 'understand' the meaning of a text by estimating how close the vocabulary in the text is to a targeted vocabulary set. Van Moere & Downey (2016) use the following example to explain the mechanism of LSA: (1) Surgery is often performed by a team of doctors. (2) On many occasions, several physicians are involved in an operation. Although the two sentences contain no words in common, their meanings are approximately the same based on the contexts of the words that comprise them. For example, the words 'physicians' and 'doctors' appear in similar contexts in English. In an LSA vector space, these two sentences would describe effectively the same 'vector' because their underlying meaning is the same.

Zupanc & Bosnic (2015: 387) compared 21 automated essay scoring systems that 'have predominance in this field – and are consequently more complex and have attracted greater publicity'. All the systems they reviewed 'work by extracting a set of attributes (system-specific) and using some machine learning algorithm to model and predict the final score' (ibid.). To be specific, an automated scoring system consists of the following components essential to ensuring the quality of scoring: (1) feature extraction: identifying features relevant to the test construct; (2) feature merging: clustering and weighting the features; (3) model building: building and validating the model using human-scored responses; (4) operational scoring of all the responses. In cases of paper-form administration of writing assessments where handwritten essays are to be scored, the written responses are scanned by high-quality digital scanners, recognised by computer systems and saved as text files before being scored by computer (e.g., Jin, Zhu & Wang, 2017; Shermis, 2014). The flow chart in Figure 6.2 is an illustration of the automated essay scoring process, which includes the components of image scanning and text recognition.

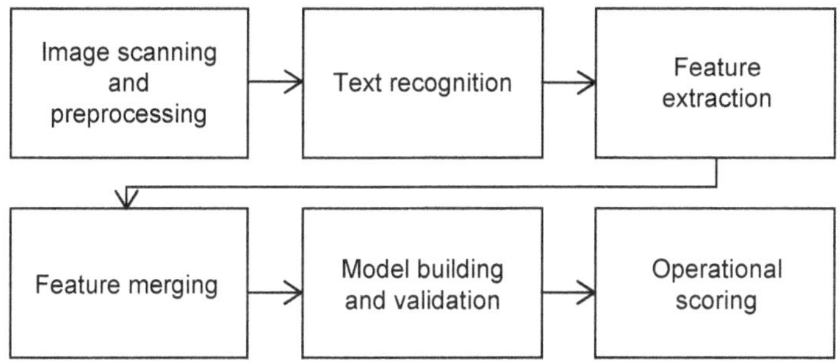

Figure 6.2: An illustration of the automated essay scoring process

Automated writing evaluation

The terms 'automated essay scoring' (AES) and 'automated writing evaluation' (AWE) are sometimes used interchangeably. However, a useful distinction could be made between the system or program developed solely for producing a holistic score and the one that provides evaluative feedback in addition to scores. Van Moere & Downey (2016: 343) recognise such a distinction by using AES to refer to 'computer scoring of writing in high-stakes tests' and AWE to describe 'a more formative, feedback-rich use of the technology for purposes of language learning'.

When Page started to work on automated scoring over fifty years ago, the aim was to free classroom teachers from scoring stacks of students' papers. The PEG program was actually a typical automated evaluation system, which was able to identify and measure 30 proxies (i.e., textual features) such as length of essay in words, average sentence length, number of commas, number of prepositions, number of spelling errors, number of common words, average word length (Page, 1968). The PEG system was acquired by Measurement, Inc. in 2002 and developed into a web-based writing practice program. Examples are provided in Shermis, Burstein, Higgins & Zechner (2010) to demonstrate the type of feedback provided by PEG. Take essay length as an example. Empirical evidence has suggested that the longer an essay, the more highly valued it is by a human rater. The relationship of course is not linear, but logarithmic. The length of an essay is important up to a point, but beyond a certain threshold it carries little additional weight. A more complex feature is the number of times the word 'because' is used in an essay. The feature could be taken as an indicator of 'sentence complexity' and is also a characteristic of 'style'. When similar features are clustered, the scoring engine could provide so-called trait scores for the intrinsic characteristics of writing such as content, style, organisation, mechanics, and so on.

In the 1990s, with the advent of computers and the internet, research of automated scoring and evaluation was revitalised. Criterion, an internet-based online writing practice service developed by ETS (www.ets.org/criterion), for example, was designed to provide descriptive feedback of student writing. Critique, one of the components of Criterion, identifies those aspects of writing that need improvement and reports content-irrelevant errors such as grammatical errors, usage problems and mechanics errors as well as more complex features such as undesirable stylistic features, discourse structure issues, off-topic content, and so on. The online writing practice service also incorporates an online planning (pre-writing) activity, which helps students to produce essays of a better quality. IntelliMetric, similarly, provides diagnostic feedback on organisation, conventions as well as sentence-by-sentence feedback on grammar, usage, spelling and mechanics. The scoring engine also has a complementary tool, IntelliMetric Mentor, that helps writers to edit and revise their drafts. AEW programs, therefore, are more of an instructional application than a scoring tool for large-scale assessments.

Automated speech scoring

The crucial difference between the automated scoring of essays and speech-based performances is the additional processing required of speech data: spoken responses need to be recognised and digitised before being scored by an automated scoring system. Since the 1990s, with the technological development in the field of speech recognition, automated scoring engines of spoken responses have made their way into the stage of practical applications.

Early versions of automated speech scoring systems were developed for scoring performances on controlled speaking tasks. Pearson's Versant English Test (VET), originally called PhonePass and delivered via telephones, was probably the first fully automated L2 speaking assessment commercially available for high-stakes uses. The test was developed in the 1990s by researchers at Stanford University (Bernstein, 1999). The tasks of PhonePass, however, were highly constrained, including for example, read-aloud, word repetition, sentence repetition. Open-ended and spontaneous speaking tasks are much more difficult to score automatically. Speaking performance such as that elicited by TOEFL iBT® 'has presented much greater challenges, owing to the difficulty and complexity in both recognising and scoring unpredictable speech' (Xi, Higgins, Zechner & Williamson, 2012: 371–372).

Before looking at wider speech features scored by automated scoring engines, we will first describe the scoring of pronunciation in some detail. According to Van Moere & Suzuki (2018: 139), an automated scoring system using automatic speech recognition (ASR) requires 'four main underlying components' for assessing pronunciation: the acoustic model, the language model, the pronunciation dictionary and the scoring model. An acoustic model deals with the sound system of the target language. The task of this component is to recognise and transcribe the speech data to be scored. To improve the accuracy of ASR, an acoustic model needs to be trained on a large sample representative of the target test population. A language model processes the vocabulary and grammar of the language in the speech data. This model facilitates speech recognition by anticipating what the speaker will say in a speaking task. To develop a language model, speaking tasks are trialled among a representative sample of the target test population and performances on the tasks are collected. The pronunciation dictionary lists the most common ways of pronouncing the words in the language model. The fourth component is the scoring model, which selects features from the speech data and applies them to predict human scores.

In recent decades, ASR technology has advanced to the point that the speech recogniser could be adapted to the speech of non-native speakers from different first language backgrounds if sufficient data have been fed into the machine for training purposes. The accuracy rate of recognition is satisfactory in testing contexts where students are highly motivated to perform to their full potential and the testing conditions are standardised (e.g., Isaacs, 2008; Zechner, Higgins & Williamson, 2009).

When the assessment construct is oral communication, instead of pronunciation, the automated scoring system extracts a different set of features, that is, features of oral proficiency. For example, powered by Ordinate technology, the VET automatically scores test takers' performances on a number of speaking tasks and reports an overall score and four sub-scores: Sentence Mastery, Vocabulary, Fluency and Pronunciation (Pearson, 2009: 12). Bernstein, Van Moere & Cheng (2010: 358) admit that the construct (called 'facility-in-L2') measured in the VET or the speaking tasks of the PTE 'is not directly related to the context or scoring of functional communication or extra-linguistic goals'; instead, facility-in-L2 tests measure 'performance outside the setting of language in use for communicative tasks'. Evidence however has been produced to support 'a mediated link between the facility-in-L2 test scores and real world spoken performance in L2' (ibid.: 371). It is therefore believed that fully automated spoken language tests, though imperfect, offer 'a starting point for a generation of more accurate measurement methods' (ibid.: 374).

The overall processes of automated scoring of speech-based data share many similarities with those of automated essay scoring: a scoring model extracts and merges features from the data and uses them to predict human scores; the model will be validated using a separate sample of speech performances scored by experienced human raters before being put into operational use. Processes unique to automated speech scoring are speech recognition and transcription. Figure 6.3 is an illustration of the automated speech scoring process.

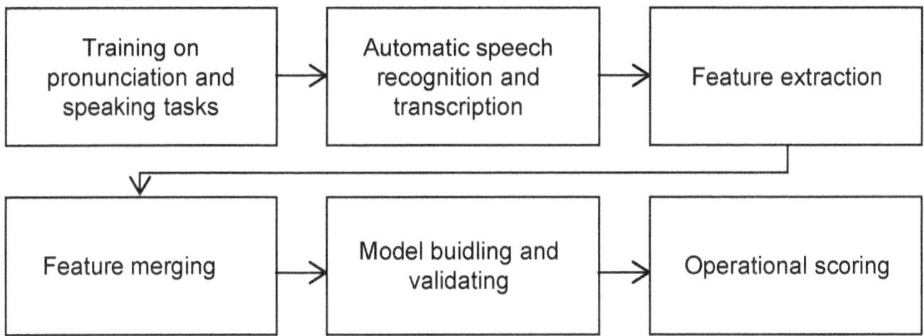

Figure 6.3: An illustration of the automated speech scoring process

Automated speech evaluation

This section describes applications of automated speech scoring that provide training or evaluative feedback to learners. ASR technology, for example, has been used extensively for training L2 learners' pronunciation. In such a tutoring program, learners are provided with opportunities to practice pronunciation and receive evaluative feedback in 'a flexible and private learning practice environment' (Van Moere & Suzuki, 2018: 137). Learners read words, phrases or sentences shown on a computer screen and the system identifies and points out mispronounced words. Learners can keep trying until 'their pronunciation aligns with a given target waveform, spectrogram, or prosodic contour' (ibid.).

In addition to pronunciation training, some automated scoring systems of speaking are able to provide diagnostic information in the form of component or trait scores (e.g., the four sub-scores of the VET). SpeechRater, for example, is one of the early engines developed for scoring and evaluating speaking performances. Similar to an automated essay scoring system like e-rater, the scoring engine of SpeechRater is also a machine learning system, which extracts features to represent a response to a particular type of task, builds a scoring model by weighting the features or clusters of features and finally produces a score that best predicts human ratings.

Designed specifically for scoring and evaluating the speaking section of the low-stakes TOEFL Practice Online (TPO) test, SpeechRater is able to score spoken responses elicited by such tasks as answering questions, responding to written or audio stimuli, and making a presentation or a speech. The challenge is that these tasks require the production of extended speech in a spontaneous manner. Higgins, Xi, Zechner &

Williamson (2011) provide a comprehensive description of the architecture and the scoring procedure of SpeechRater as well as the features automatically derived by the system to score spoken responses to TPO tasks. A total of 44 predictive features were available for consideration in developing the so-called 'filtering model', which determines whether the response should receive a score. These features fall into several major categories: low-level signal processing, response length, fluency, vocabulary diversity, pronunciation, grammatical accuracy and ASR confidence (Higgins et al., 2011: 290). Based on the statistical performances of these features and the recommendation of the experts on the Content Advisory Committee, a set of five final features were selected and the weight of each feature was determined for the final scoring model: pronunciation (acoustic model score, weight=4), fluency (speech articulation rate, weight=2), vocabulary diversity (unique words normalised by speech duration, weight=2), grammatical accuracy (language model score, weight=1) and fluency (average length of speech chunks, weight=1) (ibid.: 296).

Although the precise combination of measures selected in the scoring engines that best approximate human ratings might be opaque even to test developers (Isaacs, 2018), validity analyses have shown that subscores generated by the systems in tests like the VET and TPO are reasonably distinct and therefore offer useful diagnostic feedback to test takers (Higgins et al., 2011; Pearson, 2009: 14–22).

Ginther, Dimova & Yang (2010: 394) point out that 'automated scorers display greater internal consistency because they are trained to analyze basic and easily measured aspects of performance (e.g., fluency, pronunciation, and vocabulary)'. In their study, it was found that the temporal measures of fluency provide a strong foundation for ASE systems. The question of central concern, however, remains 'the meaning of human ratings of second language proficiency' (ibid.: 395). There is, therefore, a long way to go before scoring engines can automatically generate rich, accurate and meaningful evaluative feedback in speaking assessment.

Benefits of automated scoring and evaluation

Over the past few decades, automated scoring systems have been adopted in high-volume, high-stakes testing programmes and automated evaluation systems have significant applications in low-stakes classroom assessment environments. Arguments for automated scoring and evaluation mainly include the improved efficiency (speed) of scoring, reduced cost of scoring, scoring consistency, and generation and provision of diagnostic feedback for improving teaching and learning. In this section, benefits of automated scoring and evaluation will be discussed along these lines.

Efficiency and cost-effectiveness

Automatic scoring greatly improves rating efficiency mainly because one size fits all: a single scoring model will fit all speech-based or text-based data produced in one test. Automated scoring has made it possible for testing agencies to score large volumes of texts or speeches in a timely and cost-effective manner. An example of a fully automated test is the Pearson Test of English – Academic (PTE Academic). One of the reasons for some test takers to choose PTE Academic over other internationally recognised admission tests such as TOEFL iBT or IELTS is its speedy score reporting procedure. PTE Academic results are typically available within 5 business days (www.pearsonpte.com) whereas it takes 10–13 days for online preview of TOEFL iBT scores (www.ets.org/toefl/ibt) or IELTS scores (www.ielts.org).

Before the availability of computer-based language testing, students' written texts had to be translated to machine-readable form by punching the texts onto computer-readable cards, or later, keyboarding students' handwritten texts into the computer. Nowadays, with advanced text-recognition technology, texts produced in a paper-based language test can be scanned and recognised in an efficient manner and with a satisfactory level of accuracy (Jin et al., 2017). When testing is computerised, this time-consuming process is no longer necessary. Once written texts are digitised, the rating process is automatically completed using the model that has been established in the training phase. Similarly, ASR technology has developed to the extent that random or impromptu responses are recognisable using phoneme-level models and lengthy speeches produced by test takers in response to a highly controlled task are also recognisable using sentence-level models that involve machine training. The initial development of text- or speech-recognition systems could be costly. Once the technology is developed and becomes mature, however, its widespread application could dramatically reduce the cost.

Scoring objectivity and consistency

Automated scoring systems are trained to score learner performance by internalising 'the pooled wisdom of many expert scorers' (Vantage

Learning, 2005). The most significant gain in using automated scoring, therefore, is its scoring objectivity and consistency.

For constructed-response items, rating reliability is an important criterion of assessment quality. When speaking or writing assessments are scored by human raters, there are two criteria to evaluate the reliability of scoring: inter- and intra-rater consistency. Inter-rater consistency refers to the agreement among different raters and could be improved through rigorous rater training in which raters are calibrated to the same standards by studying carefully rating criteria and benchmark scripts. Even so, inconsistency among raters is ever-present given the subjective nature of judgement. In speech rating, for example, due to the intangible and transient nature of speech, subjectivity in human scoring is inevitable. Intra-rater consistency refers to the internal consistency of a particular rater, whose rating might be affected by such factors as fatigue, halo effect or emotions. Intra-rater inconsistency is also unavoidable but could be improved by randomly distributing test takers' speech or scripts and controlling the speed of rating (see also Chapter 1 for rater effects).

The issue of consistency can be better handled in automated scoring, which enjoys the benefit of learning from the scores derived from more than two experienced human raters. The agreement between the computer and human raters therefore is usually as high as or higher than among human raters themselves (e.g., Attali & Powers, 2009; Shermis & Hamner, 2013) and an automated scoring system does not have the issue of inter- or intra-rater consistency. On the one hand, the computer does not have idiosyncratic preferences or interpretations of students' writing or speaking and therefore is free from bias. That is, individual rater idiosyncrasies that are inevitably present in human ratings can be avoided by using automated scoring systems. Once a scoring model is built, the same essay will be awarded the same score by the same engine no matter when it is scored and how many times it is scored. In such a case, one model will fit all scripts: the computer will rate all the essays or speeches based on exactly the same sets of criteria and following the same algorithm.

On the other hand, computer scoring systems do not have the issue of subjectivity involved in human scoring because scoring engines are not affected by such human factors as fatigue, emotion or halo effects, rendering intra-rater consistency irrelevant to the reliability of speaking or writing assessments. Take L2 learners' accents as an example. When speaking performances are scored, accents have always been an issue with human raters, who are sensitive to learners' foreign accents but also bring their own experiences to the table (e.g., finding it easier to understand Indian English if they have taught many Indian students or have lived in India). Judging the degree of intelligibility could also present a great challenge to human raters due to the lack of objective criteria of intelligibility. The development of ASR technology and the training of ASR engines on corpora of both native and non-native speakers have made it possible for scoring systems to diminish or eliminate the influence of raters' familiarity with or their attitudes towards learner accents. Therefore, when properly trained, the computer is able to recognise, transcribe and score human speech in a faster and more accurate manner.

Opportunities to learn

Automated scoring systems are often criticised for lacking transparency because their scoring criteria are not known to users. Van Moere & Downey (2016), however, argue that there is no quantifiable way for us to measure how human raters weight various aspects of scoring criteria and combine the various pieces of information into a final score. It is further argued that 'in some ways machine scores are more transparent than human judgements. … it is possible to achieve something replicable with machine scoring: every piece of data analyzed, and its precise weighting in the scoring model, is verifiable in the machine algorithms' (ibid.: 352). This view is shared by Xi et al. (2012: 372), who point out that '… the scoring logic and rules utilized by an automated scoring system, although complex, are objective and thus more traceable than the decision process engaged by human raters'. The replicability or traceability of the decision-making process engaged in machine scoring makes automated writing or speaking evaluation possible.

The most significant application of automated scoring or evaluation technology, as claimed by the developer of such programs as Criterion, MyAccess! and IntelliMetric, has been in the teaching and learning of writing and speaking. When evaluating students' responses, the features that finally enter the scoring function can be used to compute so-called trait scores, that is, dimensions of the construct measured by the scoring system. By so doing, much more attention can be paid to each individual student and nuanced feedback is provided to their writing or speaking performance. Equally important, the feedback can be provided within a much shorter period of time. For speaking instruction, feedback on pronunciation can be provided to improve learners' production of targeted phonemes, although the effectiveness of such feedback remains to be evaluated (Isaacs, 2018).

Automated evaluation has begun to have a major impact on both classroom instruction and large-scale assessment. Writing instructors can now be freed from reading a large number of student essays, and accordingly, students will gain more opportunities to practise writing. When writing on a platform of automated evaluation service, students are motivated to revise their drafts based on machine-generated feedback. For high-stakes writing assessments, automated scoring often plays the role of a second or check scorer. Scoring reliability can be improved while the cost and time of scoring is reduced.

Issues to be resolved with automated scoring and evaluation

Efficient, reliable and useful as it is, the application of automated scoring technology is not without its critics. In fact, since its inception half a century ago, automated essay scoring has been a topic of controversy. Quoting Bennett (2006), Deane (2013: 12) argued that 'AES involves all the issues that arise when any assessment is validated'. In particular, there are three major issues arising from the use of automated scoring in language assessment: (1) the knowledge that essays will be machine-scored may lead to changes in behaviour that undermine the intended construct; (2) the construct measured by an AES system which cannot interpret meaning, infer communicative intent, evaluate factual correctness and quality of argumentation, or take the writing process into account, leading to the danger that an AES system can be gamed; (3) technical inadequacies of an automated scoring system that may fail to achieve complete accuracy in error identification (ibid.: 15). In this section, issues concerning the application of automated scoring in language education will be discussed from the perspectives of humanistic concerns with machine scoring, the construct validity of automatically scored assessments and the impact of automated scoring and evaluation on teaching and learning.

Humanistic concerns

Although current technology (e.g., artificial intelligence) is able to train machines to 'converse' with humans or 'understand' written texts, language communication is essentially viewed as a communicative activity between humans. As noted by Deane (2013), automated scoring systems evaluate the quality of the text whereas human raters care about the writing proficiency of the learner as a writer. There has always been a humanistic concern about using machines rather than humans to score spoken or written responses. Machines cannot think like humans, nor can they appreciate expressions and ideas appropriate to the cultural and social contexts in which we live. In assessment contexts, instead of encouraging students to use rhetorical knowledge and think critically, teachers might coach students to avoid using such knowledge or skills for fear that their responses might be misunderstood by the machine scorer. There are also sentiments among teachers that if a machine can do their job then they are somehow devalued and that anything which diminishes the profoundly communicative nature of writing or speaking is worthy of a teacher's resistance.

Among the opponents to automated scoring, Conference on College Composition and Communication (CCCC Committee on Assessment, 2006) is probably the most direct and strongest. In its position statement, CCCC explicitly voices its opposition: 'We oppose the use of machine-scored writing in the assessment of writing.' The statement further explains:

> Writing is by definition social. Learning to write entails learning to accomplish a range of purposes for a range of audiences in a range of settings. ... Automated assessment programs do not respond as human readers. While they may promise consistency, they distort the very nature of writing as a complex and context-rich interaction between people. They simplify writing in ways that can mislead writers to focus more on structure and grammar than on what they are saying by using a given structure and style. (p. 1)

Deane (2013: 11) noted that in direct, on-demand, timed writing assessments to be scored by human raters, some aspects of writing skill have already been emphasised whereas others de-emphasised: 'Explicit text features and content are foregrounded, while social and process elements of writing expertise are backgrounded.' As the standardised situation has already changed the audience and the purpose of writing, it was argued that 'objections to automated scoring are actually objections to the assumptions of standardized testing' (ibid.: 12). In other words, the humanistic concern does not arise from automated scoring. Rather, the issue is an intrinsic problem inherent to standardised testing.

Writing takes various forms, some as a way of written communication, others as a means of learning content knowledge or a language. Weigle (2013) made a distinction between writing by different learner populations and for different purposes. Learners are categorised based on their learning environment: learners in English-medium educational contexts and learners of English as a second or foreign language. Assessments of writing are designed for three main purposes: assessing writing skills (AW), assessing content through writing (ACW), and assessing language through writing (ALW). Most existing automated essay scoring systems, according to Weigle (2013: 90), were designed 'with a primarily native English speaker/writer population and an AW purpose in mind'. When native writers' writing skills are assessed, the communicative nature of writing presents an even greater challenge to automated scoring systems.

Construct validity

Related to the humanistic concern of automated scoring, construct validity of automatically scored speaking or writing assessments has also been an issue of debate. While admitting that automated speech evaluation is attractive because of potential cost reduction and increased consistency in score assignment, Ginther et al. (2010: 380) note that 'consistency becomes less appealing if based on a restricted set of variables that only partially represent the construct'. In the review of the PTE Academic, a fully automated language proficiency test for non-native speakers of English, it was found that there was a lack of evidence supporting the correspondence between what is scored and the use of language in the TLU (target language use) domain (Wang, Choi, Schmidgall & Bachman, 2012). The reviewers, therefore, felt an urgent need for test developers and users to understand precisely how constructs have been operationalised in a scoring system.

According to Messick (1989), the major threats to construct validity are construct irrelevance and construct under-representation. If a test contains excess reliable variance that is irrelevant to the interpreted construct, the score interpretation of the test is likely to be contaminated, posing a threat to the test's validity. On the other hand, when the construct of an assessment is under-represented, something important has been missing in the construct of the assessment. In high-stakes environments, if test takers know that their writing or speaking is to be assessed by machines instead of human raters, they are likely to adopt test-wise strategies in order to get a high score, introducing construct-irrelevant variances to the assessment. A more direct threat to the validity of automated scoring is construct under-representation. With current technology, certain types of features, particularly meaning-oriented and content-related features, cannot be captured by an automated scoring engine. An automated scoring system may find it easy to identify mistakes or errors common to language learners such as determiner, preposition or collocation errors, but it is much more difficult for the system to assess originality of ideas and creativity in thinking. In other words, the construct coverage of automated scoring models might not be adequate to yield scores that represent the speaking or writing construct.

The recent debate among the International Language Testing Association (ILTA) membership on the high-stakes use of automated scoring in PTE Academic is an example of construct representation. The case is of an Irish vet who took PTE Academic as a requirement of immigration by the Australian government. It is true that an unreasonably high score is required, but the fact that the test taker, as a native speaker of English having a career in an English-speaking environment, failed the PTE Academic speaking test has still aroused concern among the general public and the language testing community. A major concern is that the automated scoring engine fails to tap into the construct of spoken interaction. It is of course also likely that the Irish vet was not prepared for the test format and spoke too slowly with many pauses.

In automated speaking assessments, technological constraints may dictate the nature of the assessment (Isaacs, 2018). The accuracy of word recognition, a fundamental component of automated speech recognition, for example, tends to be affected by task types: highly controlled tasks (e.g., sentence repetition, read-aloud) would result in better recognition than open-ended tasks (e.g., an oral presentation on a given topic) in which test-taker output is unpredictable. Isaac (2018) considers construct under-representation as a limitation of technological capability of automated scoring, which relies heavily on spectral (i.e., frequency-based) and durational (i.e., time-based) measures associated with segmental accuracy and temporal fluency. Higher-order features such as discourse organisation, lexical resource, grammatical accuracy, prosody and content development are largely ignored. The state-of-the-art technology may have expanded the construct representation and gone beyond 'fluency markers' in automated speech scoring, but there is nonetheless a very long way to go before scoring engines can automatically comprehend and evaluate spoken interactions.

Impact on teaching and learning

When speaking or writing to an audience of machines, students are likely to pay heed to the features they consider are machine-comprehensible. An unfortunate consequence is that students and teachers would focus their efforts on these features in teaching and learning because they believe performances with the features would be awarded a higher score. For example, students may produce well organised, nicely phrased speeches or texts without meaningful or creative thinking. In such a case, normal classroom teaching could be replaced by coaching students to 'game' the machine.

The use of automated scoring in NAPLAN (the National Assessment Program – Literacy and Numeracy), an annual assessment for students in Australia (http://www.nap.edu.au/naplan), has caused serious concern among Australian teachers. Apart from the lack of confidence in the technology, teachers are also worried over the impact of automated scoring on teaching and learning. Major criticisms include the possibility of teaching to the test or ignoring learners' creativity in teaching. The teachers also share the notion that essays are written to stimulate readers, not machines, and that it is a disservice to the writer to have their prose processed by unfeeling computers. Some language testers voiced their concern about the power relationship in the automated scoring 'business': we are essentially putting more power into the hands of these private companies, who are making a lot of money and holding a lot of influence in terms of research output, etc. Teachers, in their view, would feel disempowered when deprived of the right to provide relevant and constructive feedback to learners.

Research of automated scoring and evaluation

Automated scoring 'is typically subject to greater scrutiny than human scoring' because of the inevitable suspicion associated with the scores produced by automated scoring systems (Xi et al., 2012: 372). Research is needed to establish the validity of automated scoring and increase public confidence in scores automatically produced by the machine. In this section, we will first provide an overview of approaches to validating automated scoring systems. We will then review studies of automated scoring on correspondence of machine- and human-generated scores, the construct validity of automated scoring, and automated writing and speaking evaluation.

Approaches to validating automated scoring systems

Automated scoring systems pose 'some distinctive validity challenges such as the potential to under- or misrepresent the construct of interest, vulnerability to cheating, impact on examinee behavior, and score users' interpretation and use of scores' (Williamson et al., 2012: 4). An evaluation framework was proposed for 'operational deployment of automated scoring in an assessment for high-stakes purposes' (ibid.). The framework consists of five areas of emphasis: construct relevance and representation, association with human scores, association with independent measures, generalisability of scores and impact on decisions and consequences, each corresponding to one inferential step of an argument-based validity framework, i.e., explanation, evaluation, extrapolation, generalisation and utilisation (ibid.: 5). Detailed guidelines and criteria associated with each area are also provided in the framework.

Using Williamson et al.'s (2012) framework, Xi et al. (2012) compared two scoring methods of an automated speech scoring system SpeechRater 1.0, which is used for scoring the speaking section of the TOEFL Practice Online (TPO). The focuses of the study were on the first two inferential steps proposed in the framework: explanation and evaluation. Evidence was produced and presented to demonstrate the correspondence in scores produced by automated scoring systems and human scorers and to understand the construct represented within the scoring processes that automated scoring systems use. The findings of the study support a multiple regression model with expert weights determined by content experts when the TPO automated scoring model was established. To build such a model, content experts' judgements were used as the basis for evaluating the construct representation of the features to be included in the model.

Weigle (2013) also adopted an interpretive argument when framing thinking about how automated scoring impacts assessment, from task design through the use of test scores. The framework outlined the evidence needed to support interpretations of test scores and their use. Drawing on Williamson et al. (2012) and Xi (2010a), Weigle (2013) proposed five inferences that are particularly relevant to automated scoring, corresponding with different areas of emphasis in validity research: evaluation, generalisation, explanation, extrapolation and utilisation. The value of laying out a validity argument, according to Weigle (2013: 92), is that it 'allows practitioners to prioritize the importance of different types of validity evidence, to integrate multiple types of validity evidence into a coherent narrative, and to monitor the progress of the validation process'.

When the focus of validation is on assessment use and consequences of assessment use, an assessment use argument (AUA; Bachman & Palmer, 2010) approach is often adopted. The review of the PTE Academic, for example, adopted such an approach. In the review, an AUA was constructed for evaluating the use of the PTE Academic for making admission decisions at tertiary-level institutions and organisations where English is used for communication (Wang et al., 2012). The AUA consists of four claims, along with warrants that are associated with each claim. The evidence that was available to support these claims and warrants was analysed and potential rebuttals were articulated. Many of the warrants are closely related to automated scoring. Examples of consistency warrants examined in the review are:

(1) 'The automated scoring algorithms for scoring written and spoken test responses were developed through trialing and comparison with multiple human ratings' (Consistency Warrant 3); and
(2) 'The automated scoring algorithms for written and spoken test responses were developed through trialing with several different groups of test takers' (Consistency Warrant 4) (Wang et al., 2012: 606).

Evidence supporting the two warrants is that both Intelligent Essay Assessor and Ordinate Scoring System, the automated scoring systems employed by PTE Academic, 'went through rigorous training and norming stages using large numbers of essays and speech samples that were rated by two trained human raters and by an adjudicator who provided a third score in the case of disagreement' (ibid.: 606). There are, however, potential rebuttals to the warrants. Evidence of the frequency and the results of ongoing training and calibration of the automated scoring systems, for example, is needed to further validate their consistencies.

An interpretive argument or AUA approach is useful when an automated scoring system is to be validated. There are, however, so many levels of inferences to be supported in order to link test performance to score-based decisions. How should we determine the prioritisation of the emphasis areas as suggested by Williamson et al. (2012)? As the strength of the chain of inferences is more likely to be affected by its weakest links, it is suggested that when setting priorities of a research agenda, we should start from the weakest links, that is, the inferences that are least likely to be supported by evidence (Chapelle, Enright & Jamieson, 2010). Xi (2012) noted that the prioritisation of validation studies also needs to be determined by the method of automated scoring implementation and the intended use of the assessment scores. For automated scoring of assessments for making high-stakes decisions, construct relevance and representation probably constitute the most important consideration in validation research.

Correspondence in machine and human-generated scores

Automated scoring engines are often claimed to be sufficiently reliable or even more reliable than human raters. Reliability, however, is not a sufficient requirement for the operational use of automated scoring systems. When the quality of an automated scoring system is evaluated, one question most frequently asked is '(C)an machine scoring produce scores similar to those of human raters?' (Shermis, 2014: 55). That is, human scores are used as the 'gold standard'. Automated scoring systems are evaluated based on how closely the scores produced by the scoring systems are correlated to those of human raters. This line of research addresses the emphasis on the inferential link of evaluation in Williamson et al.'s (2012) framework.

In large-scale testing environments, correlational studies are usually conducted by the developers of automated scoring systems in order to support their application in operational contexts. The correlations between machine and human scores typically range from 0.7 to 0.9 for total scores and slightly lower for trait scores. The Versant tests, which use the same scoring engine as the ones used for PTE Academic, for example, report machine-to-human correlation of 0.97 for overall scores and 0.88–0.97 at the trait level (Pearson, 2009). The strong correlations of human and machine scores are partly due to the constrained task formats adopted by the Versant tests. In the context where test tasks are open-ended and require spontaneous responses, the correlations are less strong than those of the fully automated Versant tests. Xi et al. (2008) reported a correlation of 0.68 for its automated speech scoring engine SpeechRater 1.0 in a TOEFL iBT field test. In Bridgeman, Powers, Stone & Mollaun (2011), the correlations between trained TOEFL raters' operational ratings and SpeechRater's scores range from 0.65 to 0.69. Shermis (2014) conducted a study of eight existing commercial automated scoring systems and one university laboratory system. Through detailed analyses of human and machine scores, the study reached the conclusion that 'with the appropriate qualifications to the validity argument, in a high-stakes testing environment machine-predicted scores came close to matching the distributional and agreement characteristics of scores assigned by human raters' (ibid.: 75).

The limitation of human scoring as a yardstick for automated scoring is underscored in Shermis (2014: 74): 'A predictive model may do a good job of matching human scoring behavior, but for reasons unrelated (or unsatisfactorily related) to the construct of interest.' In the next section, we will discuss efforts to understand the construct of automated scoring, i.e., the emphasis on the inferential link of explanation in Williamson et al.'s (2012) framework.

The construct validity of automated scoring

Although moderate to strong correlations between human and machine scores have been achieved in most existing programs, as described above, opponents of automated scoring have raised fundamental objections to the construct measured by an automated scoring system. Empirical studies of automated scoring, however, have seldom been explicitly focused on the construct of writing or speaking measured by an automated scoring system. Wang et al. (2012: 618) comment on the expanded use of automated scoring for high-stakes tests: 'it is increasingly important for some stakeholders to understand precisely how constructs have been operationalized in a scoring system. For these stakeholders, the benefits of a well-designed computer scoring system – speed, efficiency, and consistency – need to be weighed against the possibility of a narrower construct.'

Xi et al. (2012) is one of the few empirical studies that address the issue of construct relevance and representation of automatically scored speaking assessments. The study investigated the construct validity of TOEFL Practice Online (TPO), which is scored by SpeechRater 1.0, by evaluating the appropriateness of two scoring models (i.e., multiple regression and classification trees) to measuring the construct of TPO. In human-scored performance-based language assessments, scoring rubrics represent assessment constructs. The TPO rubric consists of three major categories of features: 'delivery, language use, and topic development' (Xi et al., 2012: 379). The relevance and coverage of the features present in the scoring models were evaluated by investigating 'the extent to which the features in the scoring models are linked to and cover the construct; and the extent to which the way the features are combined to produce scores captures the expected relationships between the features and the speaking scores' (ibid.: 381). The conclusion of the study was that '(T)he construct representation of the multiple regression model with expert weights was adequate to justify its use in a low-stakes application' (ibid.: 389). Although content-related features were not represented in the models, this was considered not a serious issue because test takers are less likely to trick the system with off-topic responses in a practice testing environment.

The construct of an automated scoring system can also be explored by employing external measures of the same intended construct to investigate the relationship between automated scores and criterion measures external to the assessment of interest. Weigle (2010, 2011), for example, compares machine-scored TOEFL iBT writing tests with other indicators of writing ability such as self-assessment, instructor assessment and scores on non-test writing samples. It was found that e-rater scores were moderately correlated with these external indicators of writing ability. The study also identified mismatches between the features of writing measured by e-rater and the features of writing that human raters are sensitive to when evaluating non-native writing.

Weigle (2013) highlighted the importance of contextualised construct conceptualisation for automatically scored writing assessments. The contextual factors taken into consideration are learning environment and assessment purpose. The e-rater system, for example, is used for scoring an ALW (assessing language through writing) assessment for non-native speakers learning English as a second or foreign language. Version 11.1 of the e-rater system employs 12 high-level features, grouped into nine major categories: organisation (number of discourse elements), development (length of discourse elements), positive features (preposition usage and good collocation density), lexical complexity (average word length and sophistication of word choice), topic-specific vocabulary usage, grammar, usage, mechanics and style. These features were grouped again and labelled with such headings as organisation and development, vocabulary, content, grammar, usage, mechanics and style (Deane, 2013: 13–14). With such a design, e-rater is strong in measuring 'writing as knowledge-telling' or 'fundamental control of text production processes', but weak in measuring 'quality of argumentation, sensitivity to audience, and other such elements'. The implication of contextualised construct conceptualisation for understanding the construct of automated scoring, according to Weigle (2013: 96), is that 'different aspects of writing (rhetorical/genre knowledge, content knowledge, linguistic knowledge) may be more salient in different assessment contexts, and thus different expertise may be more relevant in setting human standards – and thus AES algorithms'.

Automated writing and speaking evaluation

Since automated evaluation systems gained popularity about a decade ago, studies have been conducted to explore their usefulness for generating multiple trait scores and performance or corrective feedback for learners. Lee, Gentile & Kantor (2010), for example, examined micro text feature variables used in e-rater for scoring writing performances on the computer-based TOEFL (TOEFL CBT). The study investigated whether various features 'can be clustered or re-organized in such a meaningful way that they form a basis for computing automated trait scores (i.e. scores on organization, vocabulary, language use, mechanics, etc.) and composite scores' (Lee et al., 2010: 393). The study proved 'reasonably strong associations between several e-rater variables and multi-trait rating dimensions in some areas of essay quality, such as organization, vocabulary, and mechanics' (ibid.: 411). In the discussion, quoting Ben-Simon & Bennett (2007), the authors pointed out that 'it is critical to judge the theoretical and practical relevance of the automated essay feature variables to the target construct of writing, identify irrelevant features as well as missing ones, and evaluate the appropriateness of the weights assigned to the selected set of features for the AES systems' (Lee et al., 2010: 412).

Wang & Wang (2012) investigated the usefulness of Writing RoadMap 2.0 (WRM) for improving Chinese tertiary-level learners' English writing. WRM is an AWE system that provides a holistic score as well as analytic scores on six aspects of writing: ideas and content, organisation, voice, word choice, fluency and conventions. The study demonstrated that the feedback given by the WRM helped improve learners' writing proficiency, especially with respect to word choice, syntax, spelling and grammar. But the system failed to provide useful suggestions on broader aspects of writing such as 'ideas and content' and 'organisation'.

Dikli & Bleyle (2014) investigated the use of Criterion, a classroom-based AES system supported by ETS's e-rater scoring engine, in a college ESL writing classroom. The system provides feedback on five traits of writing: grammar, usage, mechanics, style, and organisation and development. Instructor feedback on student essays was compared to AES feedback in terms of Criterion's categories of grammar (e.g., subject-verb agreement), usage (e.g., incorrect articles, prepositions) and mechanics (e.g., spelling, capitalisation). Data were triangulated with opinion surveys regarding student perceptions of the feedback received. The results show that 'the instructor provided both more (i.e., a higher total number of coded errors) and better quality (i.e., a higher percentage of coded errors judged as accurate) feedback on form compared to the AES system used in this study (Criterion)' (Dikli & Bleyle, 2014: 12). It was also found that Criterion did not provide any feedback on some of the error categories that the instructor did and that Criterion tended to incorrectly label some types of errors (e.g., non-fragment errors). The findings of the study, according to the authors, corroborates those of their previous study which compared instructor feedback with feedback provided by an AWE system MyAccess! (Dikli, 2010). It was suggested that teachers should use automated evaluation systems as a support tool for writing instruction in full awareness of the limitations of such systems, particularly with regard to second language writers, and that students who use the tool should be informed of the limitations.

In countries where the number of English language learners (ELLs) is huge, automated evaluation is becoming increasingly popular. In China, for example, millions of ELLs are using automated scoring systems developed by commercial companies for Chinese ELLs (e.g., www. pigai.org; www.liulishuo.com). Studies have been conducted to develop and validate automated systems for scoring read-aloud (e.g., Li, Yang, Chen, Wu, Chen & Hu, 2008), essays (e.g., Liang, 2005) and translation from English to Chinese (e.g., Jiang & Wen, 2010; Tian, 2013). Research has also been conducted to demonstrate the effectiveness (or ineffectiveness) of automated evaluation on teaching and learning (e.g., Lu, Li & Li, 2015; Tang & Wu, 2012).

Conclusion

In today's rapidly changing world, high-speed networks and digital communications mean that the ability to adapt and collaborate is critical. Apart from team work, people need to learn to work with machines and collaborate with machines. To facilitate a smooth transition from human scoring to machine scoring or human-machine collaboration, we need to improve the literacy of technology-enhanced language assessment among stakeholders. Teachers and learners are the most important stakeholders and their understanding and acceptance of automated scoring will have a major effect on teaching and learning. Research of automated scoring and evaluation, therefore, needs to provide accessible explanations to such questions as:

(1) What can computers do (and not do)? How do computers do their jobs?
(2) In what ways can automated scoring and evaluation promote or negatively impact teaching, learning and assessment?
(3) How can the computer and humans collaborate to do a better job?

To address the implications of technological innovations for language assessment and balance the benefits and risks of incorporating machines into assessment practices, language assessment practitioners need to equip themselves with new knowledge, skills and competencies in machine-mediated language assessment. The challenge is how to promote better understanding of automated scoring and facilitate the acceptance of technology in language testing and assessment. Xi (2017) commented on the need for opening the black box of AI for assessment and reiterated the importance of understanding test developers' responsibilities and users' rights in situations where humans collaborate with machines.

Although automated scoring will remain controversial for a long time, in an increasingly digital world and with the fast development of AI technology, there is no doubt it is a promising area of research and practice in applied linguistics. Meanwhile, bearing in mind that the ultimate purpose of technology-enhanced language assessment is to promote teaching and learning, language testers should take the responsibility of conducting serious research of the impact of automated scoring and evaluation on language teaching, learning and assessment.

CHAPTER 7

VALIDATING SCORING PROCESSES

Introduction

Validation lies at the very heart of what language testers do and it is therefore no surprise that this topic has received considerable attention in the published literature over the years. As the notion of validity has changed over the years (Chapelle, 2012), approaches to validation have followed suit. As we will describe in more detail in this chapter, conceptualisations of validity have moved from merely focusing on test properties to examining the uses of tests, the interpretations that are made based on the test and the resulting consequences. Different methods of validation have incorporated a focus on the scoring processes, which we define as any aspects of the assessment situation that relate to the scoring of the assessment. A validation of the scoring processes therefore requires a focus on the raters, the scoring criteria and any interaction between these. However, as we will see, the focus in relation to the scoring processes of some of the frameworks put forward has been relatively narrow and we are hoping that readers will gain a deeper understanding of how the scoring processes (or aspects thereof) can be validated. We will describe the historical evolution of validity and validation and will examine how validation of the scoring processes has been integrated into these conceptualisations. We will conclude by looking at two specific cases of scoring processes: automated scoring and classroom-based assessment.

Historical development of the notion of validity

Conceptualisations of validity and the accompanying approaches to validation have changed over recent decades (see, e.g., Chapelle, 1999, 2012). In the 1960s, validity was seen as one of two aspects of a test (reliability was the other). Subsequently, up until the late 1980s, work was done on a number of different types of validity, which were all seen as separate. Construct validity was seen as an indication of how representative the assessment is of an underlying theory of language use and how well the tasks measure this trait. Content validity examines whether the test appropriately samples the domain of the target language use situation. Criterion-related validity refers to how a test score relates to other similar measures. Criterion-related validity could be further subdivided into concurrent validity, which measures how the test scores compare with other comparable test measures, and predictive validity, which is collected some time after the test (Alderson, Clapham & Wall, 1995; Hamp-Lyons, 1990) to see how well a test score predicts performance on an external criterion measure.

The view of validity changed drastically after Messick's (1989) paper on validity which proposed a more integrated view of validity. He argued that not only the assessment or the assessment scores should be the focus of the investigation but rather the inferences we draw about students. He also argued that relevance, utility, value implications and social consequences also need to be investigated. He defined validity as 'an integrated judgement of the degree to which empirical evidence and theoretical rationales support the adequacy and appropriateness of inferences and actions based on test scores' (1989: 13). He further argued that construct validity unifies all the other types of validity described up to that point and that the other types of validity should be seen as contributing to construct validity. While reliability was previously seen as distinct from validity (although as a necessary pre-condition), it was now seen as one aspect of validity.

Validation

The changes in the conceptualisations of validity described above also impacted approaches to validation. In this section, we will examine how approaches to validation have changed over time and which approaches are most common in the language testing literature. In particular, we will discuss how the validation of scoring processes has been included into each of the approaches.

Pre-Messick concepts of validation

Prior to Messick's seminal chapter in 1989, validity was established through a number of quite separate methods of validation. To establish construct validity, a test developer would have to show that an assessment is tapping into the kind of behaviour that the test construct represents and that this is related to an underlying theory of language use. Content validity, which examines whether the test tasks are similar and relevant to the target language use domain, could be established through a needs analysis of the target language use domain. Criterion-related validity was commonly collected through correlations of test scores with scores on a comparable instrument or test scores that represent measures that the original test may want to predict. Reliability, on the other hand, was seen as a separate property of the test, which, while a necessary pre-condition, was not seen as directly contributing to the test.

So how was the validation of scoring processes integrated into this approach to validation? Rater quality, as described in Chapter 2, would have been investigated under reliability, and therefore separately from validity. Examinations of the functioning of the scoring rubric would have been limited. The scoring rubric may have been the focus of investigation under construct validity, if a researcher would have examined the congruence between the operational construct and the rating criteria. The focus during this time was not on the consequences or decisions made based on the scores and the different types of evidence collected were in no way integrated into a larger argument for the use of the test for a specific purpose.

Following Messick (1989), there was a shift in thinking about validity and also the approaches to validation up to that point. But although Messick's model which integrated the different facets of validity was influential, there was little guidance for researchers or practitioners on how to proceed with validation research. To address this problem, a number of researchers put forward approaches to validation which attempted to address some of the shortcomings of the earlier methods of validation. It is important to note that these approaches were put forward by researchers in both educational assessment as well as language testing. In the following sections, we introduce three of these approaches and discuss how scoring processes are integrated into each of these.

Weir's (2005) socio-cognitive framework

In 2005, Weir proposed the socio-cognitive framework for test validation and this model has been further applied, extended or changed in a number of more recent publications (e.g., O'Sullivan & Weir, 2011). In this framework, there are five key elements: context validity, theory-based validity, scoring validity, consequential validity and criterion-related validity. Context validity and theory-based validity are considered a priori validity evidence as evidence is collected before the test, while scoring, consequential and criterion-related validity are a posteriori evidence because evidence is collected after the test event. Context, theory-based and scoring validity combine to form construct validity. In contrast to other validation frameworks we will present later in this chapter, the socio-cognitive framework has four different versions, one each for speaking, listening, reading and writing. For the purpose of this chapter, we are mostly concerned with the frameworks for speaking and writing as these relate to the concerns of this monograph, in that they include issues of scoring, more directly.

Figure 7.1 presents a graphical representation of Weir's framework taken from O'Sullivan (2010). We have reproduced this version as it is a more generic representation of the framework. It is important to note, however, that some changes in how different elements in the framework relate to each other have occurred in these more recent versions (compared to the representation in Weir, 2005). For example, context validity is now directly related to scoring validity through two-way arrows. In more recent versions, the authors have also argued for a 'symbiotic' relationship between context validity, cognitive validity and scoring validity which together form construct validity (Shaw & Weir, 2007).

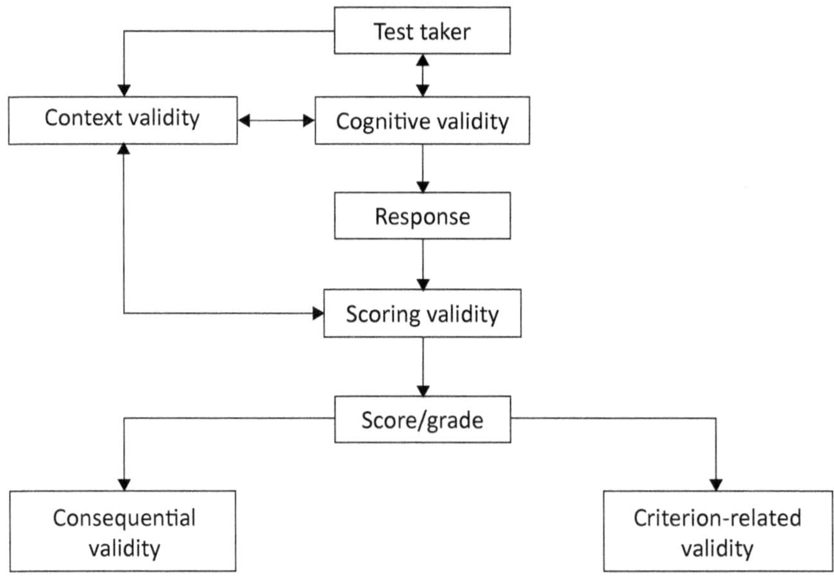

Figure 7.1: Socio-cognitive framework for test validation (from O'Sullivan, 2010)

Weir's framework has a number of advantages. Firstly, it is easy to understand. It includes the component of consequential validity, which examines aspects such as washback or the effect on the test taker. This is an advance from the previous conceptualisations of validity we described above. The framework also attempts to acknowledge interaction of different elements by using directional or bi-directional arrows although these seem to often relate to the sequence of evidence collection rather than the relationship of the different elements to each other. What Weir's framework lacks, however, is a clear structure of how validation researchers would go about making a case for validity and there is little guidance on how validation research is created and what questions would be asked to ensure that the inferences we draw about test takers and the decisions we made based on those inferences are defensible. The temporal aspect described above, where the first two boxes relating to context and cognitive (theory-based) validity are classed as a priori evidence and the other types of validity as a posteriori evidence can also be challenged as presumably all these validities should be considered a priori and investigated at different stages of the test development and validation cycle.

So how are the scoring processes validated in the socio-cognitive framework for test validation? One of the key elements in this framework focuses on scoring validity which is an element investigated after test development. Overview graphs in Weir (2005) and Shaw & Weir (2007) include the following aspects in the scoring validity box: criteria/rating scale, rating procedures (including rater training, standardisation, rating conditions), rater characteristics, rating process, rating, moderation, statistical analysis, post-exam adjustment, grading and awarding. Shaw & Weir (2007: 143) define scoring validity as being:

> concerned with all the aspects of the testing process that can impact on the reliability of test scores. It accounts for the extent to which test scores are based on appropriate criteria, exhibit consensual agreement in marking, are free as possible from measurement error, stable over time, consistent in terms of content sampling and engender confidence as reliable decision-making indicators.

Interestingly, however, there is not much information in either Weir (2005) or Shaw & Weir (2007) about the exact questions researchers should ask and how evidence could best be collected and evaluated. For less experienced practitioners, this does not provide guidance on how to go about investigating scoring validity and what type of evidence may be 'sufficient' in different areas of enquiry. The chapter on scoring validity in Shaw & Weir (2007), for example, describes test development concerns related to scoring and presents a range of test development and research projects conducted on the Cambridge suite of exams, but the actual questions to ask in a validation project are left implicit. A careful reading of the chapter shows that scoring validity in the socio-cognitive framework is concerned with the following issues:

- The appropriate type of rating scale is used, which
  - Measures different aspects of language proficiency
  - Contributes consistently to a candidate's final score
  - Is consistently interpreted by raters
- Rater variability is systematically controlled, i.e.,
  - Rater characteristics which may influence scoring are sufficiently understood and controlled
  - Rater cognitive processes are investigated to understand possible rater variability
- Rater training is effective
- Rating conditions are appropriate
- The test format (e.g., handwritten vs word-processed) is conducive to reliable scoring
- Rater variability is appropriately accounted for at post-rating stage
- Standard-setting to award grades has been appropriate
- Results reporting is conducted appropriately.

As mentioned above, all of these statements were created by our reading of the relevant chapter and are therefore a reflection of our understanding of the research and test development practice described in Shaw & Weir (2007) and do not form an official part of the framework. The type of work reported represents an indirect way into understanding what type of questions the researchers posed in their validation efforts.

The argument-based approach to validation

The argument-based approach to validation originates in Kane and his colleagues (Kane, 1992, 2001, 2006, 2012, 2013; Kane, Crooks & Cohen, 1999) has been applied and further developed for language testing validation contexts by a number of researchers, most notably by Chapelle and colleagues (Chapelle, Enright & Jamieson, 2008). It is currently the most prominent and most theorised approach to validation in the area of language assessment and is appealing as it provides a clear structure to validation work. Following Messick's work, in the argument-based approach to validation, validity is seen as a property of the proposed interpretation and use of the test score, not the assessment instrument itself. Therefore, validation entails evaluating the evidence collected and examining the plausibility of the proposed interpretations and the appropriateness of the intended uses of the test scores (Kane, 2013, 2016). Validity is not an all-or-nothing property, but rather a matter of degree which depends on how well the evidence substantiates the proposed inferences drawn about test takers and the use of scores.

Kane's approach requires the development of two, interconnected arguments. First, during the design phase of the assessment, an interpretive/use argument is developed in which the proposed interpretations and uses of the test score are specified. When developing this argument, the researcher states a series of inferences and assumptions, further described below, which are interconnected with each other. The second argument is the validity argument for the proposed interpretation and use of the test score. The justification for the proposed interpretations and uses of the test scores is then evaluated based on the coherence and completeness and the empirical analysis of the inferences and assumptions inherent in the proposed interpretations and uses (Kane, 2013, 2016). The process, therefore, can be summarised as follows. The researcher decides on the statements and decisions to be based on the test scores, specifies the inferences and assumptions leading from the test score to these statements and decisions, identifies potential competing interpretations and seeks evidence supporting the inferences and assumptions in the proposed interpretative argument and refuting potential counter-arguments. As a result, proposed interpretations that are sound and supported by evidence have a higher degree of validity than those that are not well substantiated by evidence.

As mentioned above, the argument-based approach to validation relies on a series of inferences, connecting one fact or proposition to the next (Chapelle et al., 2010), starting from the test performance and leading to the decisions made based on the test scores as well as the consequences. This network of inferences has been likened to a series of bridges (Kane et al., 1999) which link the performance on a test to the decisions and consequences. The number of inferences included in an argument depends on the type of score interpretation and uses proposed by the test developer, although language assessment researchers have mostly drawn on a very similar set of inferences. Figure 7.2 sets out one possible network of inferences (which are shown in the white boxes).

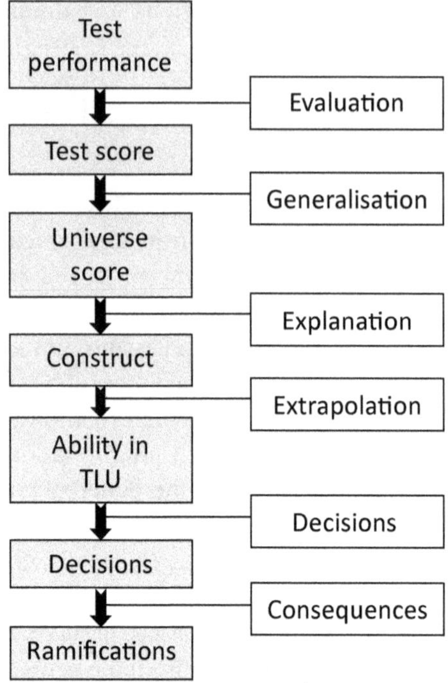

Figure 7.2: Network of inferences in an argument-based approach to validation

The claim underlying the *evaluation inference* is that the test performance is evaluated using procedures that provide observed scores that reflect the targeted language abilities. Typically, backing is required to ensure that the scoring rubrics, test administration conditions and statistical characteristics of the test items are appropriate. The *generalisation inference* is justified if observed test scores are shown to be estimates of expected scores (universe scores) across parallel tasks, raters and test administrations. The *explanation inference*, which leads from the universe score to the construct of the test, is supported if performance on the test reflects the operational test construct as defined by the test developer. The *extrapolation inference* is justified if performances on the test reflect language required for performance in the target language use domain of interest. The *decisions inference* is supported if the decisions made based on the language assessment are appropriate. Finally, the *consequences inference* is warranted if test consequences are intended to promote the interests of key stakeholders. It should be noted here that the consequences inference was later added by researchers in language assessment who felt a need for greater attention to test consequences (see, e.g., Bachman & Palmer, 2010). Chapelle et al. (2008) also added a first inference, *domain description*, which is warranted if the observations on an assessment reveal language abilities relevant to those in the target language use domain.

So how are the scoring processes integrated into an argument-based approach to validation? Knoch & Chapelle (2018) set out to clarify this relationship after showing that in the majority of the frameworks, scoring processes were mostly relegated to the evaluation inference. Their review of studies relating to scoring in the language assessment literature showed that aspects relating to scoring span the full range of inferences presented in Figure 7.2. Based on the studies they identified, they set out the warrants, assumptions and sources of backing relating to the rating processes for each inference in the figure. For example, assumptions which require backing for the explanation inference are that 'the rating scale is based on a defensible theoretical or pedagogical model of proficiency and/or development', that 'the rating criteria and descriptors cover the construct' and that 'raters' cognitive processes are consistent with the theoretical model of proficiency and/or development' (Knoch & Chapelle, 2018: 13). Similarly, one of the assumptions relating to the extrapolation inference requires researchers to collect backing to show that 'the scale criteria reflect the evaluation criteria used in the TLU domain' (ibid.: 15). To be able to 'cross' the decision inference bridge, support is required for the assumption that the 'scale differentiates test takers into levels needed for decision-making' (ibid.: 17). Aspects of scoring that relate to the consequences inference are that 'test users are able to interpret the rating scale to inform future teaching and learning' and that 'the rating scale has positive washback' (ibid.: 18). It is important to note at this point that we have only reproduced a small number of the assumptions set out in Knoch & Chapelle (2018) and we refer interested users to the full description in the original source.

As can be seen by the discussion of the argument-based approach to validation above, this approach has the advantage of providing a connected network of inferences which can be applied to a large range of assessment situations. While it may be slightly technical to apply for new users, the body of work drawing on this approach in language assessment is growing and this previous work, as well as papers like the one described by Knoch & Chapelle (2018), makes it possible for practitioners and researchers to draw on this principled approach and apply it to their own context.

Bachman & Palmer's (2010) assessment use argument

Bachman & Palmer (2010), drawing on earlier work by Bachman (2005), criticised the work by Kane for not sufficiently emphasising consequences and for not foregrounding the consequences of an assessment when they suggested that 'we need to begin the process of assessment development with a consideration of consequences' (Bachman & Palmer 2010: 158). Bachman & Palmer (2010) present a generic assessment use argument which can be adapted to different contexts and assessment use situations.

As can be seen in Figure 7.3, the assessment use argument is structured around four claims which lead from the intended consequences to the performance and assessment tasks. Bachman and Palmer therefore reversed the direction of the focus of the argument when compared to Kane, who started with the performance and led to the decisions and utilisation of the assessment. This reversal is purposeful, to ensure assessment practitioners start with a focus on consequences.

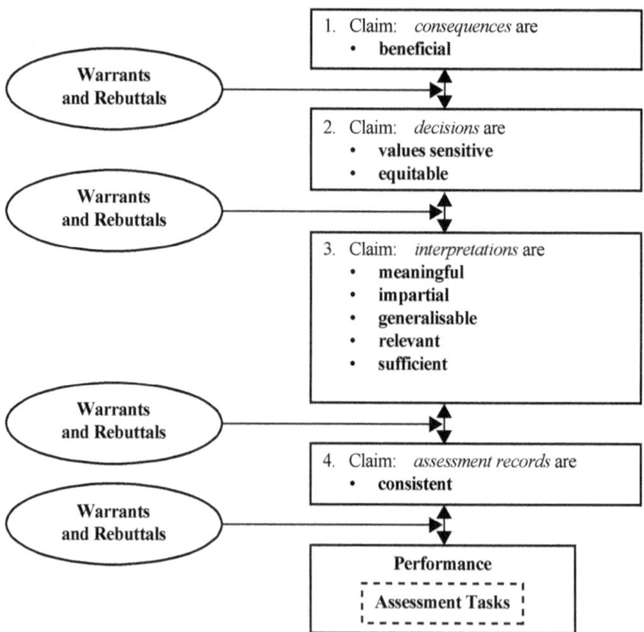

Figure 7.3: Structure of Bachman and Palmer's (2010) assessment use argument

Claim 1 states that the *consequences* of using an assessment and of the decisions that are made are beneficial to stakeholders. Underlying this claim are two warrants, one about the consequences of using the assessment and the other about the consequences of the decisions that are made. Claim 2 states that the *decisions* made on the basis of the interpretations take into consideration educational and societal values and relevant laws, rules and regulations, and are equitable for those stakeholders who are affected by the decisions. Claim 3 relates to the meaningfulness, impartiality, generalisability, relevance and sufficiency of the *interpretations*. The final claim states that the *assessment records* need to be consistent across assessment tasks, across different aspects of the assessment procedure and across different groups of test takers. Underlying each claim are warrants and possible rebuttals, a structure comparable to that proposed by Kane (2013).

When compared to Kane's argument-based approach, Bachman & Palmer's (2010) assessment use argument is simpler, following a slightly less complicated structure with fewer inferences. So where are issues of the rating processes addressed in this framework? A review of the list of warrants presented by the authors, aspects of the scoring process can be found across most claims, with the majority being located in the assessment records claim (Claim 4). Here issues relating to rater training and rating quality are situated. In Claim 3, interpretations, Bachman & Palmer deal with the meaningfulness of the construct (although not directly relating this to the rating scale criteria), and the correspondence between the criteria and test procedures to those used in the target language use domain. Claim 2, decisions, includes a number of warrants focusing on the quality and implementation of the cut scores, and while these are not directly related to the scoring processes by the authors, these warrants may be relevant to our discussion. Finally, in Claim 1, consequences, one warrant focuses on the washback, that is, whether the assessment promotes good instructional practice and effective learning. This warrant may be related to assessment scales and scoring practices in classroom-assessment settings, and we have therefore included it here.

While the assessment use argument provides a simpler structure than the argument-based approach to validation put forward by Kane, the warrants put forward by Bachman & Palmer do not quite cover the depth of aspects relating to scoring processes as those listed by Knoch & Chapelle (2018). It is however, important to remember that the structure provided by Bachman & Palmer is merely a generic structure which leaves room for additional warrants to be added when required and it is therefore up to the individual researcher/team to expand or adjust this framework to their needs.

Validation of specific scoring contexts

The validation frameworks we discussed above have generally been applied to high-stakes pen-and-paper tests. Two language testing contexts, automated scoring and classroom-based assessment, require slightly different questions to be asked, and for this reason we have dedicated specific sections to these types of assessments.

Validation of automated assessments

Since the early 1990s, there has been an increase in the development of automated scoring systems, due to a demand for 'more efficient, affordable and reliable scoring approaches' (Xi, 2012: 438). These scoring systems are at times also accompanied by automated feedback systems which are designed to reduce the marking load on teachers and to increase the speed at which test takers receive feedback. Automated assessments, just like more traditional pen-and-paper tests, have been used in a range of contexts to fulfil different purposes and to answer different questions, and the types of validation questions that can be asked are therefore different to more traditional pen-and-paper tests. While validation of these traditional assessments often focuses on the raters and the rating criteria, the validation of automated scoring requires the researcher to ask different questions.

Xi (2010a, 2012) draws on the argument-based approach to validation to frame validation questions for this context. For the *domain description inference*, she recommends the following question be asked:

- *Does the use of assessment tasks constrained by automated scoring technologies lead to construct under- or misrepresentation?*

Evidence to answer this question needs to carefully examine the trade-off between task type design and automated scoring capabilities. Many automated assessments draw on highly constrained tasks (e.g., dictation, sentence repetition), which are easier to score, but do not sample the target language use domain sufficiently. The scoring of less constrained tasks, such as constructed responses, is in its infancy for making high-stakes decisions, and therefore the scoring mechanism may rely on a very simplified construct. For this reason, some agencies use automated scoring technologies in combination with human raters to draw on the capabilities of both types of scoring.

For the *evaluation inference*, Xi poses the following questions:

- *Does automated scoring yield scores that are accurate indicators of the quality of a test performance sample?*
- *Would examinees' knowledge of the scoring logic of an automated scoring system impact the way they interact with the test tasks, thus negatively affecting the accuracy of the scores?*

The first question relies on the kind of evidence mostly used to support automated scoring systems – associations between automated scores and human ratings. Xi also points out that it is important, when comparing automated scores and human ratings, to ensure whether the test takers knew based on what construct or logic their performances were scored – simply using pen-and-paper essays which were previously scored by human raters and then inputting these into an automated scoring system to collect validity evidence may result in misleading statistical results. In fact, test takers' understanding of the scoring mechanism is an important part of the validity investigations. Test takers may attempt to 'trick' or unduly influence the scoring algorithm of automated scoring systems which may introduce construct-irrelevant variance.

The question asked in relation to the *generalisation inference* is not much different to that of tests scored by humans – evidence needs to be collected to show that the scoring mechanism produces consistent results across test forms and tasks:

- *Does automated scoring yield scores that are sufficiently consistent across measurement contexts (e.g., across test forms, across tasks in the same form)?*

Xi (2012) suggests collecting two types of information in relation to this question. First, it is important to examine how the scoring model was developed, including the representativeness (the similarity and size) of the sample used for training the model. Second, scoring reliability across parallel forms and tasks needs to be established and compared to those of human raters.

For the *explanation inference*, Xi (2012) poses three questions:

- *Do the automated scoring features under- or misrepresent the construct of interest?*
- *Is the way the scoring features are combined to generate automated scores consistent with theoretical expectations of the*

> *relationships between the scoring features and the construct of interest?*
>
> • *Does the use of automated scoring change the meaning and interpretation of scores provided by trained raters?*

The capabilities of the automated scoring mechanisms are still limited – they often draw on relatively easy computable measures and are therefore limited in the construct they can assess, despite many advances in the past two decades. More complicated aspects such as coherence, interactional competence or task fulfilment are difficult to assess automatically. There is, therefore, the danger that automated scoring significantly underrepresents the construct of interest or even measures construct-irrelevant aspects of the performance.

The result of the analysis requires the creation of a composite score based on an underlying algorithm. How best to create this score is not straightforward, as shown by Xi, and human raters' decision-making processes are yet to be fully understood and are far too complex to emulate in an automated scoring system.

The *extrapolation inference* relates the test construct to the target language use domain. The following question is posed by Xi (2012):

> • *Does automated scoring yield scores that have expected relationships with other test or non-test indicators of the targeted language ability?*

This question relates to an area of investigation that has a longer history in research on automated scoring than some other questions discussed here, that is, how the scores relate to scores on other, similar tests or to non-test criterion scores. A further area of investigation in relation to the extrapolation inference could be to examine how well the construct that is scored relates to scoring in the target language use domain. That is, do stakeholders in the target language use domain evaluate performances in a similar manner?

Finally, Xi (2012) presents two questions in relation to the *utilisation inference*:

> • *Do automated scores lead to appropriate score-based decisions?*
> • *Does the use of automated scoring have a positive impact on examinees' test preparation, teaching and learning practices?*

This final area of validity evidence is one that, we feel, requires more study. It is not yet clear how users interact with these tests, in particular in high-stakes settings. Studies on score interpretation and preparation activities in different contexts would shed light on this and provide us with an insight into users' decision-making, and teaching and learning activities.

The questions we presented above, taken from Xi (2012), show that concerns about automated scoring also permeate all the inferences in a validity argument. This mirrors what Knoch & Chapelle (2018) described when relating rating processes to the argument-based approach to validation. While many of the questions asked are similar to those asked of rating processes involving human raters, some questions above are specific to automated scoring and the evidence needed for backing is not always the same in these two contexts.

Validation of scoring in classroom-based assessment

The validation frameworks we presented above were developed for high-stakes assessment contexts. Classroom-based assessment, on the other hand, does not share all characteristics of standardised assessments and for that reason, such frameworks cannot be easily applied to instructional contexts (see, e.g., Black & Wiliam, 1998; Brookhart, 2003; Moss, 2003). To date, few similar frameworks for classroom assessments have been proposed, which may be partly due to the fact that the frameworks proposed above may be difficult to implement for classroom teachers. One attempt at creating a framework for classroom assessments by Bachman & Damboek (2018) has mainly focused on high-stakes classroom assessments, rather than examining assessments and their progression and relationship to learning objectives more broadly. It is important to discuss what features of classroom-based assessment may not be well served by the current frameworks. While we comment below on issues beyond the scoring processes, we will conclude the section by focusing on the implications for the scoring processes in classroom-based assessment.

So what are the features of classroom-based assessment that are currently difficult to include in a validation framework? First of all, classroom assessment is usually designed to document student learning or progress within a certain time period while more standardised assessments document proficiency at one point in time. Because of this need for measuring development, teachers usually base their judgement on a range of information, rather than just one formal assessment. These multiple forms of evidence that inform consequential interpretations or decisions may be assessments conducted by the teacher, by peers or by the learners themselves. These activities are often designed to build on each other and should be seen in progression for a better understanding of the assessment practices in a classroom. Activities might be based on classroom questioning or observations or on other sources and therefore not all scored in the way that standardised assessments are. How these different pieces of evidence are then combined to result in the consequential interpretations and decisions is an important aspect of classroom assessment that is not often documented.

Assessments in the classroom or any other less formal evidence used to draw inferences about learners and make subsequent decisions are often linked to external frameworks or standards or internal teaching syllabi. A validity framework investigating the assessment practices used in a course would need to investigate the strength of the link to any external or internal frameworks or guidelines. However, this may be at times difficult because classroom-assessment is often not separable from teaching and learning taking place in the classroom.

Unlike in standardised assessments, where all students answer the same test items, students in classrooms at different learning levels may be given assessments that differ from those of other students in the class. In this way, the teacher is able to gain a deeper insight into learners' abilities at their specific learning levels.

Moss (2003) argues that consequences are the single most important aspect of classroom-based assessment as the success of a class depends on how well students are moved along the learning continuum. Consequences, therefore, would need to be a key aspect in a validation framework applied to classroom-based assessment practices.

Finally, one aspect of classroom learning and assessment can be that teachers may want to investigate the students' ability to transfer skills to similar tasks as well as completely new, related tasks. This notion of transfer is not commonly included in standardised assessment, but provides important information to teachers and other stakeholders about the type of inferences they may be able to draw about students' success after finishing a certain course of study.

There are a number of issues relating to the scoring processes that are specific to classroom contexts. Unlike in standardised assessments, the scoring of performances in classrooms is usually conducted by the classroom teacher who knows the students well. Second (or even third) ratings are rare in these contexts and training in scoring is also not common.

Scales in use may be adopted from other contexts or be prepared by others. Teachers may draw on peer assessment or self-assessment but may not have received training in implementing these techniques. At the end of the term, they are usually required to integrate scores from their own scoring, as well as the scoring from other sources such as peers and their own observations over a term of unscored performances. In certain contexts, teachers are also required to link their scores/observations about students to standardised frameworks, which can be a challenging task. As can be seen, the issues relating to the scoring processes in classroom contexts differ from those described above and therefore validation activities may need to be altered.

Conclusion

This chapter set out to describe the historical changes in validity leading up to the most recent conceptualisation which sees validity as a unified concept. We have reviewed the most commonly applied validation frameworks in language assessment, the argument-based approach to validation, Weir's socio-cognitive framework and Bachman & Palmer's assessment use argument. We examined how the scoring processes are integrated into each of these frameworks. At the end of the chapter, we examined two specific scoring contexts, automated scoring and classroom-based assessment, and discussed the implications for validation of scoring processes in these contexts.

CONCLUSIONS

In this monograph, we set out to present a comprehensive overview of the current knowledge on scoring second language performance assessment, focusing on rater-mediated performance assessment as well as automated scoring. Throughout the chapters we have shown the complexity of this topic and the ever-changing research base available. While scoring is a subject that has attracted much attention in the language testing and educational assessment literature, this monograph is the first to combine all the topics, from both research and practice, into one volume. We hope to have achieved two aims: (1) to provide a volume that is useful for new researchers and practitioners starting out in the field, and (2) to highlight various areas that require more attention in future work in this field.

In Chapter 1, we provided a visual model of the various factors influencing rating quality, depicting the complex interaction of these factors. The factors are drawn from our review of the literature. We hope that this model can act as a starting point for researchers and practitioners alike, and that future work will expand and adjust the various relationships we show. Chapter 1 also provides a detailed catalogue of rater effects that have been described in work on rater-mediated assessment.

Chapter 2 summarises measures of rating quality following two traditions, those measuring rating quality in relation to other raters and those examining quality with respect to previously established agreed benchmarks. The chapter is the first to catalogue all the latest statistical methods available to researchers and practitioners and explicitly link each to the rater effects described in Chapter 1, providing a complete toolset for rater quality research.

In Chapter 3, we discussed how insights into raters' cognitive processes can shed light on interactions between various factors affecting rating quality, as outlined in Chapter 1. We argued that this kind of research is helpful and needed to underpin studies into rater quality. The chapter also explores various methodological considerations in rater cognition research and argued that future research needs to link this kind of work more closely to theoretical models of cognition.

Very few publications provide a detailed introduction into best practice in rater recruitment, training, moderation and standardisation. Chapter 4 attempts to fill this gap. The chapter uncovers a lack of research base for common practices in rater recruitment and we hope that more work will be done in this area to ensure that the ever-growing need of human raters is filled by raters from more varied backgrounds than is currently the case. The second half of the chapter provides a catalogue of score resolution techniques and presents the underlying research comparing the various techniques available.

After a focus on raters and scores in the previous chapters, Chapter 5 discusses rating scales, an integral aspect of rater-mediated assessment. We described the key types of rating scales used in L2 assessment and documented the various design methods used to develop scales. While the design method is often chosen based on convenience, we would like to argue that decisions on scale design are more complex and should always keep the score use in mind, as well as the types of inferences test developers claim to make about students.

In Chapter 6 we then turned to an increasingly important topic – automated scoring. We presented an in-depth exploration of automated scoring of L2 performances, both in written and spoken format, as well as automated feedback systems which have been built around these scoring technologies to benefit learners. The chapter essentially focuses on validity issues concerning automated scoring, in particular construct validity and score quality.

Chapter 7, then, draws together the work of the previous chapters in describing various traditions focusing on the validation of scoring processes. It focuses on rater-mediated assessment, automated scoring and scoring in classroom contexts.

A way forward

In this monograph we have summarised the latest knowledge-base on scoring L2 performance assessments. Essentially, this text is about validation and the various factors that influence the quality of the scores we report to learners and the inferences that can be made about learners based on these scores. We have presented a complex picture, which is bound to evolve in future years as research in this area is likely to continue to proliferate. More work in the various areas we have introduced is clearly needed. It is likely that, in particular, the focus on automated scoring systems will increase in the future, and we as researchers and practitioners need to ensure that the emphasis on producing and reporting valid scores is continued. This view is essentially inward-facing, that is, we are focusing attention on the test and how scores are produced.

But we also urge researchers and practitioners to continue looking outward towards our clients, who are the test takers, and policy makers. We hope that the future will bring a stronger emphasis on the communication with stakeholder groups like the ones mentioned above, and that this will bring clearer, more comprehensible descriptions and explanations of what Macqueen has referred to as the stated construct (Knoch & Macqueen, 2019). The stated construct is the information that about the test construct that can be accessed by the public. Testing companies communicate this information in various forms, for example on websites or in handbooks. How we explain score meaning in this kind of documentation is important, as this may be the only information that can be accessed by those who are making policy decisions about which tests to accept for various purposes or who are setting cut-scores for different score uses. As language testing experts, it is important we ensure that key groups of stakeholders are provided clear and understandable information about score validity, score meaning and the types of inferences that can be made about students based on their scores. So while the bulk of the monograph has looked inward at understanding how we can ensure valid scores, and while we are sure that work in this arena will continue as one of the main activities of language testers, we also need to ensure that we look outwards at the score users and communicate scoring decisions and score meaning clearly to these stakeholder groups.

REFERENCES

Agresti, A. (1996). *An introduction to categorical data analysis* (2nd edition). New York: John Wiley.

Alderson, J. C. (2000). Technology in testing: The present and the future. *System, 28*(4), 593–603.
https://doi.org/10.1016/S0346-251X(00)00040-3

Alderson, J. C., Clapham, C. & Wall, D. (1995). *Language test construction and evaluation*. Cambridge: Cambridge University Press.

Anastasi, A. (1988). *Psychological testing*. New York: Macmillan.

Attali, Y. (2016). A comparison of newly-trained and experienced raters on a standardized writing assessment. *Language Testing, 33*(1), 99–115. https://doi.org/10.1177/0265532215582283

Attali, Y. & Powers, D. (2009). Validity of scores for a developmental writing scale based on automated scoring. *Educational and Psychological Measurement, 69*(6), 978–993.
https://doi.org/10.1177/0013164409332217

Babaii, E., Taghaddomi, S. & Pashmforoosh, R. (2016). Speaking self-assessment: Mismatch between learners' and teachers' criteria. *Language Testing, 33*(3), 411–437.
https://doi.org/10.1177/0265532215590847

Bachman, L. (2005). Building and supporting a case for test use. *Language Assessment Quarterly, 2*(1), 1–34.
https://doi.org/10.1207/s15434311laq0201_1

Bachman, L. & Cohen, A. D. (Eds.). (1998). *Interfaces between second language acquisition and language testing research*. Cambridge: Cambridge University Press.
https://doi.org/10.1017/CBO9781139524711

Bachman, L. & Damboek, B. (2018). *Language assessment for classroom teachers*. Oxford: Oxford University Press.

Bachman, L. & Palmer, A. S. (1996). *Language testing in practice*. Oxford: Oxford University Press.

Bachman, L. & Palmer, A. S. (2010). *Language assessment in practice*. Oxford: Oxford University Press.

Bae, J., Bentler, P. M. & Lee, Y.-S. (2016). On the role of content in writing assessment. *Language Assessment Quarterly, 13*(4), 302–328. https://doi.org/10.1080/15434303.2016.1246552

Baird, J.-A., Greatorex, J. & Bell, J. (2004). What makes marking reliable? Experiments with UK examinations. *Assessment in Education: Principles, Policy & Practice, 11*(3), 331–348. https://doi.org/10.1080/0969594042000304627

Baker, B. A. (2012). Individual differences in rater decision-making style: An exploratory mixed-methods study. *Language Assessment Quarterly, 9*(3), 225–248. https://doi.org/10.1080/15434303.2011.637262

Banerjee, J., Yan, X., Chapman, M. & Elliott, H. (2015). Keeping up with the times: Revising and refreshing a rating scale. *Assessing Writing, 26*, 5–19. https://doi.org/10.1016/j.asw.2015.07.001

Barkaoui, K. (2007). Rating scale impact on EFL essay marking: A mixed-method study. *Assessing Writing, 12*(2), 86–107. https://doi.org/10.1016/j.asw.2007.07.001

Barkaoui, K. (2010). Variability in ESL essay rating processes: The role of the rating scale and rater experience. *Language Assessment Quarterly, 7*(1), 54–74. https://doi.org/10.1080/15434300903464418

Barkaoui, K. (2011a). Effects of marking method and rater experience on ESL essay scores and rater performance. *Assessment in Education: Principles, Policy & Practice, 18*(3), 279–293. https://doi.org/10.1080/0969594X.2010.526585

Barkaoui, K. (2011b). Think-aloud protocols in research on essay rating: An empirical study of their veridicality and reactivity. *Language Testing, 28*(1), 51–75. https://doi.org/10.1177/0265532210376379

Barnwell, D. (1989). 'Naive' native speakers and judgements of oral proficiency in Spanish. *Language Testing, 6*, 152–163. https://doi.org/10.1177/026553228900600203

Becker, A. (2016). Student-generated scoring rubrics: Examining their formative value for improving ESL students' writing performance. *Assessing Writing, 29*, 15–24. https://doi.org/10.1016/j.asw.2016.05.002

Bejar, I. I. (2012). Rater cognition: Implications for validity. *Educational Measurement: Issues and Practice, 31*(3), 2–9. https://doi.org/10.1111/j.1745-3992.2012.00238.x

Beltran, J. (2016). The effects of visual input on scoring a speaking achievement test. *Teachers' College Columbia University Working Papers in TESOL & Applied Linguistics, 16*(2), 1–23.

Bennett, R. E. (2006). Moving the field forward: Some thoughts on validity and automated scoring. In D. Williamson, R. J. Mislevy & I. I. Bejar (Eds.), *Automated scoring of complex tasks in computer-based testing* (pp. 403–412). Hillsdale, NJ: Lawrence Erlbaum.

Ben-Simon, A. & Bennett, R. E. (2007). Toward more substantively meaningful automated essay scoring. *Journal of Technology, Learning, and Assessment 6*(1). Retrieved 27 February 2019 from https://ejournals.bc.edu/index.php/jtla/article/view/1631

Berge, K. L., Skar, G. B., Matre, S., Solheim, R., Evensen, L. S., Otnes, H. & Thygesen, R. (2017). Introducing teachers to new semiotic tools for writing instruction and writing assessment: Consequences for students' writing proficiency. *Assessment in Education: Principles, Policy & Practice, 26*(1), 6–25. https://doi.org/10.1080/0969594X.2017.1330251

Bernstein, J. (1999). *PhonePass testing: Structure and construct.* Ordinate Corporation.

Bernstein, J., Van Moere, A. & Cheng, J. (2010). Validating automated speaking tests. *Language Testing, 27*(3), 355–377. https://doi.org/10.1177/0265532210364404

Black, B., Suto, I. & Bramley, T. (2011). The interrelations of features of questions, mark schemes and examinee responses and their impact on marker agreement. *Assessment in Education: Principles, Policy & Practice, 18*(3), 295–318. https://doi.org/10.1080/0969594X.2011.555328

Black, P. & Wiliam, D. (1998). Assessment and classroom learning. *Assessment in Education: Principles, Policy & Practice, 5*(1), 7–74. https://doi.org/10.1080/0969595980050102

Borman, W. C. (1977). Consistency of rating accuracy and rating errors in the judgement of human performance. *Organizational Behaviour and Human Performance, 20*, 238–252. https://doi.org/10.1016/0030-5073(77)90004-6

Bramley, T. (2007). Paired comparison methods. In P. E. Newton, J.-A. Baird, H. P. Goldstein & P. Tymms (Eds.), *Techniques for monitoring the comparability of examination standards* (pp. 246–294). London: QCA.

Bramley, T. (2015). *Investigating the reliability of Adaptive Comparative Judgement. Cambridge Assessment Research Report*. Retrieved 19 October 2019 from Cambridge, UK: https://www.cambridgeassessment.org.uk/Images/232694-investigating-the-reliability-of-adaptive-comparative-judgment.pdf

Brennan, R. L. (2001). *Generalizability theory*. New York: Springer.
https://doi.org/10.1007/978-1-4757-3456-0

Bridgeman, B., Powers, D., Stone, E. & Mollaun, P. (2011). TOEFL iBT speaking test scores as indicators of communicative language proficiency. *Language Testing, 29*(1), 91–108.
https://doi.org/10.1177/0265532211411078

Brindley, G. (1991). Defining language ability: The criteria for criteria. In S. Anivan (Ed.), *Current developments in language testing*. Singapore: SEAMEO Regional Language Centre.

Brindley, G. (1998). Describing language development? Rating scales and SLA. In L. F. Bachman & A. D. Cohen (Eds.), *Interfaces between second language acquisition and language testing research*. Cambridge: Cambridge University Press.
https://doi.org/10.1017/CBO9781139524711.007

Brookhart, S. M. (2003). Developing measurement theory for classroom assessment purposes and uses. *Educational Measurement: Issues and Practice, 22*(4), 5–12.
https://doi.org/10.1111/j.1745-3992.2003.tb00139.x

Brown, A. (1995). The effect of rater variables in the development of an occupation-specific language performance test. *Language Testing, 12*, 1–15. https://doi.org/10.1177/026553229501200101

Brown, A. (2000). *An investigation of the rating process in the IELTS oral interview*. Retrieved 12 March 2018 from IELTS Australia Pty Ltd, Canberra: https://www.ielts.org/teaching-and-research/research-reports/volume-03-report-3

Brown, A. (2003a). Interviewer variation and the co-construction of speaking proficiency. *Language Testing, 20*(1), 1–25.
https://doi.org/10.1191/0265532203lt242oa

Brown, A. (2003b). *Legibility and the rating of second language writing: An investigation of the rating of handwritten and word-processed IELTS task two essays*. Retrieved 13 May 2019 from IELTS Australia Pty Ltd, Canberra: https://www.ielts.org/teaching-and-research/research-reports/volume-04-report-4

Brown, A. (2005). *Interviewer variability in oral proficiency interviews*. Frankfurt: Peter Lang.

Brown, A. (2006). An examination of the rating process in the revised IELTS speaking test. *IELTS Research Reports, 6*, 41–70.

Brown, A. (2012). Interlocutor and rater training. In Fulcher, G. & Davidson, F. (Eds.) *The Routledge handbook of language testing* (pp. 413–425). Abingdon: Routledge.

Brown, A. & Hill, K. (1998). Interviewer style and candidate performance in the IELTS oral interview. In S. Woods (Ed.), *Research Reports 1997, Volume 1* (pp. 173–191). Sydney: ELICOS.

Brown, A., Iwashita, N. & McNamara, T. (2005). *An examination of rater orientation and test-taker performance on English-for-academic-purposes speaking tasks*. Retrieved 23 April 2018 from https://www.ets.org/Media/Research/pdf/RR-05-05.pdf. https://doi.org/10.1002/j.2333-8504.2005.tb01982.x

Brown, A. & Jaquith, P. (2011). *The development and validation of an on-line rater training and marking system: Promises and pitfalls*. Basingstoke: Palgrave Macmillan.

Brown, G., Glasswell, K. & Harland, D. (2004). Accuracy in the scoring of writing: Studies of reliability and validity using a New Zealand writing assessment system. *Assessing Writing, 9*, 105–121. https://doi.org/10.1016/j.asw.2004.07.001

Bygate, M., Skehan, P. & Swain, M. (Eds.). (2001). *Researching pedagogic tasks: Second language learning, teaching and testing*. Harlow: Longman.

Cai, H. (2015). Weight-based classification of raters and rater cognition in an EFL speaking test. *Language Assessment Quarterly, 12*(3), 262–282. https://doi.org/10.1080/15434303.2015.1053134

Carey, M. D. & Mannell, R. H. (2009). The contribution of interlanguage phonology accommodation to inter-examiner variation in the rating of pronunciation in oral proficiency interviews. In P. Thompson (Ed.), *IELTS Research Reports, Volume 9*. IDP: IELTS Australia.

Carey, M. D., Manell, R. H. & Dunn, P. K. (2011). Does a rater's familiarity with a candidate's pronunciation affect the rating in oral proficiency interviews? *Language Testing, 28*(2), 201–219. https://doi.org/10.1177/0265532210393704

CCCC Committee on Assessment. (2006). *Writing assessment: A position statement (revised March 2009, reaaffirmed November 2014)*. Retrieved 12 October 2018 from http://www.ncte.org/cccc/resources/positions/writingassessment

Chalhoub-Deville, M. (1995). Deriving oral assessment scales across different tests and rater groups. *Language Testing, 12*, 16–33. https://doi.org/10.1177/026553229501200102

Chalhoub-Deville, M. (1997). Theoretical models, assessment frameworks and test construction. *Language Testing, 14*, 3–22. https://doi.org/10.1177/026553229701400102

Chalhoub-Deville, M. & Wigglesworth, G. (2005). Rater judgement and English language speaking proficiency. *World Englishes, 24*(3), 383–391. https://doi.org/10.1111/j.0083-2919.2005.00419.x

Chan, S., Inoue, C. & Taylor, L. (2015). Developing rubrics to assess the reading-into-writing skills: A case study. *Assessing Writing, 26,* 20–37. https://doi.org/10.1016/j.asw.2015.07.004

Chapelle, C. (1999). Validity in language assessment. *Annual Review of Applied Linguistics, 19,* 254–272.
https://doi.org/10.1017/S0267190599190135

Chapelle, C. (2012). Conceptions of validity. In G. Fulcher & F. Davidson (Eds.), *The Routledge handbook of language testing* (pp. 21–33). New York: Routledge.

Chapelle, C., Enright, M. & Jamieson, J. (Eds.). (2008). *Building a validity argument for the Test of English as a Foreign Language.* New York: Routledge.

Chapelle, C., Enright, M. & Jamieson, J. (2010). Does an argument-based approach to validity make a difference? *Educational Measurement: Issues and Practice, 29*(1), 3–13.
https://doi.org/10.1111/j.1745-3992.2009.00165.x

Chen, Y.-S. & Liu, J. (2016). Constructing a scale to assess L2 written speech act performance: WDCT and email tasks. *Language Assessment Quarterly, 13*(3), 231–250.
https://doi.org/10.1080/15434303.2016.1213844

Cherry, R. & Meyer, P. (1993). Reliability issues in holistic assessment. In M. Williamson & B. Huot (Eds.), *Validating holistic scoring for writing assessment: Theoretical and empirical foundations* (pp. 109–141). Cresskill, NJ: Hampton.

Cohen, J. (1960). A coefficient for agreement for nominal scales. *Educational and Psychological Measurement, 20,* 37–46.
https://doi.org/10.1177/001316446002000104

Cohen, J. (1968). Weighted kappa: Nominal scale agreement with provision for scaled disagreement or partial credit. *Psychological Bulletin 70,* 213–220.

Coniam, D. (2009). A comparison of onscreen and paper-based marking in the Hong Kong public examination system. *Educational Research and Evaluation, 15*(3), 243–263.
https://doi.org/10.1080/13803610902972940

Coniam, D. (2011). A qualitative examination of the attitudes of liberal studies markers towards onscreen marking. *British Journal of Educational Technology, 42*(6), 1042–1054.
https://doi.org/10.1111/j.1467-8535.2010.01136.x

Coniam, D. (2013). The increasing acceptance of onscreen marking – The 'table computer' effect. *Educational Technology & Society, 16*(3), 119–129.

Coniam, D. & Yeung, A. (2010). Markers' perceptions regarding the onscreen marking of liberal studies in the Hong Kong public examination system. *Asia Pacific Journal of Education, 30*(3), 249–271. https://doi.org/10.1080/02188791.2010.495836

Connor-Linton, J. (1995). Crosscultural comparison of writing standards: American ESL and Japanese EFL. *World Englishes, 14*, 99–115. https://doi.org/10.1111/j.1467-971X.1995.tb00343.x

Cooper, W. H. (1981). Ubiquitous halo. *Psychological Bulletin, 90*, 218–244. https://doi.org/10.1037/0033-2909.90.2.218

Cooze, M. (2011). Assessing writing tests on scores: The introduction of online marking. *Cambridge ESOL Research Notes, 43*, 12–15.

Council of Europe. (2001). *Common European Framework of Reference for Languages: Learning, teaching, assessment*. Strasbourg: Council of Europe.

Crick, J. E. & Brennan, R. L. (1983). *GENOVA: A general purpose analysis of variance system. Version 2.1*. Iowa City, IA: American College Testing Program.

Crocker, L. & Algina, J. (1986). *Introduction to classical and modern test theory*. Fort Worth: Harcourt Brace.

Cronbach, L. J. (1955). Processes affecting scores on 'understanding of others' and 'assumed similarity'. *Psychological Bulletin, 52*, 177. https://doi.org/10.1037/h0044919

Cronbach, L. J. (1990). *Essentials of psychological testing* (5th edition). New York: Harper and Row.

Cronbach, L. J., Gleser, G. C., Nanda, H. & Rajaratnam, N. (1972). *The dependability of behavioral measurements: Theory of generalizability for scores and profiles*. New York: Wiley.

Cumming, A. (1990). Expertise in evaluating second language compositions. *Language Testing, 7*(1), 31–51. https://doi.org/10.1177/026553229000700104

Cumming, A., Kantor, R. & Powers, D. E. (2001). *Scoring TOEFL essays and TOEFL 2000 prototype writing tasks: An investigation into raters' decision making and development of a preliminary analytic framework*. TOEFL Monograph Series 22. Princeton, NJ: Educational Testing Service.

Cumming, A., Kantor, R. & Powers, D. E. (2002). Decision making while rating ESL/EFL writing tasks: A descriptive framework. *The Modern Language Journal, 86*, 67–96. https://doi.org/10.1111/1540-4781.00137

Cumming, A., Kantor, R., Powers, D. E., Santos, T. & Taylor, C. (2000). *TOEFL 2000 writing framework: A working paper. TOEFL Monograph Series 18*. Retrieved 30 August 2018 from Princeton, NJ: https://www.ets.org/research/policy_research_reports/publications/report/2000/icix

Davies, A. (1999). Standard English: Discordant voices. *World Englishes, 18*(2), 171–186. https://doi.org/10.1111/1467-971X.00132

Davies, A., Brown, A., Elder, C., Hill, K., Lumley, T. & McNamara, T. (1999). *Dictionary of language testing*. Cambridge: Cambridge University Press.

Davis, L. (2012). *Rater expertise in a second language speaking assessment: The influence of training and experience*. Unpublished doctoral dissertation, University of Hawai'i at Manoa.

Davis, L. (2016). The influence of training and experience on rater performance in scoring spoken language. *Language Testing, 33*(1), 117–135. https://doi.org/10.1177/0265532215582282

Deane, P. (2013). On the relation between automated essay scoring and modern views of the writing construct. *Assessing Writing, 18*(1), 7–24. https://doi.org/10.1016/j.asw.2012.10.002

DeRemer, M. L. (1998). Writing assessment: Raters' elaboration of the rating task. *Assessing Writing, 5*, 7–29. https://doi.org/10.1016/S1075-2935(99)80003-8

Deygers, B. & Van Gorp, K. (2015). Determining the score validity of a co-constructed CEFR-based rating scale. *Language Testing, 32*(4), 521–541. https://doi.org/10.1177/0265532215575626

Dikli, S. (2010). Nature of automated essay scoring feedback. *CALICO Journal, 28*(1), 99–134. https://doi.org/10.11139/cj.28.1.99-134

Dikli, S. & Bleyle, S. (2014). Automated essay scoring feedback for second language writers: How does it compare to instructor feedback? *Assessing Writing, 22*(1), 1–17. https://doi.org/10.1016/j.asw.2014.03.006

DiPardo, A., Storms, B. A. & Selland, M. (2011). Seeing voices: Assessing writerly stance in the NWP Analytic Writing Continuum. *Assessing Writing, 16*(3), 170–188. https://doi.org/10.1016/j.asw.2011.01.003

Douglas, D. & Selinker, L. (1992). Analyzing oral proficiency test performance in general and specific-purpose contexts. *System, 20*, 317–328. https://doi.org/10.1016/0346-251X(92)90043-3

Drave, N. (2011). *Marker 'fatigue' and marking reliability in Hong Kong's Language Proficiency Assessment for Teachers of English (LPATE)*. Paper presented at IAEA 2011. Retrieved from http://www.iaea.info/documents/paper_30171b739.pdf

Ducasse, A. (2010). *Interaction in paired oral proficiency assessment in Spanish: Rater and candidate input into evidence-based scale development and construct definition*. Frankfurt: Peter Lang. https://doi.org/10.3726/978-3-653-05393-7

Ducasse, A. & Brown, A. (2009). Assessing paired orals: Raters' orientation to interaction. *Language Testing, 26*(3), 423–443. https://doi.org/10.1177/0265532209104669

Duijm, K., Schoonen, R. & Hulstijn, J. (2017). Professional and non-professional raters' responsiveness to fluency and accuracy in L2 speech: An experimental approach. *Language Testing, Online First*. https://doi.org/10.1177/0265532217712553

East, M. (2009). Evaluating the reliability of a detailed analytic scoring rubric for foreign language writing. *Assessing Writing, 14*(2), 88–115. https://doi.org/10.1016/j.asw.2009.04.001

Eckes, T. (2005). Examining rater effects in TestDaF writing and speaking performance assessments: A many-facet Rasch analysis. *Language Assessment Quarterly, 2*(3), 197–221. https://doi.org/10.1207/s15434311laq0203_2

Eckes, T. (2008). Rater types in writing performance assessments: A classification approach to rater variability. *Language Testing, 25*(2), 155–185. https://doi.org/10.1177/0265532207086780

Eckes, T. (2011). *Introduction to many-facet Rasch measurement*. Frankfurt: Peter Lang. https://doi.org/10.3726/978-3-653-04844-5

Eckes, T. (2012). Operational rater types in writing assessment: Linking rater cognition to rater behavior. *Language Assessment Quarterly, 9*(3), 270–292. https://doi.org/10.1080/15434303.2011.649381

Eckes, T. (2015). *Introduction to many-facet Rasch measurement – Analyzing and evaluating rater-mediated assessments* (2nd edition). Frankfurt: Peter Lang.

Educational Testing Service. (2019). TOEFL iBT: About the Test. Retrieved 20 October 2019 from https://www.ets.org/toefl/ibt/about

Elder, C. (1993). How do subject specialists construe classroom language proficiency? *Language Testing, 10*(3), 235–254. https://doi.org/10.1177/026553229301000303

Elder, C., Barkhuizen, G., Knoch, U. & Von Randow, J. (2007). Evaluating rater responses to an online training program for L2 writing assessment. *Language Testing, 24*(1), 37–64. https://doi.org/10.1177/0265532207071511

Elder, C. & Davies, A. (1998). Performance on ESL examinations: Is there a language distance effect? *Language and Education, 12*, 1–17. https://doi.org/10.1080/09500789808666736

Elder, C., Knoch, U., Barkhuizen, G. & Von Randow, J. (2005). Individual feedback to enhance rater training: Does it work? *Language Assessment Quarterly, 2*(3), 175–196. https://doi.org/10.1207/s15434311laq0203_1

Ellis, R. (2003). *Task-based language learning and teaching*. Oxford: Oxford University Press.

Engelhard, G. (1996). Evaluating rater accuracy in performance assessments. *Journal of Educational Measurement, 33*, 56–70. https://doi.org/10.1111/j.1745-3984.1996.tb00479.x

Engelhard, G. (2013). *Invariant measurement: Using Rasch models in the social, behavioral and health sciences*. New York: Routledge. https://doi.org/10.4324/9780203073636

Engelhard, G., Wang, J. & Wind, S. (2018). A tale of two models: Psychometric and cognitive perspectives on rater-mediated assessments using accuracy ratings. *Psychological Test and Assessment Modeling, 60*(1), 33–52.

Erdosy, M. U. (2003). Exploring variability in judging writing ability in a second language: A study of four experienced raters of ESL compositions. In *TOEFL Research Report 70*. Princeton: Educational Testing Service. https://doi.org/10.1002/j.2333-8504.2003.tb01909.x

Ericsson, K. A. & Simon, H. A. (1993). *Protocol analysis: Verbal reports as data* (Revised edition). Cambridge, MA: MIT Press. https://doi.org/10.7551/mitpress/5657.001.0001

Ewert, D. & Shin, S.-Y. (2015). Examining instructors' conceptualizations and challenges in designing a data-driven rating scale for a reading-to-write task. *Assessing Writing*, 38–50. https://doi.org/10.1016/j.asw.2015.06.001

Fairbairn, J. (2015). *An examination of how analystic raters adapt to holistic marking*. Unpublished MA dissertation, University of Lancaster.

Fayer, J. M. & Krasinski, E. (1987). Native and nonnative judgements of intelligibility and irritation. *Language Learning, 37*, 313–326. https://doi.org/10.1111/j.1467-1770.1987.tb00573.x

Ford, A. (1931). Neutralizing inequalities in ratings. *Personnel Journal, 9*, 466–469.

Fowles, D. (2011). *Literature review on effects on assessment of e-marking. Centre for Education Research and Policy.* Accessed 27 February 2019 at www.cerp.org.uk

Fox, J. (2004). Biasing for the best in language testing and learning: An interview with Merrill Swain. *Language Assessment Quarterly, 1*(4), 235–251. https://doi.org/10.1207/s15434311laq0104_3

Freedman, S. W. & Calfee, R. C. (1983). Holistic assessment of writing: Experimental design and cognitive theory. In J. Mosenthal, L. Tamor & S. Walmsley (Eds.), *Research in writing: Principles and methods.* New York: Longman.

Fritz, E. & Ruegg, R. (2013). Rater sensitivity to lexical accuracy, sophistication and range when assessing writing. *Assessing Writing, 18*, 173–181. https://doi.org/10.1016/j.asw.2013.02.001

Fulcher, G. (1996). Does thick description lead to smart tests? A data-based approach to rating scale construction. *Language Testing, 13*(2), 208–238. https://doi.org/10.1177/026553229601300205

Fulcher, G. (2003). *Testing second language speaking.* London: Pearson.

Fulcher, G. (2015). Assessing second language speaking. *Language Teaching, 48*(2), 198–216.
https://doi.org/10.1017/S0261444814000391

Fulcher, G. & Davidson, F. (2007). *Language testing and assessment: An advanced resource book.* Abingdon: Routledge.
https://doi.org/10.4324/9780203449066

Fulcher, G., Davidson, F. & Kemp, J. (2011). Effective rating scale development for speaking tests: Performance decision trees. *Language Testing, 28*(1), 5–29. https://doi.org/10.1177/0265532209359514

Furneaux, C. & Rignall, M. (2007). The effect of standarization-training on rater judgements for the IELTS writing module. In L. Taylor & P. Falvey (Eds.), *IELTS Collected Papers: Research in speaking and writing assessment* (pp. 422–445). Cambridge: Cambridge University Press.

Galaczi, E. D. (2004). *Peer-peer interaction in a paired speaking test: The case of the First Certificate in English.* Unpublished PhD dissertation, Teachers' College, Columbia University, New York.

Galaczi, E. D., ffrench, A., Hubbard, C. & Green, A. (2011). Developing assessment scales for large-scale speaking tests: A multiple-method approach. *Assessment in Education: Principles, Policy & Practice, 18*(3), 217–237. https://doi.org/10.1080/0969594X.2011.574605

Gass, S. & Mackey, A. (2000). *Stimulated recall methodology in second language research*. Mahwah, NJ: Lawrence Earlbaum Associates.

Gebril, A. & Plakans, L. (2014). Assembling validity evidence for assessing academic writing: Raters reactions to integrated tasks. *Assessing Writing, 21*, 56–73. https://doi.org/10.1016/j.asw.2014.03.002

Geranpayeh, A. (2011). The impact of online marking on examiners' behaviour. *Cambridge ESOL Research Notes, 43*, 15–20.

Ginther, A., Dimova, S. & Yang, R. (2010). Conceptual and empirical relationships between temporal measures of fluency and oral English proficiency with implications for automated scoring. *Language Testing, 27*(3), 379–399. https://doi.org/10.1177/0265532210364407

Graesser, A. C., McNamara, D. & Kulikowich, J. M. (2011). Coh-Metrix: Providing multilevel analyses of text characteristics. *Educational Researcher, 40*(5), 223–234.
https://doi.org/10.3102/0013189X11413260

Green, A. (Ed.) (1998). *Verbal protocol analysis in language testing research: A handbook* (Vol. 5). Cambridge: Press Syndicate of the University of Cambridge.

Hall, K. & Harding, A. (2002). Level descriptions and teacher assessment in England: Towards a community of assessment practice. *Educational Research, 44*(1), 1–16. https://doi.org/10.1080/00131880110081071

Hamp-Lyons, L. (1990). Second language writing: Assessment issues. In B. Kroll (Ed.), *Second language writing: Research insights for the classroom* (pp. 69–87). New York: Cambridge University Press. https://doi.org/10.1017/CBO9781139524551.009

Hamp-Lyons, L. (1991). Scoring procedures for ESL contexts. In L. Hamp-Lyons (Ed.), *Assessing second language writing in academic contexts*. Norwood, NJ: Ablex Publishing Corporation.

Hamp-Lyons, L. (1995). Rating nonnative writing: The trouble with holistic scoring. *TESOL Quarterly, 29*(4), 759–762.
https://doi.org/10.2307/3588173

Hamp-Lyons, L. (2011). Writing assessment: Shifting issues, new tools, enduring questions. *Assessing Writing, 16*(1), 3–5.
https://doi.org/10.1016/j.asw.2010.12.001

Hamp-Lyons, L. & Matthias, S. P. (1994). Examining expert judgments of task difficulty on essay tests. *Journal of Second Language Writing, 3*(1), 49–68. https://doi.org/10.1016/1060-3743(94)90005-1

Han, Q. (2016). Rater cognition in L2 speaking assessment: a review of the literature. *Teachers' College Columbia University Working Papers in TESOL & Applied Linguistics, 16*(1), 1–24.

Harsch, C. & Martin, G. (2012). Adapting CEF-descriptors for rating purposes: Validation by a combined rater training and scale revision approach. *Assessing Writing, 17*(2), 228–250. https://doi.org/10.1016/j.asw.2012.06.003

Haswell, R. H. & Haswell, J. T. (1996). Gender bias and critique of student writing. *Assessing Writing, 3*, 31–83. https://doi.org/10.1016/S1075-2935(96)90004-5

Hawkey, R. & Barker, F. (2004). Developing a common scale for the assessment of writing. *Assessing Writing, 9*(2), 122–159. https://doi.org/10.1016/j.asw.2004.06.001

Higgins, D., Xi, X., Zechner, K. & Williamson, D. (2011). A three-stage approach to the automated scoring of spontaneous spoken responses. *Computer Speech and Language, 25*, 282–306. https://doi.org/10.1016/j.csl.2010.06.001

Hirai, A. & Koizumi, R. (2013). Validation of empirically derived rating scales for a story retelling speaking test. *Language Assessment Quarterly, 10*(4), 398–422. https://doi.org/10.1080/15434303.2013.824973

Hong Kong Examinations and Assessment Authority. (2015). *Onscreen marking system*. Retrieved 27 February 2019 from www.hkeaa.org

Hopkins, K. D. (1998). *Educational and psychological measurement and evaluation* (8th edition). Boston: Allyn and Bacon.

Hoskens, M. & Wilson, M. (2001). Real-time feedback on rater drift in constructed-response items: An example from the Golden State examination. *Journal of Educational Measurement, 38*(2), 121–145. https://doi.org/10.1111/j.1745-3984.2001.tb01119.x

Hsieh, C.-N. (2011). Rater effects in ITA testing: ESL teachers' versus American undergraduates' judgements of accentedness, comprehensibility, and oral proficiency. *Spaan Fellow Working Papers in Second or Foreign Language Assessment, 9*, 47–74.

Hsu, T. H. (2016). Removing bias towards World Englishes: The development of a rater attitude instrument using Indian English as a stimulus. *Language Testing, 33*(3), 367–389. https://doi.org/10.1177/0265532215590694

Huang, B. H. (2013). The effects of accent familiarity and language teaching experience on raters' judgements of non-native speech. *System, 41*, 770–785. https://doi.org/10.1016/j.system.2013.07.009

Huang, B. H., Alegre, A. & Eisenberg, A. (2016). A cross-linguistic investigation of the effect of raters' accent familiarity on speaking assessment. *Language Assessment Quarterly, 13*(1), 25–41. https://doi.org/10.1080/15434303.2015.1134540

Huang, J. (2008). How accuracte are ESL students' holistic writing scores on large-scale assessments? A generalizability theory approach. *Assessing Writing, 13,* 201–218.
https://doi.org/10.1016/j.asw.2008.10.002

Huang, J. (2012). Using generalizability theory to examine the accuracy and validity of large-scale ESL writing assessment. *Assessing Writing, 17*(3), 123–139. https://doi.org/10.1016/j.asw.2011.12.003

Huang, Y. (2007). A survey of the CET online marking system. *Foreign Language World, 2,* 82–96.

Huot, B. (1990). Reliability, validity, and holistic scoring: What we know, what we need to know. *College Composition and Communication, 41*(2), 201–213. https://doi.org/10.2307/358160

In'nami, Y. & Koizumi, R. (2016). Task and rater effects in L2 speaking and writing: Asynthesis of generalizability studies. *Language Testing, 33*(3), 341–366. https://doi.org/10.1177/0265532215587390

Isaacs, T. (2008). Towards defining a valid assessment criterion of pronunciation proficiency in non-native English-speaking graduate students. *The Canadian Modern Language Review, 64*(4), 555–580. https://doi.org/10.3138/cmlr.64.4.555

Isaacs, T. (2018). Fully automated speaking assessment: Changes to proficiency testing and the role of pronunciation. In O. Kang, R. I. Thomson & J. M. Murphy (Eds.), *The Routledge handbook of contemporary English pronunciation* (pp. 570–584). Abingdon: Routledge. https://doi.org/10.4324/9781315145006-36

Isaacs, T. & Thomson, R. I. (2013). Rater experience, rating scale length, and judgements of L2 pronunciation: revisiting research conventions. *Language Assessment Quarterly, 10*(2), 135–159.
https://doi.org/10.1080/15434303.2013.769545

Isaacs, T., Trofimovich, P. & Foote, J. A. (2017). Developing a user-oriented second language comprehensibility scale for English-medium universities. *Language Testing, 35*(2), 193–216.
https://doi.org/10.1177/0265532217703433

Jacobs, H., Zinkgraf, S., Wormuth, D., Hartfield, V. & Hughey, J. (1981). *Testing ESL composition: A practical approach.* Rowley, MA: Newbury House.

Jacoby, S. (1998). *Science as performance: Socializing scientific discourse through conference talk rehearsals.* Unpublished doctoral dissertation, University of California, Los Angeles.

Jacoby, S. & McNamara, T. (1999). Locating competence. *English for Specific Purposes, 18*(3), 213–241.
https://doi.org/10.1016/S0889-4906(97)00053-7

Jamieson, J. (2014). Defining constructs and assessment design. In A. Kunnan (Ed.), *The companion to language assessment*. London: John Wiley & Sons. https://doi.org/10.1002/9781118411360.wbcla062

Janssen, G., Meier, V. & Trace, J. (2015). Building a better rubric: Mixed methods rubric revision. *Assessing Writing, 26*, 51–66. https://doi.org/10.1016/j.asw.2015.07.002

Jiang, J. & Wen, Q. (2010). A comparative study of Ngram and translation unit alignment in automated scoring of students' English-Chinese translation. *Modern Foreign Languages Quarterly, 33*(2), 177–184.

Jin, T., Mak, B. & Zhou, P. (2012). Confidence scoring of speaking performance: How does fuzziness become exact? *Language Testing, 29*(1), 43–65. https://doi.org/10.1177/0265532211404383

Jin, Y. & Yang, H. R. (2011). *Quality control for the marking of constructed-response items: The CET Online Marking System*. Paper presented at the 13th Academic Forum on English Language Testing in Asia, Hong Kong, 24–26 November 2011.

Jin, Y., Zhu, B. & Wang, W. (2017). *Writing to the machine: Challenges facing automated scoring in the College English Test in China*. Paper presented at the Symposium on human-machine teaming up for language assessment: The need for extending the scope of assessment literacy, Language Testing Research Colloquium, Bogota, Colombia, 21–24 July 2017.

Joe, J. N., Harmes, J. C. & Hickerson, C. A. (2011). Using verbal reports to explore rater perceptual processes in scoring: A mixed methods application to oral communication assessment. *Assessment in Education: Principles, Policy & Practice, 18*(3), 239–258. https://doi.org/10.1080/0969594X.2011.577408

Johnson, D. & Van Brackle, L. (2012). Linguistic discrimination in writing assessment: How raters react to African American 'errors', ESL errors, and standard English errors on a state-mandated writing exam. *Assessing Writing, 17*, 35–54. https://doi.org/10.1016/j.asw.2011.10.001

Johnson, J. & Lim, G. S. (2009). The influence of rater language background on writing performance assessment. *Language Testing, 26*(4), 485–505. https://doi.org/10.1177/0265532209340186

Johnson, M. & Nadas, R. (2009). Marking essays on screen: An investigation into the reliability and some qualitative aspects of on-screen essay marking. *Research Matters: A Cambridge Assessment Publication, 8*, 2–9.

Johnson, R. L., Penny, J., Fisher, S. & Kuhs, T. (2003). Score resolution: An investigation of the reliability and validity of resolved scores. *Applied Measurement in Education, 16*(4), 299–322. https://doi.org/10.1207/S15324818AME1604_3

Johnson, R. L., Penny, J. & Gordon, B. (2000). The relation between score resolution methods and interrater reliability: An empirical study of an analytic scoring rubric. *Applied Measurement in Education, 13*(2), 121–138. https://doi.org/10.1207/S15324818AME1302_1

Johnson, R. L., Penny, J., Gordon, B., Shumate, S. R. & Fisher, S. P. (2005). Resolving score differences in the rating of writing samples: Does discussion improve the accuracy of scores? *Language Assessment Quarterly, 2*(2), 117–146. https://doi.org/10.1207/s15434311laq0202_2

Jolle, L. (2014). Pair assessment of pupil writing: A dialogic approach for studying the development of rater competence. *Assessing Writing, 20* (April), 37–52. https://doi.org/10.1016/j.asw.2014.01.002

Kachru, B. B. (1982). *The other tongue: English across cultures*. Urbana, IL: University of Illionois Press.

Kachru, B. B. (1985). Standards, codification and sociolinguistic realism: The English language in the outer circle. In R. Quirk & H. Widdowson (Eds.), *English in the world: Teaching and learning the language and literatures* (pp. 11–30). Cambridge: Cambridge University Press.

Kane, M. (1992). An argument-based approach to validity. *Psychological Bulletin, 112*(3), 527–535. https://doi.org/10.1037/0033-2909.112.3.527

Kane, M. (2001). Current concerns in validity theory. *Journal of Educational Measurement, 38*, 319–342. https://doi.org/10.1111/j.1745-3984.2001.tb01130.x

Kane, M. (2006). Validation. In R. L. Brennan (Ed.), *Educational measurement* (pp. 17–64). Westport, CT: American Council on Education/ Praeger.

Kane, M. (2012). Validating score interpretations and uses. *Language Testing, 29*(1), 3–17. https://doi.org/10.1177/0265532211417210

Kane, M. (2013). Validating the interpretations and uses of test scores. *Journal of Educational Measurement, 50*(1), 1–73. https://doi.org/10.1111/jedm.12000

Kane, M. (2016). Validity as the evaluation of the claims based on test scores. *Assessment in Education: Principles, Policy & Practice, 23*(2), 309–311. https://doi.org/10.1080/0969594X.2016.1156645

Kane, M., Crooks, T. & Cohen, A. (1999). Validating measures of performance. *Educational Measurement: Issues and Practice, 12*, 5–17. https://doi.org/10.1111/j.1745-3992.1999.tb00010.x

Kim, H. J. (2011). *Investigating raters' development of rating ability on a second language speaking assessment.* Unpublished Ed.D. dissertation, Teachers' College, Columbia University, New York.

Kim, Y.-H. (2009). An investigation into native and non-native teachers' judgments of oral English performance: A mixed methods approach. *Language Testing, 26*(2), 187–217. https://doi.org/10.1177/0265532208101010

Kim, Y.-H. (2011). Diagnosing EAP writing ability using the reduced reparameterized unified model. *Language Testing, 28*(4), 509–541. https://doi.org/10.1177/0265532211400860

Kneeland, N. (1929). That lenient tendency in rating. *Personnel Journal, 7*, 356–366.

Knoch, U. (2009). *Diagnostic assessment of writing: The development and validation of a rating scale.* Frankfurt: Peter Lang.

Knoch, U. (2011). Investigating the effectiveness of individualized feedback to rating behaviour – A longitudinal study. *Language Testing, 28*(2), 179–200. https://doi.org/10.1177/0265532210384252

Knoch, U. & Chapelle, C. (2018). Validation of rating processes within an argument-based framework. *Language Testing, 35*(4), 477–499. https://doi.org/10.1177/0265532217710049

Knoch, U., Deygers, B. & Khamboonruang, A. (in press). Revising rating scale development for rater-mediated language performance assessment: Modelling construct and contextual choices made by scale developers. *Language Testing.*

Knoch, U., Elder, C., Woodward-Kron, R., Flynn, E., Manias, E., McNamara, T., … Huisman, A. (2017). *Towards improved quality of written patient records: Development and validation of language proficiency standards for writing for non-native English speaking health professionals.* Melbourne: Language Testing Research Centre, University of Melbourne.

Knoch, U., Fairbairn, J. & Huismann, A. (2015). An evaluation of the effectiveness of training Aptis raters online. *British Council Validation Series, VS/2015/001.* London: British Council.

Knoch, U., Fairbairn, J. & Huismann, A. (2016). An evaluation of an online rater training program for the speaking and writing sub-tests of the Aptis test. *The Association for Language Testing and Assessment of Australia and New Zealand, Volume 5, Issue 1.*

Knoch, U. & Macqueen, S. (2019). *Assessing English for professional purposes: Language and the workplace*. London: Routledge. https://doi.org/10.4324/9780429340383

Knoch, U., Macqueen, S. & O'Hagan, S. (2014). *An investigation of the effect of task type on the discourse produced by students at various score levels in the TOEFL iBT writing test*. TOEFL iBT Report – 23, ETS Research Report RR-14-43. Retrieved from Princeton, NJ: https://doi.org/10.1002/ets2.12038

Knoch, U., Read, J. & von Randow, J. (2007). Re-training writing raters online: How does it compare with face-to-face training? *Assessing Writing, 12*(1), 26–43. https://doi.org/10.1016/j.asw.2007.04.001

Kondo-Brown, K. (2002). A FACETS analysis of rater bias in measuring Japanese second language writing performance. *Language Testing, 19*(1), 3–31. https://doi.org/10.1191/0265532202lt218oa

Krippendorff, K. (2004). Reliability in content analysis: Some common misconceptions and recommendations. *Human Communication Research, 30*(3), 411–433.
https://doi.org/10.1111/j.1468-2958.2004.tb00738.x

Kuiken, F. & Vedder, I. (2017). Functional adequacy in L2 writing: Towards a new rating scale. *Language Testing, 34*(3), 321–336. https://doi.org/10.1177/0265532216663991

Kunnan, A. (2018). *Evaluating language assessments*. New York: Routledge. https://doi.org/10.4324/9780203803554

Lallmamode, S. P., Daud, M. D. & Abu Kassim, N. L. (2016). Development and initial argument-based validation of a scoring rubric used in the assessment of L2 writing electronic portfolios. *Assessing Writing, 30*, 44–62. https://doi.org/10.1016/j.asw.2016.06.001

Leckie, G. & Baird, J.-A. (2011). Rater effects on essay scoring: Amultilevel analysis of severity drift, central tendency, and rater experience. *Journal of Educational Measurement, 48*, 399–418. https://doi.org/10.1111/j.1745-3984.2011.00152.x

Lee, H. K. (2009). Native and nonnative rater behaviour in grading Korean students' English essays. *Asia Pacific Education Review, 10*, 387–397). https://doi.org/10.1007/s12564-009-9030-3

Lee, Y.-W., Gentile, C. & Kantor, R. (2010). Toward automated multi-trait scoring of essays: investigating links among holistic, analytic and test feature scores. *Applied Linguistics, 31*(3), 391–417. https://doi.org/10.1093/applin/amp040

Lee, Y.-W. & Kantor, R. (2007). Evaluating prototype tasks and alternative rating schemes for a new ESL writing test through G-theory. *International Journal of Testing, 7*(4), 353–385. https://doi.org/10.1080/15305050701632247

Li, H. & He, L. (2015). A comparison of EFL raters' essay-rating processes across two types of rating scales. *Language Assessment Quarterly, 12*(2), 178–212. https://doi.org/10.1080/15434303.2015.1011738

Li, M., Yang, X., Feng, G., Wu, M., Chen, J. & Hu, G. (2008). Feasibility and practice of automated scoring of read-aloud in large-scale college Engish testing. *Foreign Language World, 4*, 88–95.

Liang, M. (2005). *Constructing a scoring model for automated scoring of Chinese English language learners' essay writing.* Unpublished PhD dissertation, Nanjing University, Nanjing.

Lim, G. (2011). The development and maintenance of rating quality in performance writing assessments: A longitudinal study of new and experienced raters. *Language Testing, 28*(4), 543–560. https://doi.org/10.1177/0265532211406422

Linacre, J. (2002). Judge ratings with forced agreement. *Rasch Measurement Transactions, 16*, 857–858.

Linacre, J. M. (1999). Investigating rating scale category utility. *Journal of Outcome Measurement, 3*(2), 103–122.

Linacre, J. M. (2016). Facets Rasch measurement computer program. Chicago: Winsteps.com.

Lindhardsen, V. (2018). From independent ratings to communal ratings: A study of CWA raters' decision-making behaviours. *Assessing Writing, 35*(2), 12–25. https://doi.org/10.1016/j.asw.2017.12.004

Ling, G., Mollaun, P. & Xi, X. (2014). A study on the impact of fatigue on human raters when scoring speaking responses. *Language Testing, 31*(4), 479–499. https://doi.org/10.1177/0265532214530699

Lu, Z., Li, X. & Li, Z. (2015). AWE-based corrective feedback on developing EFL learners' writing skill. In F. Helm, M. Guarda, & S. Thouesny (Eds.), *Critical CALL – Proceedings of the 2015 EUROCALL conference, Padova, Italy* (pp. 375–380). Dublin: Research-publishing-net. https://doi.org/10.14705/rpnet.2015.000361

Lumley, T. (1998). Perceptions of language-trained raters and occupational experts in a test of occupational English language proficiency. *English for Specific Purposes, 17*(4), 347–367. https://doi.org/10.1016/S0889-4906(97)00016-1

Lumley, T. (2002). Assessment criteria in a large-scale writing test: What do they really mean to the raters? *Language Testing, 19*(3), 246–276. https://doi.org/10.1191/0265532202lt230oa

Lumley, T. (2005). *Assessing second language writing. The rater's perspective*. Frankfurt: Peter Lang.

Lumley, T. & McNamara, T. (1995). Rater characteristics and rater bias: Implications for training. *Language Testing, 12*(1), 54–71. https://doi.org/10.1177/026553229501200104

Lynch, B. & McNamara, T. (1998). Using G-theory and many-facet Rasch measurement in the development of performance assessments of the ESL speaking skills of immigrants. *Language Testing, 15*(2), 158–180. https://doi.org/10.1177/026553229801500202

Marefat, F. & Heydari, M. (2016). Native and Iranian teachers' perceptions and evaluation of Iranian students' English essays. *Assessing Writing, 27*, 24–36. https://doi.org/10.1016/j.asw.2015.10.001

Martin, G. (2012). *Assessing coding quality: Agreement measures and quality control designs for large scale system monitoring assessments*. Hamburg: International Association for the Evaluation of Educational Achievement.

May, L. (2006). An examination of rater orientations on a paired candidate discussion task through stimulated verbal recall. *Melbourne Papers in Language and Testing, 11*(1), 29–51.

May, L. (2009). Co-constructed interaction in a paired speaking test: The rater's perspective. *Language Testing, 26*(3), 397–421. https://doi.org/10.1177/0265532209104668

May, L. (2011). *Interaction in a paired speaking test: The rater's perspective*. Frankfurt: Peter Lang.

McIntyre, R. M., Smith, D. & Hassett, C. E. (1984). Accuracy of performance ratings as affected by rater training and perceived purpose of rating. *Journal of Applied Psychology, 69*, 147–156. https://doi.org/10.1037/0021-9010.69.1.147

McNamara, T. (1996). *Measuring second language performance*. London & New York: Longman.

McNamara, T. (2001). Language assessment as social practice: Challenges for research. *Language Testing, 18*(4), 333–350. https://doi.org/10.1177/026553220101800402

McNamara, T. (2002). Discourse and assessment. *Annual Review of Applied Linguistics, 22*, 221–242. https://doi.org/10.1017/S0267190502000120

McNamara, T. & Knoch, U. (2012). The Rasch wars: The emergence of Rasch measurement in language testing. *Language Testing, 29*(4), 553–574. https://doi.org/10.1177/0265532211430367

McNamara, T., Knoch, U. & Fan, J. (2019). *Fairness, justice and language assessment*. Oxford: Oxford University Press.

McNamara, T. & Lumley, T. (1997). The effect of interlocutor and assessment mode variables in overseas assessments of speaking skills in occupational settings. *Language Testing, 14*, 140–156. https://doi.org/10.1177/026553229701400202

Meiron, B. E. (1998). *Rating oral proficiency tests: A triangulated study of rater thought processes*. Unpublished MA thesis, California State University Los Angeles, CA.

Meisel, J., Clahsen, H. & Pienemann, M. (1981). On determining developmental stages in natural second language acquisition. *Studies in Second Language Acquisition, 3*, 109–135. https://doi.org/10.1017/S0272263100004137

Mendoza, A. & Knoch, U. (2018). Examining the validity of an analytic rating scale for a Spanish test for academic purposes using the argument-based approach to validation. *Assessing Writing, 35*, 41–55. https://doi.org/10.1016/j.asw.2017.12.003

Messick, S. (1989). Validity. In R. L. Linn (Ed.), *Educational measurement* (3rd edition, pp. 13–103). New York: Macmillan.

Mickan, P. (2003). *'What's your score?' An investigation into language descriptors for rating written performance*. Retrieved 2 October 2019 from Canberra: https://www.ielts.org/teaching-and-research/research-reports/volume-05-report-3

Milanovic, M., Saville, N. & Shen, S. (1996). A study of the decision-making behaviour of composition markers. In M. Milanovic & N. Saville (Eds.), *Studies in Language Testing 3: Performance, cognition and assessment*. Cambridge: Cambridge University Press.

Miller, G. A. (1956). The magical number seven, plus or minus two: Some limits on our capacity for processing information. *Psychological Review, 63*(2), 81–97. https://doi.org/10.1037/h0043158

Mislevy, R. J. & Yin, C. (2012). Evidence-centred design in language testing. In G. Fulcher & F. Davidson (Eds.), *The Routledge handbook of language testing* (pp. 208–222). London & New York: Routledge.

Morgan, G. B., Zhu, M., Johnson, R. L. & Hodge, K. J. (2014). Interrater reliability estimators commonly used in scoring language assessments: A Monte Carlo investigation of estimator accuracy. *Language Assessment Quarterly, 11*(3), 304–324. https://doi.org/10.1080/15434303.2014.937486

Morozov, A. (2011). Student attitudes toward the assessment criteria in writing-intensive college courses. *Assessing Writing, 16*(1), 6–31. https://doi.org/10.1016/j.asw.2010.09.001

Moss, P. (1992). Shifting conceptions of validity in educational measurement: Implications for performance assessment. *Review of Educational Research, 62*, 229–258. https://doi.org/10.3102/00346543062003229

Moss, P. (2003). Reconceptualizing validity for classroom assessment. *Educational Measurement: Issues and Practice, 22*(4), 13–25. https://doi.org/10.1111/j.1745-3992.2003.tb00140.x

Mun, E. Y. (2005). Rater agreement – Weighted kappa. In B. S. Everitt & D. Howell (Eds.), *Encyclopedia of statistics in behavioral science* (Vol. 3, pp. 1714–1715). New York: Wiley. https://doi.org/10.1002/0470013192.bsa544

Murphy, K. R. (1982). Difficulties in the statistical control of halo. *Journal of Applied Psychology, 74*, 161–164. https://doi.org/10.1037/0021-9010.67.2.161

Myford, C. M. & Wolfe, E. W. (2002). When raters disagree, then what: Examining a third-rating discrepancy resolution procedure and its utility for identifying unusual patterns of ratings. *Journal of Applied Measurement, 3*(3), 300–324.

Myford, C. M. & Wolfe, E. W. (2003). Detecting and measuring rater effects using many-facet Rasch measurement: Part I. *Journal of Applied Measurement, 4*(4), 386–422.

Myford, C. M. & Wolfe, E. W. (2004). Detecting and measuring rater effects using many-facet Rasch measurement: Part II. *Journal of Applied Measurement, 5*(2), 189–227.

Nakatsuhara, F. (2004). *An investigation into conversational styles in paired speaking tests*. Unpublished MA dissertation, University of Essex, Colchester.

Nakatsuhara, F. (2008). Inter-interviewer variation in oral interview tests. *ELT Journal, 62*(3), 266–275. https://doi.org/10.1093/elt/ccm044

Nakatsuhara, F., May, L., Lam, D. & Galaczi, E. D. (2018). Learning-oriented feedback in the development and assessment of interactional competence. *Cambridge Research Notes, 70*, 4–67.

Neumann, H. (2014). Teacher assessment of grammatical ability in second language academic writing: A case study. *Journal of Second Language Writing, 24*, 83–107. https://doi.org/10.1016/j.jslw.2014.04.002

North, B. (1995). The development of a common framework scale of descriptors of language proficiency based on a theory of measurement. *System, 23*(4), 445–465. https://doi.org/10.1016/0346-251X(95)00032-F

North, B. (2003). Scales for rating language performance: Descriptive models, formulation styles, and presentation formats. *TOEFL Monograph 24*.

North, B. & Schneider, G. (1998). Scaling descriptors for language proficiency scales. *Language Testing, 15*(2), 217–263. https://doi.org/10.1177/026553229801500204

O'Loughlin, K. (1994). The assessment of writing by English and ESL teachers. *Australian Review of Applied Linguistics, 17*, 23–44. https://doi.org/10.1075/aral.17.1.02olo

O'Loughlin, K. (2007). An investigation into the role of gender in the IELTS oral interview. In L. Taylor & P. Falvey (Eds.), *IELTS Collected papers: Research in speaking and writing assessment* (pp. 63–95). Cambridge: Cambridge University Press.

O'Sullivan, B. (2010). Validity and validation. Invited Talk, Lancaster University, February.

O'Sullivan, B. (Ed.) (2011). *Language testing: Theories and practice*. Basingstoke: Palgrave Macmillan.

O'Sullivan, B. & Dunlea, J. (2015). Aptis General Technical Manual Version 1.0. *Aptis Techical Report, TR/2015/002*. London: British Council.

O'Sullivan, B. & Rignall, M. (2007). Assessing the value of bias analysis feedback to raters for the IELTS writing module. In L. Taylor & P. Falvey (Eds.), *IELTS Collected Papers* (pp. 446–476). Cambridge: Cambridge University Press.

O'Sullivan, B. & Weir, C. (2011). Test development and validation. In B. O'Sullivan (Ed.), *Language testing: Theories and practice* (pp. 13–32). Basingstoke: Palgrave Macmillan.

Orr, M. (2002). The FCE speaking test: Using rater reports to help interpret test scores. *System, 30*, 143–154. https://doi.org/10.1016/S0346-251X(02)00002-7

Page, E. B. (1966). The imminence of grading essays by computer. *Phi Delta Kappan, 48*, 238–243.

Page, E. B. (1968). Analyzing student essays by computer. *International Review of Education, 14*, 210–255. https://doi.org/10.1007/BF01419938

Patterson, B. F., Wind, S. A. & Engelhard, G. (2017). Incorporating criterion ratings into model-based rater monitoring procedures using latent-class signal detection theory. *Applied Psychological Measurement, 41*(6), 472–491. https://doi.org/10.1177/0146621617698452

Pearson. (2009). *Versant English test: Test description and validation summary*. Menlo Park, CA: Pearson. Retrieved from www.versanttest.com/technology/VersantEnglishTestValidation.pdf

Penny, J. (2003). My life as a reader. *Assessing Writing, 8*, 192–215. https://doi.org/10.1016/j.asw.2003.08.001

Penny, J. A. & Johnson, R. L. (2011). The accuracy of performance task scores after resolution of rater disagreement: A Monte Carlo study. *Assessing Writing: An International Journal, 16*(4), 221–236. https://doi.org/10.1016/j.asw.2011.06.001

Penny, J., Johnson, R. L. & Gordon, B. (2000). The effect of rating augmentation on inter-rater reliability: An empirical study of a holistic rubric. *Assessing Writing, 7*(2), 113–194. https://doi.org/10.1016/S1075-2935(00)00012-X

Perkins, K. (1983). On the use of composition scoring techniques, objective measures, and objective tests to evaluate ESL writing ability. *TESOL Quarterly, 17*(4), 651–671. https://doi.org/10.2307/3586618

Pinot de Moira, A., Massey, C., Baird, J.-A. & Morrissy, M. (2002). Marking consistency over time. *Research in Education, 67*, 79–87. https://doi.org/10.7227/RIE.67.8

Pollatsek, A., Reichle, E. D. & Rayner, K. (2006). Test of the E–Z reader model: Exploring the interface between cognition and eye-movement control. *Cognitive Psychology, 52*(1), 1–56. https://doi.org/10.1016/j.cogpsych.2005.06.001

Pollitt, A. (2012). Comparative judgement for assessment. *International Journal of Technology and Design Education, 22*(2), 157–170. https://doi.org/10.1007/s10798-011-9189-x

Pollitt, A. & Murray, N. L. (1996). What raters really pay attention to. In M. Milanovic & N. Saville (Eds.), *Performance testing, cognition and assessment: Selected papers from the 15th Language Testing Research Colloquium (LTRC), Cambridge and Arnhem* (Vol. 3). Cambridge: Cambridge University Press.

Powers, D. & Farnum, M. (1997). Effects of mode of presentation on essay scores. *ETS RM-97-08*. Princeton, NJ: Educational Testing Service.

Powers, D., Farnum, M., Grant, M. & Kubota, M. (1997). A pilot test of online essay scoring. *ETS RM-97-07*. Princeton, NJ: Educational Testing Service.

Purpura, J. (2012). *What is the role of strategic competence in a processing account of L2 learning or use?* Paper presented at the American Association for Applied Linguistics Conference, Boston, MA.

Purpura, J. (2014). Cognition and language assessment. In A. Kunnan (Ed.), *The companion to language assessment* (pp. 1452–1476). Hoboken, NJ: Wiley-Blackwell. https://doi.org/10.1002/9781118411360.wbcla150

Raczynski, K., Cohen, A. S., Engelhard, G. & Lu, Z. (2015). Comparing the effectiveness of self-paced and collaborative frame-of-reference training on rater accuracy in a large-scale writing assessment. *Journal of Educational Measurement, 52*(3), 301–318. https://doi.org/10.1111/jedm.12079

Raikes, N., Greatorex, J. & Shaw, S. (2004). *From paper to screen: Some issues on the way*. Paper presented at the IAEA Conference, Manchester.

Rakedzon, T. & Baram-Tsabari, A. (2017). To make a long story short: A rubric for assessing graduate students' academic and popular science writing skills. *Assessing Writing, 32*, 28–42. https://doi.org/10.1016/j.asw.2016.12.004

Repp, A. C., Nieminen, G. S., Olinger, E. & Brusca, R. (1988). Direct observation: Factors affecting the accuracy of observers. *Exceptional Children, 55*, 29–36. https://doi.org/10.1177/001440298805500103

Roever, C. & Kasper, G. (2018). Speaking in turns and sequences: Interactional competence as a target construct in testing speaking. *Language Testing, 35*(3), 331–355. https://doi.org/10.1177/0265532218758128

Ruth, L. & Murphy, S. (1984). *Designing writing tasks for the assessment of writing*. Norwood, NJ: Ablex.

Sadler, D. R. (1987). Specifying and promulgating achievement standards. *Oxford Review of Education, 13*(2), 191–209. https://doi.org/10.1080/0305498870130207

Sadler, D. R. (2011). Academic freedom, achievement standards and professional identity. *Quality in Higher Education, 17*(1), 85–100. https://doi.org/10.1080/13538322.2011.554639

Sakyi, A. A. (2000). Validation of holistic scoring for ESL writing assessment: How raters evaluate compositions. In A. J. Kunnan (Ed.), *Fairness and validation in language assessment: Selected papers from the 19th Language Testing Research Colloquium, Orlando, Florida*. Cambridge: Cambridge University Press.

Santos, T. (1988). Professors' reactions to the academic writing of nonnative-speaking students. *TESOL Quarterly, 22*, 69–90. https://doi.org/10.2307/3587062

Sawaki, Y. (2007). Construct validation of analytic rating scale in speaking assessment: Reporting a score profile and a composite. *Language Testing, 24*(3), 355–390. https://doi.org/10.1177/0265532207077205

Schoonen, R. (2005). Generalizability of writing scores: An application of structural equation modeling. *Language Testing, 22*(1), 1–30. https://doi.org/10.1191/0265532205lt295oa

Schoonen, R., Vergeer, M. & Eiting, M. (1997). The assessment of writing ability: Expert readers versus lay readers. *Language Testing, 14*(2), 157–184. https://doi.org/10.1177/026553229701400203

Scott, S. G. & Bruce, R. A. (1995). Decision-making style: The development and assessment of a new measure. *Educational and Psychological Measurement, 55*, 818–831.
https://doi.org/10.1177/0013164495055005017

Seamster, T. L., Redding, R. E. & Kaempf, G. L. (2000). A skill-based cognitive task analysis framework. In J. M. Schraagen, S. F. Chipman & V. L. Shalin (Eds.), *Cognitive task analysis* (pp. 135–145). Mahwah, NJ: Lawrence Erlbaum Associates.

Seedhouse, P. & Egbert, M. (2006). The interactional organisation of the IELTS Speaking Test. *International English Language Testing System (IELTS) Research Reports 2006: Volume 6.* Canberra: IELTS Australia and British Council.

Seedhouse, P., Harris, A., Naeb, R. & Ustunel, E. (2014). The relationship between speaking features and band descriptors: A mixed methods study. *IELTS Research Reports Online Series, 2014*(2), 1–30.

Shavelson, R. J. & Webb, N. M. (1991). *Generalizability theory: A primer.* Newbury Park, CA: Sage.

Shaw, S. (2002). The effect of training and standardisation on rater judgement and inter-rater reliability. *Cambridge Research Notes, 8*(5), 13–17.

Shaw, S. (2004). Creating a virual community of assessment practice: Towards 'on-line' rater reliabilty. *Cambridge Research Notes, 15*(6), 18–20.

Shaw, S. & Weir, C. (2007). *Examining writing.* Cambridge: Cambridge University Press.

Shermis, M. D. (2014). State-of-the-art automated essay scoring: Competition, results, and future directions from a United States demonstration. *Assessing Writing, 20*, 53–76.
https://doi.org/10.1016/j.asw.2013.04.001

Shermis, M. D. & Burstein, J. (Eds.). (2003). *Automated essay scoring: A cross-disciplinary perspective.* Mahwah, NJ: Lawrence Erlbaum. https://doi.org/10.4324/9781410606860

Shermis, M. D. & Burstein, J. (Eds.). (2013). *Handbook of automated essay evaluation: Current applications and new directions.* New York: Routledge. https://doi.org/10.4324/9780203122761

Shermis, M. D., Burstein, J., Higgins, D. & Zechner, K. (2010). Automated essay scoring: Writing assessment and instruction. In M. E. Peterson, E. Baker & B. McGraw (Eds.), *International encyclopedia of education* (pp. 20–26). Oxford: Elsevier. https://doi.org/10.1016/B978-0-08-044894-7.00233-5

Shermis, M. D. & Hamner, B. (2013). Contrasting state-of-the-art automated scoring of essays: Analysis. In M. D. Shermis & J. Burstein (Eds.), *Handbook of automated essay evaluation: Current applications and new directions* (pp. 313–346). New York: Routledge. https://doi.org/10.4324/9780203122761

Shi, L. (2001). Native- and nonnative-speaking EFL teachers' evaluation of Chinese students' English writing. *Language Testing, 18*(3), 303–325. https://doi.org/10.1177/026553220101800303

Shin, S.-Y. & Ewert, D. (2015). What accounts for integrated reading-to-write task scores. *Language Testing, 32*, 259–281. https://doi.org/10.1177/0265532214560257

Shohamy, E., Gordon, C. M. & Kraemer, R. (1992). The effects of raters' background and training on the reliability of direct writing tests. *The Modern Language Journal, 76*(1), 27–33. https://doi.org/10.1111/j.1540-4781.1992.tb02574.x

Skehan, P. (2000). Tasks and language performance assessment. In M. Swain (Ed.), *Researching pedagogic tasks: Second language learning, teaching and testing.* Harlow: Longman.

Sloan, C. & McGinnis, I. (1982). The effect of handwriting on teachers' grading of high school essays. *Journal of the Association for the Study of Perception, 17*(2), 15–21.

Smith, D. (2000). Rater judgments in the direct assessment of competency-based second language writing ability. In G. Brindley (Ed.), *Studies in immigrant English language assessment.* Sydney: National Centre for English Language Teaching and Research.

Song, B. & Caruso, I. (1996). Do English and ESL faculty differ in evaluating the essays of native English-speaking and ESL students? *Journal of Second Language Writing, 5*(2), 163–182. https://doi.org/10.1016/S1060-3743(96)90023-5

Steedle, J. T. & Ferrara, S. (2016). Evaluating comparative judgment as an approach to essay scoring. *Applied Measurement in Education, 29*(3), 211–223. https://doi.org/10.1080/08957347.2016.1171769

Stemler, S. E. (2001). An overview of content analysis. *Practical Assessment, Research & Evaluation, 7*(17), 1–6.

Stemler, S. E. (2007). Interrater reliability. In N. Salkind (Ed.), *Encyclopedia of measurement and statistics* (pp. 484–486). Thousand Oaks, CA: Sage.

Stemler, S. E. & Tsai, J. (2008). Best practices in interrater reliability three common approaches. In J. Osborne (Ed.), *Best practices in quantitative methods* (pp. 29–35). Thousand Oaks, CA: Sage. https://doi.org/10.4135/9781412995627.d5

Struthers, L., Lapadat, J. & MacMillan, P. D. (2013). Assessing cohesion in children's writing: Development of a checklist. *Assessing Writing, 18*, 187–201. https://doi.org/10.1016/j.asw.2013.05.001

Sulsky, L. M. & Balzer, W. K. (1988). Meaning and measurement of performance rating accuracy: Some methodological and theoretical concerns. *Journal of Applied Psychology, 73*, 497–506. https://doi.org/10.1037/0021-9010.73.3.497

Suto, I., Crisp, V. & Greatorex, J. (2008). Investigating the judgemental marking process: An overview of our recent research. *Research Matters: A Cambridge Assessment Publication, 5*, 6–8.

Suto, I. & Greatorex, J. (2008). What goes through an examiner's mind? Using verbal protocols to gain insights into the GCSE marking process. *British Educational Research Journal, 34*(2), 213–233. https://doi.org/10.1080/01411920701492050

Swain, M. (2001). Examining dialogue: Another approach to content specification and to validating inferences drawn from test scores. *Language Testing, 18*(3), 275–302. https://doi.org/10.1177/026553220101800302

Sweedler-Brown, C. (1985). The influence of training and experience on holistic essay evaluation. *English Journal, 74*, 49–55. https://doi.org/10.2307/817702

Tang, J. & Wu, Y. (2012). The application of automated essay scoring systems in college English teaching. *Foreign Languages and Their Teaching, 4*, 53–59.

Thurstone, L. L. (1927). A law of comparative judgment. *Psychological Review, 34*(4), 273–286. https://doi.org/10.1037/h0070288

Tian, Y. (2013). *Online spontaneous automated scoring of translation from English to Chinese*. Beijing: Foreign Language Teaching and Research Press.

Trace, J., Janssen, G. & Meier, V. (2017). Measuring the impact of rater negotiation in writing performance assessment. *Language Testing, 34*(1), 3–22. https://doi.org/10.1177/0265532215594830

Turner, C. E. (2000). Listening to the voices of rating scale developers: Identifying salient features for second language performance assessment. *The Canadian Modern Language Review, 56*(4), 555–584. https://doi.org/10.3138/cmlr.56.4.555

Turner, C. E. & Upshur, J. A. (2002). Rating scales derived from student samples: Effects of the scale maker and the student sample on scale content and student scores. *TESOL Quarterly, 36*(1), 49–70. https://doi.org/10.2307/3588360

Uebersax, J. (2002). Statistical methods for rater agreement. Retrieved 17 April 2018 from http://www.john-uebersax.com/stat/agree.htm

Upshur, J. A. & Turner, C. E. (1995). Constructing rating scales for second language tests. *ELT Journal, 49*(1), 3–12. https://doi.org/10.1093/elt/49.1.3

Upshur, J. A. & Turner, C. E. (1999). Systematic effects in the rating of second-language speaking ability: Test method and learner discourse. *Language Testing, 16*(1), 82–111. https://doi.org/10.1177/026553229901600105

Van Moere, A. & Downey, R. (2016). Technology and artificial intelligence in language assessment. In D. Tsagari & J. Banerjee (Eds.), *Handbook of Second Language Assessment* (pp. 341–357). New York: De Gruyter Mouton.

Van Moere, A. & Suzuki, M. (2018). Using speech processing technology in assessing pronunciation. In O. Kang & A. Ginther (Eds.), *Assessment in second language pronunciation* (pp. 137–152). New York: Routledge. https://doi.org/10.4324/9781315170756-8

Vantage Learning. (2005). *How IntelliMetric works*. Retrieved October 2019 from http://www.vantagelearning.com/products/intellimetric/intellimetric-how-it-works/

Vaughan, C. (1991). Holistic assessment: What goes on in the rater's mind? In L. Hamp-Lyons (Ed.), *Assessing second language writing in academic contexts* (pp. 111–125). Norwood, NJ: Ablex Publishing Corporation.

Wagner, M. (2015). *The centrality of congnitively diagnostic assessment for advancing secondary school ESL students' writing: A mixed methods study*. Available from ProQuest Central; ProQuest Dissertations & Theses Global; Social Science Premium Collection (1719259603). Retrieved from http://search.proquest.com.ezp.lib.unimelb.edu.au/docview/1719259603?accountid=12372

Wang, F. & Wang, S. (2012). A comparative study on the influence of automated evaluation system and teaching grading on students' English writing. *Procedia Engineering, 29*, 993–997. https://doi.org/10.1016/j.proeng.2012.01.077

Wang, H., Choi, I., Schmidgall, J. & Bachman, L. (2012). Review of Pearson Test of English Academic: Building an assessment use argument. *Language Testing, 29*(4), 603–619. https://doi.org/10.1177/0265532212448619

Wang, J., Engelhard, G., Raczynski, K., Song, T. & Wolfe, E. (2017). Evaluating rater accuracy and perception for integrated writing assessments using a mixed-methods approach. *Assessing Writing, 33*, 36–47. https://doi.org/10.1016/j.asw.2017.03.003

Wang, J., Engelhard, G. & Wolfe, E. (2016). Evaluating rater accuracy in rater-mediated assessments using an unfolding model. *Educational and Psychological Measurement, 76*(6), 1005–1025. https://doi.org/10.1177/0013164415621606

Wang, Y. (2004a). An introduction to the prototype CET online marking system. *Foreign Language World, 4*, 67–73.

Wang, Y. (2004b). An empirical investigation of the CET online marking system. *Foreign Language World, 5*, 74–79.

Wang, Y. (2005). *A reliability study of online marking of compositions produced on the National College English Test.* Unpublished PhD thesis, Shanghai Jiao Tong University,

Wang, Y. (2015). *Marking reliability and online marking of compositions produced on a large-scale English examination – An empirical study.* Shanghai: Shanghai Foreign Language Education Press.

Watts, A. (2006). *Fostering communities of practice: A rationale for developing the use of new technologies in support of raters.* Cambridge: Cambridge University Press.

Wei, J. & Llosa, L. (2015). Investigating differences between American and Indian raters in assessing TOEFL iBT speaking tasks. *Language Assessment Quarterly, 12*(3), 283–304. https://doi.org/10.1080/15434303.2015.1037446

Weigle, S. C. (1994). Effects of training on raters of ESL compositions. *Language Testing, 11*(2), 197–223. https://doi.org/10.1177/026553229401100206

Weigle, S. C. (1998). Using FACETS to model rater training effects. *Language Testing, 15*(2), 263–287. https://doi.org/10.1177/026553229801500205

Weigle, S. C. (1999). Investigating rater/prompt interactions in writing assessment: Quantitative and qualitative approaches. *Assessing Writing, 6*, 145–178. https://doi.org/10.1016/S1075-2935(00)00010-6

Weigle, S. C. (2002). *Assessing writing.* Cambridge: Cambridge University Press. https://doi.org/10.1017/CBO9780511732997

Weigle, S. C. (2010). Validation of automated scores of TOEFL iBT tasks against non-test indicators of writing ability. *Language Testing, 27*(3), 335–353. https://doi.org/10.1177/0265532210364406

Weigle, S. C. (2011). *Validation of automated scores of TOEFL iBT tasks against non-test indicators of writing ability.* Retrieved from Princeton, NJ: https://doi.org/10.1002/j.2333-8504.2011.tb02260.x

Weigle, S. C. (2013). English language learners and automated scoring of essays: Critical considerations. *Assessing Writing, 18*, 85–99. https://doi.org/10.1016/j.asw.2012.10.006

Weigle, S. C. & Boldt, H. (2003). Effects of task and rater background on the evaluation of ESL student writing: A pilot study. *TESOL Quarterly, 37*(2), 345–354. https://doi.org/10.2307/3588510

Weir, C. J. (2005). *Language testing and validation: An evidence-based approach.* Basingstoke: Palgrave Macmillan. https://doi.org/10.1057/9780230514577

Wenger, E. (1998). *Communities of practice: Learning, meaning and identity.* Cambridge: Cambridge University Press. https://doi.org/10.1017/CBO9780511803932

Wenger, E. & Snyder, W. (2000). Communities of practice: The organizational frontier. *Harvard Business Review, 78*(1), 139–145.

Wenger, E., Snyder, W. & McDermott, R. (2002). *Cultivating communities of practice: A guide to managing knowledge.* Boston, MA: Harvard Business School Press.

Wheadon, C. (2015). The opposite of adaptivity? [Blog]. Retrieved from https://blog.nomoremarking.com/the-opposite-of-adaptivityc26771d21d50

White, E. M. (1985). *Teaching and assessing writing.* San Francisco: Jossey-Bass Inc.

Wigglesworth, G. (1993). Exploring bias analysis as a tool for improving rater consistency in assessing oral interaction. *Language Testing, 10*(3), 305–323. https://doi.org/10.1177/026553229301000306

Williamson, D., Xi, X. & Breyer, F. J. (2012). A framework for evaluation and use of automated scoring. *Educational Measurement: Issues and Practice, 31*(1), 2–13. https://doi.org/10.1111/j.1745-3992.2011.00223.x

Wind, S. A. & Engelhard, G. (2014). How invariant and accurate are domain ratings in writing assessment? *Assessing Writing, 18,* 278–299. https://doi.org/10.1016/j.asw.2013.09.002

Wind, S. A. & Peterson, M. E. (2018). A systematic review of methods for evaluating rating quality in language assessment. *Language Testing, 35*(2), 161–192. https://doi.org/10.1177/0265532216686999

Winke, P., Gass, S. & Myford, C. (2013). Raters' L2 background as a potential source of bias in rating oral performance. *Language Testing, 30*(2), 231–252. https://doi.org/10.1177/0265532212456968

Winke, P. & Lim, H. (2015). ESL essay raters' cognitive processes in applying the Jacobs et al. rubric: An eye-movement study. *Assessing Writing, 25,* 37–53. https://doi.org/10.1016/j.asw.2015.05.002

Wiseman, C. (2008). *Investigating selected facets in measuring second language writing ability using holistic and analytic scoring methods.* Unpublished Ed.D. dissertation, Columbia University, New York.

Wolfe, E. (1997). The relationship between essay reading style and scoring proficiency in a psychometric scoring system. *Assessing Writing, 4*(1), 83–106. https://doi.org/10.1016/S1075-2935(97)80006-2

Wolfe, E. (2006). Uncovering rater's cognitive processing and focus using think-aloud protocols. *Journal of Writing Assessment, 2*(1), 37–6.

Wolfe, E., Jiao, H. & Song, T. (2015). A family of rater accuracy models. *Journal of Applied Measurement, 16*(2), 153–160.

Wolfe, E., Kao, C. W. & Ranney, M. (1998). Cognitive differences in proficienct and nonproficient essay scorers. *Written Communication, 15*(4), 465–492. https://doi.org/10.1177/0741088398015004002

Wolfe, E. W., Moulder, B. C. & Myford, C. M. (2001). Detecting differential rater functioning over time (DRIFT) using a Rasch multi-faceted rating scale model. *Journal of Applied Measurement, 2*(3), 256–280.

Wolfe, E. & Ranney, M. (1996). Expertise in esssay scoring. In D. C. Edelson & E. A. Domeshek (Eds.), *Proceedings of ICLS 96* (pp. 545–550). Charlottesville, VA: Association for the Advancement of Computing in Education.

Wresch, W. (1993). The imminence of grading essays by computer – 25 years later. *Computers and Composition, 10*(2), 45–58. https://doi.org/10.1016/S8755-4615(05)80058-1

Xi, X. (2010a). Automated scoring and feedback systems: Where are we and where are we heading? *Language Testing, 27*(3), 291–300. https://doi.org/10.1177/0265532210364643

Xi, X. (2010b). How do we go about investigating test fairness? *Language Testing, 27*(2), 147–170. https://doi.org/10.1177/0265532209349465

Xi, X. (2012). Validity and the automated scoring of performance tests. In G. Fulcher & F. Davidson (Eds.), *The Routledge handbook of language testing* (pp. 438–451). Abingdon: Routledge.

Xi, X. (2017). *Opening the black box of AI for assessment: Developer responsibilities and user rights*. Paper presented at the Symposium on human-machine teaming up for language assessment: The need for extending the scope of assessment literacy. Language Testing Research Colloquium, Bogota, Colombia, 21–23 July 2017.

Xi, X., Higgins, D., Zechner, K. & Williamson, D. (2008). *Automated scoring of spontaneous speech using SpeechRater v1.0*. RR-08-62. Retrieved from http://origin-www.ets.org/Media/Research/pdf/RR-08-62.pdf. https://doi.org/10.1002/j.2333-8504.2008.tb02148.x

Xi, X., Higgins, D., Zechner, K. & Williamson, D. (2012). A comparison of two scoring methods for an automated speech scoring system. *Language Testing, 29*(3), 371–394. https://doi.org/10.1177/0265532211425673

Xi, X. & Mollaun, P. (2006). *Investigating the utility of analytic scoring for the TOEFL academic speaking test (TAST)*. Retrieved from Princeton, NJ: https://doi.org/10.1002/j.2333-8504.2006.tb02013.x

Xi, X. & Mollaun, P. (2009). *How do raters from India perform in scoring the TOEFL iBT speaking section and what kind of training helps? TOEFL iBT Research Report RR-09-31)*. Retrieved from Princeton, NJ: https://doi.org/10.1002/j.2333-8504.2009.tb02188.x

Xi, X. & Mollaun, P. (2011). Using raters from India to score a large-scale speaking test. *Language Learning, 61*(4), 1222–1255. https://doi.org/10.1111/j.1467-9922.2011.00667.x

Yan, X. (2014). An examination of rater performance on a local oral English proficiency test: A mixed-methods approach. *Language Testing, 31*(4), 501–527. https://doi.org/10.1177/0265532214536171

Zechner, K., Higgins, D. X. & Williamson, D. (2009). Automatic scoring of non-native spontaneous speech in tests of spoken English. *Speech Communication, 51*(10), 883–895. https://doi.org/10.1016/j.specom.2009.04.009

Zhang, J. (2016). Same text different processing? Exploring how raters' cognitive and meta-cognitive strategies influence rating accuracy in essay scoring. *Assessing Writing, 27*, 37–53. https://doi.org/10.1016/j.asw.2015.11.001

Zhang, Y. & Elder, C. (2011). Judgments of oral proficiency by non-native and native English speaking teacher raters: Competing or complementary constructs? *Language Testing, 28*(1), 31–50. https://doi.org/10.1177/0265532209360671

Zhang, Y., Powers, D., Wright, W. & Morgan, R. (2003). *Applying the online scoring network (OSN) to advanced program placement (AP) tests.* ETS RR-03-12. Princeton, NJ: Educational Testing Service. https://doi.org/10.1002/j.2333-8504.2003.tb01904.x

Zhao, C. G. (2013). Measuring authorial voice strength in L2 argumentative writing: The development and validation of an analytic rubric. *Language Testing, 30*(2), 201–230. https://doi.org/10.1177/0265532212456965

Zupanc, K. & Bosnic, Z. (2015). Advances in the field of automated essay evaluation. *Informatica, 39*, 383–395.

INDEX

Authors